Granite Gallows

**True Tales of the Death Penalty & More from
New Hampshire's History**

Christopher Richard Benedetto

Second Edition

To Celia, Cadogan, and Camden
In memory of Nathaniel
You will never be forgotten

Table of Contents   **Page**

Introduction

There is perhaps no topic more controversial in New Hampshire today than the death penalty. While the Granite State was relatively late to begin executing criminals during the colonial era, New Hampshire is now the last state in New England with the death penalty still on the books. In October 2006, the murder of police officer Michael Briggs in Manchester by Michael Addison ignited the most recent controversy in the tragic story of capital punishment in the Granite State. Since then, calls to abolish the death penalty have once again gained momentum in the hearts and minds of New Hampshire residents. Clerics and activists have formed the New Hampshire Coalition to Abolish the Death Penalty to urge the legislature and governor to terminate capital punishment forever. But as this book will demonstrate, one of the ironies of history is that centuries ago, ecclesiastical authorities in New Hampshire legitimated the secular death penalty long before they started having second thoughts. The most recent bill to kill capital punishment failed to pass by only one vote in 2014, and certainly the debate is far from over. But how did we get here?

Unfortunately, the history of the death penalty in New Hampshire has been mostly forgotten by the public and largely neglected by historians, except for narrow studies of a few individual cases. Whether you support abolition, or want to keep the law as it is, the history of the death penalty in the Granite State is more relevant now than ever before. The origin of the capital punishment in the Granite State is perplexing, especially in comparison to its southern neighbor. New Hampshire and Massachusetts were of course colonized by Europeans within a few years of each other during the seventeenth century, and for many decades afterwards they were closely connected politically and followed essentially the same legal code which allowed the death penalty for many offenses, including rape, murder, witchcraft, and even for concealing the birth of an illegitimate child.

But curiously, Massachusetts had already executed 137 people before New Hampshire first used the death penalty. While Bay Colony hanged many for witchcraft, most notoriously in 1692, there were numerous accusations of witchcraft but no executions in New Hampshire for that offense during the colonial period. Why was there such a discrepancy? Much of it was due to chance, and sheer bad luck for the New Hampshire colonial government rather than any opposition to capital punishment. For example, between 1648 and 1738, there were at least twelve documented murders in New Hampshire which could have resulted in the death penalty. But in none of these cases was there enough evidence for a jury to convict and dispatch the accused to the gallows, which from one perspective is encouraging that the rule of law was followed. The first executions in New Hampshire nearly occurred in 1734, when two sailors were indicted but ultimately acquitted for the murder of Abigail Dent, a seventeen year old whose bruised, strangled body was found in a swamp near Portsmouth. But as we will see, in 1739 the circumstances would all come together to enable New Hampshire's first hangings, and ignite the debate over the death penalty which continues today.

The title I chose for this book is of course a play on words; there were never actual gallows constructed with granite, though it seems that early on New Hampshire residents connected their identity with the geology of the region when one newspaper asked: "We cannot believe that we shall be taunted with having hearts as hard as our Granite rocks." The image on the cover of this book is from a broadside in the Library of Congress of the execution of Robert Young in Massachusetts in 1779, though it is an accurate depiction of how the early executions in New Hampshire's history would have likely appeared.

The history of capital punishment in New Hampshire exposes many issues that our society still grapples with today, including race, reproductive rights, bankruptcy, and the highly contentious relationship between insanity and crime. But this book doesn't just examine the cases which ended with a hanging; I also examine cases that didn't end at the gallows, and these are particularly interesting because they reveal how attitudes to capital punishment changed in New Hampshire over the centuries. I have also sought to tell the stories of the victims of these tragedies, though ironically their lives are often more challenging to uncover. The book also explores other taboo topics that had a profound impact on the Granite State, including body snatching, child abuse, abortion, and suicide. These tales shed light on New Hampshire's history during eras of momentous change and stress, from the American Revolution to the Industrial Revolution and beyond.

I would like to thank the staff of the New Hampshire State Archives, the Rauner Library at Dartmouth, and the Baker Library at Harvard for their invaluable assistance during my research for this book. For those who are interested in my sources, the endnotes are conveniently placed at the end of each chapter to reduce the amount of page flipping readers will have to do. I hope this book is an illuminating and compelling journey into the dark corners of New Hampshire's past for my readers as it has been for me. Enjoy and beware!

Chapter One

Innocence Lost
Missing Infants, Ministers, and the Death Penalty

Of the twenty-four souls who have suffered capital punishment in New Hampshire's history, perhaps the most well-known today is Ruth Blay. In 1768, the twenty-five year old schoolteacher was convicted of concealing the premature birth of her stillborn illegitimate daughter under a barn in Hampton (the child was likely stillborn). Poor Ruth Blay was subsequently hanged on the outskirts of Portsmouth on December 31, 1768, and over the past two and a half centuries, the legend of Ruth Blay's hasty execution has become an integral part of New Hampshire folklore, retold in poetry, prose, and even on the stage.[1] But the records of New Hampshire's colonial government provide a tantalizing clue to what really happened that winter's day. In early 1769, Portsmouth farmer Samuel Hall sent a petition to the provincial assembly seeking compensation for damage done to his property during the Blay execution. Hall complained of a "new Fence and Stone wall, which was almost broke to pieces and thrown down by the crowd of people who attended the Execution, and other damage done to his Pasture by the Horses." Today, one can visit the South Street cemetery in Portsmouth and imagine the chaotic, tragic events which transpired there. However, a more significant episode which ignited the debate over the death penalty in New Hampshire has been nearly forgotten. To fully understand the origins of the death penalty in the Granite State, we must go back even further, before Ruth Blay herself was even born.

In colonial New Hampshire, the social stigma suffered by women who conceived illegitimate children was severe and often resulted in corporal punishment. In Portsmouth during the summer of 1673, for example, Elizabeth Oliver was severely whipped in public for "being with child before Marriage & neglecting to send for helpe...& rapping her child in a shirt...putting it into the bed denying she had any child to the women that came in after her delivery wherby ye child in appearance was dead."[2] But at the beginning of the eighteenth century, the New Hampshire government sought even harsher penalties for this social crime. In 1714, the General Assembly passed "An Act to Prevent the Destroying and Murthering of Bastard Children" which declared:

6

Whereas many lewd women that have been delivered of Bastard children, to avoid shame and escape punishment, do secretly Bury or Conceal the Death of their children, and after if the Child be found Dead, the said Women doe alleadge that the Said Child was Born dead, whereas it falleth out Sometimes (although it is hardly to be proved) that the Said Child or Children were Murthered by the Said Women their lewd Mothers or by their Assent or procurement. Be it therefore enacted . . . that if any woman be delivered of any Issue of her body, male or female, which if it were born alive should by law be a Bastard; and that she Endeavor privately either by drowning or secret burying thereof ...So to conceal the death thereof that it may not come to light, whether it were born alive or not but be concealed. In Every Such Case the Mother soe offending shall Suffer death as in the case of Murther except such Mother cann make proof by one Witness at the least, the Child whose death was by her So intended to be concealed was born dead.[3]

However, another New Hampshire statute dating from 1702 provided a legal recourse for women who conceived illegitimately. It stipulated that a man who was "accused by any woman to be the father of a Bastard Child begotten of her body, she continuing constant in her accusation being exam'd upon Oath . . . he shall be adjudged the reputed father of such child notwithstanding his denial and stand charged with the maintenance thereof." Court records from this era abound with cases of women who brought the alleged fathers of their illegitimate offspring to court for child support and often won because the magistrates did not want the community to have to support the child. But despite these legal deterrents, in December 1739, the residents of New Hampshire gathered to witness the executions of two women who had committed what local minister Arthur Browne classified as "the most unnatural murder."[4] These events shook the colony to its core, but the historical context reveals that this shocking tragedy, in the eyes of many New Hampshire colonists, may have been the culmination of a series of troubling events that had begun decades earlier.

Beginning in the 1720s, there were signs of trouble on the horizon in colonial New Hampshire. An earthquake shattered the tranquil night of October 29, 1727, which Puritan ministers across New England, including Jabez Fitch of Portsmouth, commonly interpreted as an omen of the "Wrath to come" if the populace did not engage in a "universal and constant Reformation."[5] Then in 1735, communities across New Hampshire were devastated by a "Distemper in the throat," probably an outbreak of diphtheria, which resulted in the deaths of over one thousand people in the colony, taking a particularly devastating toll on children. In Portsmouth alone in 1735, over eighty children under the age of ten perished, and Jabez Fitch discussed the broader sociological and spiritual impact of this deadly illness: "The great mortality that has been among children should make parents very sensible that they are uncertain comforts, and should quicken them to a faithful discharge of their duty towards their children. The loss of so many children, whom if had pleased God that they lived, might have built up many families, will be a great prevention of the growth and increase of the country; and ought therefore to be lookt upon as Frown of Providence upon the Land in general, as well as a sore Affliction to the Parents in particular."[6]

While it is oft repeated that infant mortality rates were much higher in colonial America than in modern times, that certainly does not mean that a child's life was valued any less. The survival of healthy children sustained hope not only for their parents, but for the future of the British colony engaged in the long colonial struggle with the French in North America. Indeed, when the healthy survival of every child was so fragile, the possibility that a mother might intentionally conceal the birth and premature death of her newborn was particularly heinous to the inhabitants of eighteenth-century New Hampshire. Tragically, the unforgiving laws, social norms, and hard economic realities of the colonial era left many women with to make this excruciating choice.[7]

Only three years after the diphtheria claimed its victims, Reverend Fitch and his community were outraged on the morning of August 11, 1739, when the body of a female newborn was found floating at the bottom of a well. Warrants were issued and "a Widow woman named Sarah Simpson who had been suspected some time before to have been with child, was apprehended and charged with being the mother of the child found in the well."[8] According to one contemporary, Simpson was "about 27 years [born] in ye parish of Oyster River," in Durham, New Hampshire and she was "put out young, and serv'd her apprenticeship in Portsmouth."[9] When she was questioned, Sarah denied that the baby in the well was hers, but then admitted she had recently given birth, and stunned provincial officials by leading them to the shallow grave where she had buried her baby's body near the Piscataqua River.

Events took an unexpected turn the following day when Penelope Kenny, a twenty-year-old native of Limerick, Ireland serving in the household of Dr. Joseph Franklin, was interrogated by authorities who now suspected her of being the mother of the baby in the well. Not satisfied with her evasive answers, they unpleasantly forced Kenny to disrobe and be physically examined by "four or five skillful Women," most likely midwives, "who reported that according to their Judgment she had been delivered of a Child within a week." But Kenny still "would not give direct Answers to questions put to her," and only after spending a night in the local jail did Penelope finally confess that she "alone delivered of a Male-Child alive the Wednesday Morning before." Kenny then confessed that she "put it alive into a tub in her Master's Cellar and then left it, till Friday-Night following, when she threw it into the River."[10]

Upon this damning evidence, Penelope and Sarah were each tried and convicted by a jury of "twelve good and lawful men" for "feloniously concealing the death of an...infant bastard child" on August 30, 1739. According to one official, the trials of Simpson and Kenny were "long, tedious and attended with much trouble and difficulty," and over thirty witnesses were summoned to testify, though their exact words have been lost.[11] There was some uncertainty, however, concerning the extent and nature of their crimes. Jabez Fitch remarked that Simpson and Kenny both "deny'd that they laid violent Hands on their children; one affirming that her Child was dead born; and the other, that hers dy'd soon after it was born." But for Fitch these claims were irrelevant because "both seem'd sensible of their Neglect of taking due care to preserve the Life of their Children: So that they tho't themselves guilty of the Breach of the sixth Commandment by omission, if not by Commission."[12]

New Hampshire authorities, following their Puritan peers in Massachusetts, considered the women's actions not only sexually deviant behavior, but also an affront to the existing social order that could not go unpunished.[13] And it is very possible that memories of the "awful Calamity" that had claimed the lives of so many innocent children three years earlier made the deeds of Sarah Simpson and Penelope Kenny that much more appalling, and convinced Chief Justice Henry Sherburne and his colleagues to condemn both women to be hanged on November 21, 1739.[14] . In the days that followed this unprecedented sequence of events, Simpson and Kenny were "persuaded by some indiscreet persons who came to visit them, that their sentence was rigorous and unjust, and . . . they might obtain a reprieve so as to be finally executed from suffering." A petition was sent to Governor Jonathan Belcher, and on November 12, he signed an order that postponed the executions until December 27.[15]

The "mournful spectacle" that unfolded in Portsmouth in December 1739 reflected a communal ritual of execution that was practiced hundreds of times across New England from the seventeenth through the mid nineteenth-centuries, when public executions were banned.[16] On the morning of December 27, Sarah Simpson was escorted from the jail to the South Church, where Reverend William Shurtleff preached an "execution" sermon, while Penelope Kenny spent her dwindling hours at Queen's Chapel perched on a hill across town listening to Reverend Arthur Browne, who had offered her spiritual guidance.[17] This was possibly because Browne, like Kenny, was a native of Ireland and felt a connection with him. Browne had served as the rector of King's Chapel in Providence, Rhode Island for six years before moving north to Queen's Chapel, the first Episcopal Church in Portsmouth, in 1736.[18]

Two paradoxical themes emerge from these epic sermons. The ministers did not hesitate to use the example of condemned women to remind the entire community of the spiritual ignorance and sins of the flesh that could damn any soul. "May her untimely End influence you all," warned Arthur Browne, "to lay fast hold on Instruction; may her Example and Sufferings answer the Intention of Law, and deter all viciously and wickedly disposed persons among you from incurring the like condemnation."[19] William Shurtleff took the opportunity to remind his parishioners that the "neglect and abuse of God's Sabbaths (which the condemned person here present reflects upon with so much regret)…very often lead to Capital Crimes." But just as the ministers portrayed Penelope Kenny and Sarah Simpson as criminals destined for eternal damnation, they also represented the young women as pitiful sinners who were eager to repent. William Shurtleff discussed the case of the "poor Prisoner" with "the tenderest Bowels of Compassion, and the deepest Concern of Soul," and Arthur Browne asked his audience, "why should I at present upbraid or insult this poor Malefactor! She is convinced I trust of the heinousness of her Sins, and may her Preparation and Repentance avail her in the Day of the Lord."[20]

Accompanied by the ministers of Portsmouth, Sarah Simpson and Penelope Kenny were then escorted about a mile to the place of execution on the outskirts of town. This possibly was the site of a gallows which had been erected in 1718 in a field between the homes of William Cotton and Edward Cates, where it stood as an intimidating reminder to the locals of the power of the royal government.[21] Although a fresh blanket of snow had shrouded the landscape the day before, "the execution of the said women drew together a vast concourse of people" and the "numerous spectators seem'd earnestly concern'd for them." In the crowd was Samuel Lane, a young cordwainer who had traveled from Hampton to see "two women Hanged at the Bank."[22] Lane's terse diary entry does not reveal his thoughts as he watched Sarah Simpson and Penelope Kenny utter their final words before Sherriff Eleazar Russell carried out his grisly task. By the time Simpson approached her final moments of earthly existence, Jabez Fitch remarked that she had "discover'd an uncommon

Composure of Mind, and gave very pertinent Answers to the Questions that were put to her." Sarah Simpson's last words were captured by Reverend Fitch:

> After she came to the place of Execution, a Writing, (That was put into one of the Ministers Hands by the Way, said to be of her dictating and which she acknowledged to be so) was publickly read at her Desire; wherein she mentions several things that were Matter of Grief and Bitterness to her, as that she had been forgetful of GOD in her Childhood and Youth, and she pass'd away her early days in light and wicked Company: To which she ascribes it, that her riper Years had been a Course of more direct Rebellion against GOD; And she fires that Parents as well as Children would received Instruction from it. She also mourns that she had improv'd no more by the Opportunities she had had in some Families in which she liv'd, or been conversant, for some little Time after she was grown up; where the Worship of GOD was upheld, and where she had receiv'd many good and wholesome Instructions. And she mentions it with Regret that when she entered into the Marriage State, it was not with one that took care to maintain the Exercise of Family Religion and advises all when they marry, to make it their great Care to marry in the LORD: She at the same Time expresses her Thankfulness to the Ministers that visited her, and that, as she express'd it, had so often carried her to the Throne of Grace, particularly to the two who had been most frequent in their Visits; And, declaring her Forgiveness of all the World, she signifies her own Hope, notwithstanding her great and manifold Sins, of obtaining Forgiveness and finding Mercy with God thro' the Blood of JESUS CHRIST his Son.

When given her opportunity, Penelope Kenny spoke "a few words by the way of Warning to others, and the Rev. Mr. Fitch having then commended them both to the Mercy of God in Christ, she and the other were executed . . . and left us not without hopes of their being delivered from the second Death."[23]

But long after the two women's bodies were buried in unmarked and long forgotten graves, one mystery refused a decent burial. If Sarah Simpson laid her poor infant to rest in a shallow grave and Penelope Kenny cast her nameless newborn into the churning waters of the Piscataqua River, then who was the mother of the dead child found in the well in August 1739? William Shurtleff was convinced "that there has been one among us thro' whose means these Persons have been remarkably detected, that is equally & it may be more heinously guilty in the sight of GOD; and could I suppose the Person to be within Hearing, I would say, *Don't encourage yourself from your present impunity*: Be assur'd that though you are as yet concealed from Men, both you and your

11

Crime are known to God."[24]   But the identity of that third woman who tossed a baby into the well in Portsmouth was apparently never discovered, and perhaps she took her secret to her grave.

An accidental archaeological discovery during the 1970s, however, revealed that the disposal of unwanted offspring in wells or privy pits was practiced in other areas of colonial America. While excavating an eighteenth-century brick privy in Philadelphia in 1973, archaeologists unexpectedly found among the assorted refuse the partial skeletal remains of two human newborns. The archaeologists determined that sometime during the second half of the eighteenth century, at least one woman had given birth and "whatever the circumstances, these infants were apparently unwanted, probably illegitimate. The mother (or mothers) either murdered them…or at least concealed their births and deaths in order to avoid stigma, threat of prosecution, loss of reputation…or at least the responsibility of mothering a bastard child."[25]

What is certain, however, is that the tragic events of 1739 ushered in a new era of crime and punishment in New Hampshire and made a profound impression on all who witnessed them. Jabez Fitch was confident that "the sad end of these women may be a Warning to all others, to take heed of the Sin of Uncleanness," echoing sentiments expressed by the famous Puritan minister Cotton Mather in Massachusetts more than forty years earlier.[26]   William Shurtleff fervently hoped that "nothing of the like Nature might again happen among us!"[27] But he was sadly mistaken.

About sixteen years passed before the next instance of capital punishment in New Hampshire. On December 12, 1754, a quarrel broke out between one Peter Clough, a mariner allegedly, and Eliphaz Dow at the home of Dow's brother, Noah, in Hampton Falls. Like many disputes at that time, it seems to have been about livestock. Noah Dow testified that Clough came to his house to accuse Eliphaz Dow of his killing his cow. "I try'd to still them", claimed Noah Dow, "and got up and told them I would have no fighting in my house." The three men then went outside, with Noah Dow between them as peacemaker. Clough allegedly said to Eliphaz Dow, "God Damn You…and my brother answered Dam You take care what you do." Noah Dow then turned around to see his brother grabbing an iron hoe and watch with horror as his brother Eliphaz struck Clough on the left side of his head with the gardening tool, killing him instantly. Eliphaz Dow went on the run, but was soon captured and indicted for the murder of Peter Clough. Dow pleaded not guilty, but in February 1755, he was easily convicted of the crime. Both in his brother and one Richard Smith testified that the summer before, that they had heard Dow "speak about Peter Clough and say he believe'd he should kill him…or he would burn him out and run to Canada." Dow was originally sentenced to hang in March 1755, but he received two reprieves from Royal Governor Benning Wentworth. Finally on May 9, 1755, Eliphaz Dow was hanged in Portsmouth. According to one eyewitness report that has surfaced, Dow was described as "one of the most stupid and hardned creatures I ever saw. Mr. Langdon preached an excellent sermon, but he would not hear it, nor has ever been to meeting till last Sabbath, and then was event forced to it. Near ten thousand people were at the Gallows, but he would neither speak nor have a Prayer, nor did he care to be spoken to."[28] Besides this, really nothing is known about the first man to be executed in New Hampshire.

Dow's hanging was to be the last execution in New Hampshire until Ruth Blay met her end in 1768, though the events of 1739 case did not mean that every woman accused of infanticide or even concealing the death of a bastard child would be sent to her death. For example, there were similar cases in New Hampshire prior to the American Revolution that have been forgotten because they did not end at the gallows. Sometime between 1739 and prior to 1744, a woman of African descent owned by Captain Samuel Banfield of Portsmouth was "try'd for her life for the murder of her bastard child" but was apparently spared the noose. In 1764, an unidentified woman in Portsmouth was suspected of murdering her baby, "having delivered alone; but after a Trial of above six Hours…it appeared the Child was still born, upon which Evidence she was immediately release."[29] After the American Revolution, there was another series of suspicious infant deaths in Portsmouth. In November 1786, the *New-Hampshire Spy* reported that the body of a male infant was found "with strokes on its head" and the child's mother was accused of committing the crime. The married woman's identity was mercifully guarded by local newspapers because the printers sought "to use the greatest tenderness-we desire not to wound the feelings of the unfortunate by exaggerating every little particular."[30] Then in May 1790, Dorothy Goss was charged with "murdering her infant child" but after a lengthy trial in Portsmouth she was found not guilty and released from custody.[31]

Although deliberate violence in these cases was evident, why did none of them result in capital punishment? It may have been due to the lack of evidence in each case, but also by the end of the eighteenth century, prevailing attitudes in New Hampshire towards sexuality and capital punishment in general had become more lenient in regards to defendants who were women. Social historians have demonstrated that across New England after the Revolution, the number of women who conceived out-of-wedlock increased dramatically as prosecution of this moral crime decreased. In 1791, this subtle change in social norms was reflected by the repeal of the archaic statute that led to the first executions in New Hampshire by lawmakers, who replaced it with a form of "symbolic" execution in which "the Mother so offending" would be compelled to stand on the gallows for one hour with a noose around her neck, and suffer public humiliation but not death.[32] However, in the following century, New Hampshire lawmakers would be compelled to reconsider whether women deserved to stand on the gallows once again.

Endnotes: Chapter One

1. The most recent and perhaps most accurate work on the Blay tragedy is by Carolyn Marvin, "The Hanging of Ruth Blay, December, 30, 1768: Separating Fact from Fiction" *Historical New Hampshire*, Spring 2009, 3-23.

2. *New Hampshire State Papers, Volume XL* (Concord: 1943) 293.

3. *Laws of New Hampshire, Volume One, Province Period 1679-1702* (Manchester: John B. Clarke Co., 1904), 678 and *Laws of New Hampshire, Volume Two, Province Period 1702-1745* (Concord: Rumford Printing Company, 1913), 127.

4. *Religious Education of Children Recommended, In a Sermon Preach'd in the Church of Portsmouth December 27th 1739 . . . by Arthur Browne, A.M.* (Boston, 1740), 13.

5. *A Discourse Shewing What regard we ought to have to the Awful Work of Divine Providence in the Earthquake, which happen'd the Night of the 29th of October, 1727 By Jabez Fitch . . .* (Boston: B. Green, 1728), 8.

6.. *An Account of the numbers that have died of the Distemper in the Throat, Within the Province of New Hampshire . . . July 26, 1736* (Boston: 1736) 13, and also Jeremy Belknap, *The History of New Hampshire . . . Volume II* (Dover: 1812), 97.

7. Peter Hoffer and N.E.H. Hull, *Murdering Mothers: Infanticide in England and New England 1558-1803* (New York: NYU Press, 1984), 115.

8. *Boston News-Letter*, August 17, 1739 and also New Hampshire Provincial Court Records, Microfilm Series, Case No. 20062.

9. "The Diary of Master Joseph Tate of Somersworth, New Hampshire," *The New England Historic and Genealogical Register* 74 (1920): 130.

10. *Boston News-Letter*, August 17, 1739. Penelope Kenny's Irish origins are also in the diary of Joseph Tate, who described her as "a servant girl about 20 years of age [born] in or near Limerick in Ireland," *Register* 74 (1920): 130. When Kenny immigrated to New Hampshire remains unknown.

11. New Hampshire Provincial Court Records, Case No. 20062, and *Boston News-Letter*, September 7, 1739 and *New Hampshire State Papers, 1725-1800, Volume XVIII* (Manchester: 1890) 130, 132, 133.

12. *The Faith and Prayer of a Dying Malefactor: A Sermon Preach'd December 27, 1739 . . . by William Shurtleff . . . to which is annexed a brief narrative concerning the said criminals and a Preface by the Reverence Mr. Fitch* (Boston: J. Draper, 1740) iii.

13. Laurel Thatcher Ulrich, *Good Wives: Image and Reality in the Lives of Women in Northern New England 1650-1750* (New York: Vintage Books, 1991), 196.

14. New Hampshire Province Court Records, Microfilm Series, Case No. 20062.

15. *The Faith and Prayer of a Dying Malefactor*, 20.

16. Stuart Banner, *The Death Penalty: An American History* (Cambridge: Harvard University Press, 2002), 24-52. Also see Deborah Navas, *Murdered By His Wife: An absorbing tale of crime and punishment in Eighteenth-century Massachusetts* (Amherst: UMass Press, 1999).

17. Shurtleff served as the minister in nearby Newcastle from 1712 until 1732, when he moved to Portsmouth, *Sibley's Harvard Graduates, Volume V, 1701-1712* (Cambridge: Harvard University Press, 1937), 396-402. Also see *The Faith and Prayer of a Dying Malefactor*, 29.

18.Mary Cochrane Rogers, *Glimpses of An Old Social Capital . . . As Illustrated By The Life of The Reverend Arthur Browne And His Circle* (Boston: 1923), 4-10.

19.*Religious Education of Children Recommended, In a Sermon Preach'd in the Church of Portsmouth, December 27ᵗʰ 1739...by Arthur Browne* (Boston:1740) 13.

20. *The Faith and Prayer of a Dying Malefactor*, 17, and *Religious Education of Children Recommended*, 14.

21. *Provincial Papers of New Hampshire . . . Volume XIX* (Manchester: John B. Clarke, 1891), 124–25; also see *The Faith and Prayer of a Dying Malefactor*, 27.

22. *The Faith and Prayer of a Dying Malefactor*, iv, and also *Almanack or a Journal for the Years 1737–1801 by Samuel Lane . . .* (Concord: New Hampshire Historical Society, 1988).

23. *The Faith and Prayer of a Dying Malefactor*, 27-29.

24. *The Faith and Prayer of a Dying Malefactor*, 20. It is believed that the woman's bodies were buried nearby the gallows, located in "the triangular ground formed by the junction of South and Middle Roads" in Portsmouth; see Helen Pearson, *Vignettes of Portsmouth . . .* (Boston: The Steson Press, 1913) 40.

25. Sharon Ann Burnston, "Babies in the Well: An Insight into Deviant Behavior in Eighteenth-Century Philadelphia," *In Remembrance: Archaeology and Death*, David Poirier and Nicholas Bellantoni eds. (London: Bergin and Garvey, 1997), 51–65.

26. Kathleen M. Brown, "Murderous Uncleanness: The Body of Female Infanticide in Puritan New England," *A Centre of Wonders: The Body in Early America*, Janet Moore Lindman and Michele Lise Tarter eds. (Ithaca: Cornell University Press, 2001), 77–94.

27. *The Faith and Prayer of a Dying Malefactor*, 20.

28. New Hampshire Provincial Court Case Files, # 27132; *Boston Evening Post*, May 19, 1755.

29. *Miscellaneous Provincial and State Papers, 1725–1800, Volume XVIII* (Manchester: 1890) 208, and also *New-Hampshire Gazette*, May 25, 1764.

30. *New-Hampshire Spy*, November 7, 1786.

31. *New-Hampshire Spy*, May 8, 1790.

32. Laurel Thatcher Ulrich, *A Midwife's Tale: The Life of Martha Ballard Based on Her Diary, 1785–1812* (New York: Vintage Books, 1991), 147–59, and also *Laws of New Hampshire . . . Volume Five, First Constitutional Period, 1784–1792* (Concord: Rumford Press, 1916), 596–597

Chapter Two

Branded for Life
Crime & Punishment in Early New Hampshire

In 1741, the decades-long dispute between New Hampshire and Massachusetts authorities over the geographic boundary between the two colonies was finally settled. Within a few years, Governor Benning Wentworth and his cronies began the process of formally incorporating the sparsely inhabited lands west of the Merrimack River into towns. In April 1746, for example, the neighboring communities of Dunstable, Merrimack, Hollis, and Monson were all chartered in a span of only three days. During the decades which followed, new sawmills, homes, and meetinghouses sprung up across a landscape irrevocably altered by European colonization.[1]

One of the many families to cross the "Province Line" into New Hampshire in hope of a prosperous future was the Wilkins' clan of Middleton, Massachusetts. Vital records reveal that Israel Wilkins married Margaret Case on July 18, 1726, and went on to have a few children, including a son Israel Jr. around 1742 and a daughter Hannah, born in 1745 in Middleton.[2] By April 1769, it appears that the Wilkins family had relocated to Monson, because that month Israel Wilkins Sr. signed a petition from the town's landowners thanking Governor John Wentworth for his assistance.[3] However, when the Wilkins moved to New Hampshire, the colony's geographic and political boundaries were still in a state of flux; if the town of Monson doesn't sound very familiar, that is because it ceased to exist on July 4, 1770, after its residents asked the provincial government to revoke their charter because the land at the center of town was "so very poor, Broken, Baron, and uneaven" and there was also "no prospect of ever Building a Meeting-House in the Center or elsewhere." Ultimately, their unusual request was granted and the rough land of Monson was divided amongst surrounding towns, including Milford and Hollis.

More changes were in store in March 1771 when New Hampshire was split up into its five original counties; Strafford, Rockingham, Grafton, Cheshire, and Hillsborough. In Hollis resided two members of the new colonial government; Samuel Hobart, one of Hillsborough county's Justices of the Peace and an elected representative in the New Hampshire General Assembly since 1768; and Benjamin Whiting, who was appointed the first Sheriff of Hillsborough County, where Amherst was chosen to host the proceedings of the Superior Court.[4]

Not all residents of the New Hampshire, however, were pleased with the administration and policies of Governor John Wentworth, who had been appointed to the post by King George III in 1767. The Wentworth family had formed a political dynasty in New Hampshire for nearly half a century; John's uncle Benning Wentworth had governed the colony for over twenty years, and Benning's father John had done so before that. But as boisterous public demonstrations against the authority of the British government and their emissaries spread across the colonies, New Hampshire was certainly no exception. In Massachusetts the destruction of tea came to symbolize the colonist's defiance of royal power, but in New Hampshire, lumber was at the center of a series of violent encounters between colonists and royal authorities.

Beginning in the 1720s, new laws in New Hampshire decreed that it was illegal to cut down any tree over a foot in diameter and use or sell the wood for their own profit without prior permission. Known as "His Majesty's Woods or Mast-Trees", these soaring white pines over 100 feet high were incised with the insignia of an arrow by the "Deputy Surveyor of the King's Woods" to mark them for the Crown and their ultimate destiny as masts or planks for the Royal Navy. Anyone caught having the trees cut in a local sawmill without the specific permission of the governor had to forfeit the fresh cut lumber to royal authorities or pay a stiff fine. Since it was neither prudent nor practical for the governor himself to enforce this naturally unpopular law, local officials often had to do the dirty work, which could be quite dangerous. For example, in 1734, when Royal Surveyor David Dunbar discovered some illegally cut timbers near Exeter and tried to enforce the law, deputies he sent to seize the lumber were assaulted by a group of angry men who also let it be known that some local Indians had been hired to assassinate Dunbar himself. While this threat was never carried out, the boldness of the locals sent shockwaves through the provincial government. [5]

Twenty years later in 1754, Governor Benning Wentworth and the colonial assembly signed "An Act for preventing and suppressing of Riots…and Unlawful Assemblies." If a group of three or more persons were found to commit any "unlawful Act with force of Violence against the Peace, or to manifest Terror of the People", they were to pay a hefty fine of fifty pounds each, and if they could not pay within twenty-four hours, the offenders were to be severely whipped publicly for challenging the authority of the Crown. Penalties for larger groups of rioters were much stiffer; "If twelve persons or more, being armed with Clubs, or other Weapons…shall be unlawfully, riotously, tumultuously or routerously assembled…shall not thereupon immediately disperse themselves [after being confronted by an official] shall…pay a fine not exceeding the sum of Five Hundred Pounds…and shall be whipt Thirty Stripes on the naked Back at the public Whipping-Post, and suffer twelve Months Imprisonment, and once every three Months…received the same Number of Stripes as aforesaid." This strong piece of legislation, however, was only in effect for three years and ultimately did little to hold back the rising tide of civil unrest in New Hampshire. The Wilkins family would witness some of these events in their own backyard.

As the 1770s began, New Hampshire citizens from all walks of life continued to openly defy royal authority like their neighbors in Massachusetts. On October 26, 1771, when the ship *Resolution* returned to Portsmouth from the Caribbean, Captain Richard Keating tried to smuggle one hundred valuable barrels of molasses into the colony without paying customs duties on them. When George Meserve, the Collector of His Majesty's Customs for the colony, discovered this, he had the vessel and its contents seized immediately. Three days later however, "between the hours of Eleven and Twelve O' Clock at night there entered on board of said Brigantine a Numerous Company of Men in disguise Armed with Clubs, and wrested said Vessel out of the hands of the proper Officers then on board, turned Some of them out of the Vessel and Confined others in the Cabbin, then proceeded to unload and Carry away the molasses aforesaid." Governor John Wentworth condemned "the illegal & riotous Transaction" and offered a reward of two hundred pounds to anyone who could help bring the culprits to justice. The Portsmouth "molasses party" preceded the Boston Tea Party by two years, but it has been largely forgotten because its political ramifications were not as severe.[6]

Only a few months later in February 1772, Deputy Surveyor John Sherburn was doing an inspection of some sawmills in Goffstown and Weare when he discovered hundreds of valuable white pine logs that had been cut down illegally. On February 7, the following notice appeared in the *New-Hampshire Gazette,* the colony's only newspaper: "All persons claiming property in the following White Pine Logs, seized by order of the Surveyor General in Goffstown and Weare, in the Province of New Hampshire, may appear at a Court of Vice-Admiralty to be held at Portsmouth, on Thursday the 27th. Instant at Ten of the clock A. M. and shew cause why the same should not be declared forfeited, agreeable to an Information filed in said Court." Ultimately, the saw mill owners in Goffstown grudgingly paid their fines, and received their lumber back in return. In Weare, however, sawmill owners led by Ebenezer Mudgett refused to go to court, pay the fines, and thus submit to royal authority.[7]

Governor Wentworth ultimately gave the order to Sheriff Benjamin Whiting of Hollis to arrest Mudgett, hopeful that would send a strong message to other rebellious merchants across the colony. On April 13, 1772, Whiting and his assistant John Quigly traveled north to Weare to give Mudgett the bad news. Being a local man, Whiting gave him a chance to raise his bond overnight "to prevent the…disagreeable Necessity of going to Gaol", or he was trying to save Mudgett the public humiliation of going to jail. Whiting and Mudgett agreed to meet the following morning at nearby Quinby's tavern, where the Sheriff planned to stay the night. But at five in the morning, Whiting awoke to see Mudgett standing over his bed. It soon became clear to the Sheriff that this was no social call, as a group of men entered the room with their faces painted black to conceal their identities and branches from pine trees in their hands. Whiting reached for his flintlock pistol, but was quickly subdued by the group of "lawless Ruffians." What came next was one of the boldest acts of defiance leading up to the American Revolution.

According to an eyewitness account, the posse held Whiting down and "stripped his Shirt, the only covering of his Body, off by Pieces, beat him in the Sides, took him entirely from the floor, then…they stretched him out, seized him by the Throat and choaked him, till they extorted such Promises from him, as their lawless Madness dictated, and menacing him in the most shocking manner!" Quigly did not fare much better. After disabling their weapons and cutting their horse's ears and tails, the two men were chased out of town at gunpoint. Though he was "chagrined almost to Madness" and injured, Whiting was not a cowardly man; within a few hours, he had raised a loyal posse to capture Mudgett and his accomplices. As soon as the Weare men caught sight of their adversaries, they fled into the nearby woods and swamps "with all possible speed." But Whiting would prove relentless in pursuit of his attackers. Eventually eight men, including Mudgett, were captured and fined before the Hillsborough County Superior Court in Amherst in September 1772.[8]

While the "Pine Tree Riot" was the most significant incident to appear in the early years of the Hillsborough County Court, the case of Israel Wilkins Jr. of Hollis a few months later was interesting in other ways. Little is known about Wilkins' early life, other than that he was around thirty years old in 1772, unmarried and still living with his parents on their farm. He apparently had severe financial problems, suggested by his frequent appearances in the county court in Amherst since December 1771, when David and Esther Farnsworth sued him over a debt which had accumulated since April 1765. In January 1772, when the court convened again, Israel Wilkins was placed in the county jail until he paid up. The surviving evidence suggests this was not done until April 1772, probably by Israel's parents, which must have added even more humiliation to his situation.[9] On the evening of Saturday November 21, 1772, the tension was palpable at the Wilkins' home in Hollis, and long-forgotten documents now preserved at Harvard University provide an intimate glimpse into the tumultuous events of that night.

According to Israel's mother Margaret, the trouble began when her son came into the house after dark and joined his family by the fireside. As shadows danced on the walls, a heated conversation between the Israel and his father commenced; apparently, Mr. Wilkins was not pleased about his son's continuing financial and legal troubles. "My son was angry", Mrs. Wilkins said a few days later, "& my husband was angry also, & sundry Angry words & expressions were utter'd by them both at each other – and one set in one Corner & the other in the other Corner before the Fire." In a matter of a few moments, the intense emotions between father and son boiled over like a pot hanging over their fire. In Mrs. Wilkins' words: "My Husband provoked my Son by his angry words & my Son rose up & shoved or threw over the Chair that my Husband set in & flung him partly on the Hearth."

Now in a full-fledged rage, the elder Mr. Wilkins grabbed his chair and held it menacingly towards his son. Mrs. Wilkins rose to her feet and stepped between her son and husband, begging them to stop their quarrel. But Israel had lost all restraint: "My Son pushed my husband & me down together on the floor & then my Son immediately went out of the Room." His sister Hannah, who was at that time seven-months pregnant, had already left the room to find her husband Israel Kenney, "that he might come in & prevent them from hurting each other", but she could not find him. She caught her brother and said to him, "For Mercy's Sake go out of Doors." By then, it may have been too late to stop this furious family quarrel from escalating further.[10]

In the early days of colonial New Hampshire, an act of physical or verbal aggression by a son towards his parents was a serious crime. When Richard Martin was brought to court in 1669 in Salisbury, Massachusetts for "abusing his father and throwing him down...and holding up an axe against him", he was fortunate to be sentenced to be severely whipped before everyone at the nearby meetinghouse in what is now Hampton, New Hampshire. In 1679, the royal government of New Hampshire stipulated, "If any man have a rebellious or stubborne son of sufficient years and understanding...w'ch shall not obey the voice of his father or the voice of his mother, that when they have chastened him will not hearken unto them, then shall his father and mother, being his natural parents, bring him before the Magistrates assembled in court, and testify unto them that their son is rebellious and stubborne, and will not obey their voice…but lives in sundry notorious crimes, such son shall be put to death, or otherwise severely punished."[11] While this legislation never resulted in the death penalty, it serves as a sobering insight into familial relationships in early New Hampshire. Even the conflict between Great Britain and the American colonies decades almost a century later was commonly described as an upstart child rebelling against the authority of its parent.

On the night of November 21, 1772, after knocking his parents to the floor, a fuming Israel Wilkins rushed outside and his mother "got up & followed as fast as I could, in order to stop my Husband & heard a Noise in the entry as tho my Husband had fell on the floor." Rushing to the doorway, Margaret Wilkins "found my Husband getting up as I believe…I stepped out at the door & said to my son you poor Child…you have killed your Father but it was dark & I did not see my son." Returning to the room where the argument began, Mrs. Wilkins and her daughter Hannah found Mr. Wilkins sitting on the floor "with a wound in his Head & bleeding." Apparently, Israel had struck his father with some blunt object, probably a piece of firewood, with considerable force and then disappeared into the dark. Now in a full-blown panic, Mrs. Wilkins asked their neighbor Edward Carter to help care for her injured husband until Doctor John Hale of Hollis arrived, who also served in the New Hampshire's General Assembly and as a Justice of the Peace for Hillsborough County.[12]

When Hale examined his patient in the dim light, he discovered that Mr. Wilkins had suffered a severe gash on the left side of his head approximately three inches long and one inch deep that probably fractured the man's skull and caused serious internal damage to his brain. With the severe limitations of eighteenth-century medicine, there was little Hale could do except attempt to clean the wound, apply fresh linen or cotton bandages, and perhaps administer opium in a glass of rum or hard cider to dull the pain. According to Margaret, her husband "seemed to be in a sort of a Stupid condition & in about an hour…he was taken with Fits…and he continued until Tuesday evening following, about 11 o'Clock & then he died."[13]

While Doctor Hale could not save his patient's life, his duty as a Justice of the Peace also required him to investigate the suspicious circumstances of Israel Wilkins' death. On November 25, after Israel Wilkins Sr. had been buried, an inquest was held in Amherst, leaving no doubt that a heated family argument had escalated into a case of patricide. A few days later, on December 4, 1772 the *New-Hampshire Gazette* reported that the fugitive Israel Wilkins "was apprehended by the order of the Worshipful Samuel Hobart, Esq; and after Examination committed to Amherst Jail." Now instead of worrying about paying off his debts, Wilkins had to face the serious possibility that his own life was in jeopardy.

From a legal standpoint, the Wilkins case was the first capital trial in the history of Hillsborough County, and as an incident of patricide, one of the few in New Hampshire's early history.[14] But the only other known case of patricide in eighteenth-century New Hampshire allegedly occurred in Exeter in the autumn of 1794, when Jack Johnson murdered his father in a drunken rage and buried the body in a barn cellar. Johnson then went to Portsmouth and joined the crew of a vessel commanded by Captain Nathaniel Boardman. Soon after leaving port, the young man was overcome by his guilty conscience, confessed his crime to the captain, and threw himself overboard, never to be seen again. According to one historian of Exeter writing nearly a century later, "no legal investigation was thought necessary, and the wretched story of this parricide and suicide does not appear on our criminal records, but has come down to us only by imperfect tradition." There are very few scraps of evidence to substantiate this legend; a John Johnson (Jack was clearly a nickname) was married in Exeter in January 1789, and contemporary newspapers reveal that Captain Boardman did indeed sail out of Portsmouth on the brig *Nancy* between 1795 and 1799.[15] But the Wilkins case remains the best documented patricide case in New Hampshire before 1800.

In December 1772, the colonial authorities wasted little time in indicting Israel Wilkins for murder of his father:

> *The Jurors for our Lord the King upon their oaths do present that Israel Wilkins late of Hollis in said County of Hillsborough, Yeoman, not having the fear of God before his Eyes but being moved and seduced by the instigation of the Devil on the twenty-first day of November A.D. 1772…with force and arms feloniously and of his Malice beforethought did make an assault upon the Body of one Israel Wilkins Senior of Hollis…with a certain billet of wood of the value of three pence did voluntarily…smite and strike in and upon his left temple thereby giving him a mortal wound…of which the said Israel Wilkins Senior thereafter languished for the space of three days…and at the expiration of said three days, the said Israel Wilkins died of the said mortal wound at Hollis aforesaid. And so the Jurors…upon their Oaths…say that…Israel Wilkins…did kill and murder against the peace of our said Lord the King his Crown and dignity.*

In response to the indictment, Wilkins' pleaded not guilty and "put himself upon the County for Trial."[17] The trial to determine Wilkins' fate, however, was delayed until the Hillsborough County Superior Court reconvened at Amherst nine months later in September 1773. By this point, the defendant was fortunate enough to be represented by twenty-nine year old lawyer John Lowell from Newburyport, Massachusetts. Despite his young age, Lowell was already a well-respected jurist of his day; he graduated from Harvard in 1760 and within several years was admitted to the bar in Massachusetts and New Hampshire, where he developed a busy practice. In 1773, Lowell's success as an attorney was demonstrated by a three-story mansion he built on High Street in Newburyport. Decades later during the 1790s, Lowell was named the Chief Judge of the First Federal Circuit Court in Boston by President Washington, and according to an obituary after his death in 1802, Lowell possessed "an understanding acute and penetrating...a mind enriched by literature and improved by observation" and "an eloquence impetuous, yet fascinating and impressive."[18]

These qualities are noticeable in Lowell's memoranda from the trial, which have survived amongst his voluminous papers at Harvard. Whether Lowell was appointed by the court to defend Wilkins or perhaps he took on the case because of its unique aspects is unclear; what also may have facilitated his travel to New Hampshire for a lengthy period of time in 1773 was that Lowell's first wife, Sarah, died in May 1772, and Lowell would not remarry until May 1774.[19] In his remarks to the jury and Judges Meseach Weare, William Parker, and Leverett Hubbard on September 16, 1773, Lowell attempted to win their sympathy:

> *May it please your Honours & you Gentlemen of the Jury...This trial has already taken up so much of your time that I am afraid you look forward with pain when you consider that you are yet to hear a further argument in behalf of the Prisoner as well as the case closed on the part of the Crown but the importance of this Trial to the Prisoner as well as the Public I hope will apologize for the length of it...'Tis indeed Gentlemen a solemn business in which we are all this day engaged...the life of a fellow Subject was metted to our Care...*

A close examination of Lowell's trial notes reveals that while he could not deny that Mr. Wilkins "came to his death by some violent means," he was determined to instill doubt into the minds of the jury exactly how that wound was inflicted and the slim evidence that Israel Wilkins' crime was premeditated "led into the field of uncertainty &

conjecture." The lack of "violent presumption" made Lowell hopeful the "killing may be reduced to that species of Homicide which is called Manslaughter." Lowell also did his best to play on the conscience of the jury and remind them of their civic duty: "Let me observe here that you are to pay regard only to the evidence offer'd you in Court…you are not to try him on any stories you may have heard abroad." In his closing statement, Lowell warned the jurors, if they allowed local gossip about the case to influence their verdict, "in my opinion you would yourselves be guilty not of Perjury only but of Murder itself."[20] Lowell's arguments were apparently persuasive, for the jury found Israel Wilkins guilty of manslaughter. At this critical juncture, John Lowell made a brilliant legal move which in all likelihood saved his client from being hanged.

According to the official record of the trial, the three judges asked Israel Wilkins why the "Sentence of Death should not be passed upon him." His attorney cleverly responded that given the circumstances of the case, Wilkins should be granted the "benefit of clergy." This was an obscure legal loophole that originated in medieval England when priests who committed a serious crime were allowed to be tried in an ecclesiastical court instead of a secular one, which often resulted in more lenient sentences. As the centuries passed and King Henry VIII broke away from the Catholic faith and established the Church of England, this exemption was extended to any defendant who was literate, a minister or clerk. During that era, it was also decreed that the "benefit of clergy" would only be granted to persons charged with their first felony, and never again, and as a result a rather gruesome and painful practice came into existence. To make sure these offenders could never again be granted the benefit of clergy, they were branded with a hot iron on the brawn of their left thumb with the letter such as "T" or M", depending what their offense was, leaving a permanent and painful reminder of their criminal past.

By the early eighteenth century, when the English colonies in America were thriving, this legal privilege had been extended to all subjects of the Crown on both sides of the Atlantic who were convicted of their first "clergyable" felonies including manslaughter, cases in which the intent to murder the victim was absent.[21] The use of the seemingly antiquated practice of "benefit of clergy" was actually quite common across colonial New Hampshire and beyond. In April 1744, two Irishmen in Portsmouth named Tolly Daniel and Daniel Bourne were convicted of manslaughter in the death of Benjamin Hill. According to the April 23, 1744 issue of the *Boston Post-Boy*, both men were "branded with the Letter T, on the brawny part of the left thumb." In September 1769 in Portsmouth, a ship's captain, Morris Cavenaugh, beat young George Henderson so severely that he died soon after. Cavenaugh was ultimately he was found guilty of manslaughter, pleaded the benefit of clergy, and was branded, according the *Boston Evening Post* on October 9, 1769.

A few years before Israel Wilkins was tried for patricide in Amherst, an even more sensational case in neighboring Massachusetts also involved the benefit of clergy. On the night of March 5, 1770 a hostile encounter between British soldiers and a rowdy group of Bostonians erupted into violence, leaving three civilians dead on the spot, and three more that eventually died from their wounds. While the "Boston Massacre" became the stuff of legend, less well-known is that months later John Adams served as the defense attorney during the trial of eight British soldiers and one officer in December 1770. Two of them, Hugh Montgomery and Matthew Kilroy, were found guilty of manslaughter and pleaded the benefit of clergy, based upon John Adams advice. The two soldiers were branded on their thumbs and returned to the ranks. That same month in Boston, a sailor named John King was also found guilty of manslaughter and "the prisoner was immediately branded in Court, and then dismissed."[22]

Three years later, on September 17, 1773, Israel Wilkins' life was spared and he was sentenced to be "burned with a hot Iron in the form of a letter T on the brawny part of the Thumb of his left hand, and it is further considered that the said Israel Wilkins forfeit all his Goods and Chattels to the King." These events naturally attracted the attention of many local citizens, including farmer Matthew Patten of Bedford, who wrote in his journal: "I stayed and heard the Tryal of Israel Wilkens for Killing his father Israel being the first Capital Tryal in the County he was found guilty of manslaughter he was branded the next day with the letter T on the...hand." Wilkins would not be the last man in colonial New Hampshire to be granted the benefit of clergy; on Christmas Day in 1775, John Patten and Thomas Shirley of Chester got into a heated argument at a local tavern and Patten cut Shirley on the head with a broken scythe blade he was taking to a blacksmith to be repaired. Shirley eventually died from his wounds on February 1, 1776 and John Patten was convicted of manslaughter in September 1776, and nearly three years to the day that Israel Wilkins found himself in the same situation, Patten was branded at the Superior Court of Hillsborough County.[23]

What was it like to be branded? According to those who have endured it, after the initial pain, the burning sensation reportedly lingered for several minutes after the hot iron was pressed to the skin, and the hand in question was sore for a few days.[24] In addition to the physical pain, this whole process was obviously intended to be humiliating; while Israel Wilkins was certainly lucky to have escaped the gallows, he was now marked for life as a criminal, and worse, a man who had killed his own father. The relationship between Israel and his mother and sister must have been strained, and it seems a logical conclusion that he was a pariah in Hollis. But the story isn't that simple. After 1772, Israel Wilkins apparently returned to Hollis and continued to have legal problems. One court document preserved at the New Hampshire State Archives from 1774 shows that Josiah Blood sued Israel and his brother-in-law, Israel Kenney, after they neglected to pay twenty pounds Blood had lent them in 1771. A tax list from January 1775 also shows that Israel Wilkins was still living on the west side of Hollis, and that year paid a hefty seven pounds and two pence in taxes to authorities. [25]

Like the majority of young able-bodied men in Hollis during the 1770s, Wilkins also served in the local militia. On the morning of April 19, 1775, word spread north to New Hampshire of a bloody engagement between colonial troops and British regulars in Lexington and Concord, Massachusetts, only about twenty-five miles to the south. Within a few hours, the Hollis militia company shouldered their flintlock muskets and began the march to join the fight against the British. Remarkably, a roster of these men has survived and Israel Wilkins' name appears on it, as does his brother-in-law Israel Kenney and older brother Bray Wilkins. Revolutionary War records show that Israel Wilkins served in the Hollis company for about six days, and in total, marched eighty-four miles to Boston and back in April 1775.[26] While Israel likely returned home, documents reveal that Bray Wilkins and Israel Kenney enlisted in the American army for eight months and like many New Hampshire soldiers, fought in the battle of Bunker Hill on June 17, 1775. Kenney even lost a knapsack during the bloody action, and served in the First New Hampshire Regiment in the Continental Army in 1776.[27]

But after this brief appearance during one of the most legendary events in American history, Israel Wilkins abruptly vanishes from the historical record, as did the practice of branding, which died out before the end of the eighteenth century in New Hampshire. Did Israel Wilkins remain in Hollis to care for his elderly mother or did he die sometime between 1775 and 1776? It is worth noting that no Israel Wilkins appears on the New Hampshire Association Test of 1776, which adult males were obligated to sign to prove their loyalty to the American cause. A search of contemporary newspapers and the first federal census in 1790 reveals nothing as well. Whatever his fate was, it is certain that the stinging mark of hot iron on his thumb followed Israel Wilkins to his grave.

Endnotes: Chapter Two

1. Samuel Thomas Worcester, *History of the Town of Hollis...* (57-58).
2. Massachusetts Vital Records to 1850 (Online Database: NewEnglandAncestors.org, New England Historic Genealogical Society, 2001-2008), accessed on December 28, 2009.
3. *New Hampshire State Papers, Volume XII* (Concord: 1943) 614-615.
4. *History of the Town of Hollis...*, 120-121 and *New-Hampshire Gazette*, May 27, 1768.
5. *New Hampshire State Papers, Volume XVIII* (Concord: 1943) 51-56.
6. *New-Hampshire Gazette*, November 8, 1771.
7. http://www.nhptv.org/wild/karnerwhitepineriot.asp, accessed December 31, 2009.
8. *New-Hampshire Gazette*, May 8, 1772.
9. Hillsborough County Court Records, Case File Numbers 000918 and 001484, New Hampshire State Archives.
10. Testimony of Margaret Wilkins and Hannah Kenney, November 25, 1772, Papers of John Lowell (MS Am 1582), Houghton Library, Harvard College Library, Harvard University.
11. *The Laws of New Hampshire, Volume One, Province Period 1679–1702* (Manchester: John B. Clarke Co., 1904) 14-15, and *Records and Files of the Quarterly Courts of Essex County, Volume IV*, 186-187.
12. Worcester, *History of the Town of Hollis*, 211, and *New-Hampshire Gazette*, February 27, 1767.
13. Mary C. Gillet, *The Army Medical Department 1775-1818* (Washington, D.C: Government Printing Office, 1981) 15-17.
14. Elaine Forman Crane, *Killed Strangely : The Death of Rebecca Cornell* (Ithaca: Cornell University Press, 2002) 98.
15. *New-Hampshire Gazette*, January 11, 1831, July 24, 1832; *Portsmouth Journal*, September 3, 1831; *Farmer's Cabinet*, January 9, 1845.
16. *New York Times*, July 8, 1869; Charles Bell, *History of the Town of Exeter New Hampshire* (Exeter: 1988) 55, 404-405 and *New-Hampshire Gazette*, June 9, 1795, November 20, 1799.
17. "Benefit of Clergy", J.E. Sargent LL.D, *The Granite Monthly* (4) 1881, 79-80.
18. Clifford K. Shipton, *Biographical Sketches of Those Who Attended Harvard College in the Classes 1756-1760 (Sibley's Harvard Graduates, Volume 14)* (Boston: Massachusetts Historical Society, 1968) 650-651; *Boston Gazette*, May 10, 1802.
19. *New-Hampshire Gazette*, May 8, 1772, and Massachusetts Vital Records to 1850 (Online Database: NewEnglandAncestors.org, New England Historic Genealogical Society, 2001-2008), accessed on January 16, 2010; Memoranda in case of Israel Wilkins, Container 764, Papers of John Lowell (MS Am 1582), Houghton Library, Harvard College Library, Harvard University.
20. Memoranda in case of Israel Wilkins, Container 764, Papers of John Lowell (MS Am 1582), Houghton Library, Harvard College Library, Harvard University.
21. George W. Dalzell, *Benefit of Clergy in America & Related Matters* (Winston-Salem, North Carolina: John F. Blair Publisher, 1955) 11-26.
22. *New-York Mercury*, March 22, 1756; *New-Hampshire Gazette*, October 6, 13, 1769; *Boston Evening Post*, December 3, 1770; *Boston Gazette*, December 17, 1770.
23. *The Diary of Matthew Patten of Bedford, NH from 1754 to 1788* (Concord: Rumford Press, 1903) 308, 355; Benjamin Chase, *History of Old Chester from 1719 to 1869* (Auburn, NH: 1869) 590-591.
24. *Benefit of Clergy*, Dalzell, 249.
25. Worcester, *History of the Town of Hollis*, 138.

26. Worcester, *History of the Town of Hollis*, 147-148, and Ezra Stearns, *Genealogical and Family History of the State of New Hampshire* (New York: Lewis Publishing Company, 1908) Volume I: 35.

27.Worcester, *History of the Town of Hollis*, 151, 155 , 164, 347

Chapter Three

"Marked out by Fate"
The Death Penalty Comes to Dover

As the fateful year 1788 began, feelings of uncertainty and restlessness pervaded the fledgling United States. While American independence had finally been won in 1783 after eight grueling years of war, how to effectively govern this new nation and simultaneously protect the liberties of the people remained a hotly contested subject. The vociferous debate to replace the inadequate Articles of Confederation with a new Constitution, drafted in Philadelphia the previous summer, echoed from the plantations of Georgia to the hardscrabble farms and bustling ports of New England. On the morning of Monday, February 4, 1788, only about a week before the delegates of New Hampshire were to gather in Exeter to discuss and vote upon this very topic, Revolutionary War veteran Elisha Thomas left his wife Sarah and their children in New Durham and began the journey south to Portsmouth to conduct some business. But Elisha would never reach his destination, and soon his entire family was plunged into a sinister course of events that must rank among the most tragic in New Hampshire's history.

Born in Newmarket around 1746, Elisha Thomas was an able young farmer when the American Revolution began. After the port of Boston was closed to trade by the British authorities in 1774 in retaliation for the infamous "tea party", Elisha was one of many Newmarket residents who signed a petition on October 31 of that year to "express their sentiments of Condolence to said Suffering Bostonians...in the Common Cause of Liberty." After hostilities officially broke out between the colonists and British regulars in April 1775, Elisha enlisted in Colonel Enoch Poor's regiment on May 27, which was the second military unit to be raised in New Hampshire that spring. The hours before Elisha's departure for military service must have also been an anxious time for his young wife Sarah. When farmer Matthew Patten's family of Bedford, New Hampshire learned his son intended to join the militia marching to Boston, Patten recorded in his diary that "our Girls sit up all night baking bread and fitting things for him." It is easy to imagine Sarah Thomas did the same for her husband the night before he marched off to war.[1]

For these citizens turned soldiers, the first challenge before entering combat with the British Regulars was finding a working flintlock musket. While some farmers did own "fowlers", guns that were for primarily for hunting and not military service, it is clear that at the beginning of the American Revolution, many aspiring soldiers did not even own their own firearm. In December 1775, for example, Matthew Patten observed in his diary that when twelve men from Bedford assembled to join the army, "there was 7 guns lacking to equip them." Consequently, many towns were forced to procure old, retooled, and poorly made weapons. While it is not known whether Elisha Thomas possessed his own musket, or received one from the colony, the substandard quality of his gun would eventually come back to haunt him.

Once they were outfitted, Elisha and the rest of Poor's regiment marched south to Massachusetts shortly after the bloody battle of Bunker Hill on June 17.[2] They spent the rest of that fateful summer with the colonial forces besieging Boston, and his enlistment ended at the end of 1775 and like many others, he returned home. Less than a year later, however, on September 20, 1776, Elisha re-enlisted as a private in the militia regiment commanded by Colonel Thomas Tash of Newmarket, which was organized to reinforce George Washington's struggling Continental Army fighting for its survival around New York City.

Thomas Tash was himself a fairly prominent figure in eighteenth-century New Hampshire. As an officer during the Seven Years' War, he commanded a battalion of 250 men at Fort No. 4 on the Connecticut River, and later engaged the French forces in combat. After that conflict, Tash lived comfortably in Newmarket, where he was affluent enough to be involved in the slave trade. In the December 22, 1758 issue of the *New-Hampshire Gazette*, the following advertisement appeared: "A Negro Woman 22 Years of Age, capable of doing any sort of Household Work, to be sold. Enquire of Major Tash of New-Market, or of the Printer hereof." Tash also played a substantial role in the settlement of New Durham during the 1760s, where a road still bears his name today.[3]

But Tash's military service was far from over. On December 15, 1774, he led a band of local minutemen in a raid on the royal garrison at Fort William and Mary in Newcastle, New Hampshire, which provided an abundance of gunpowder and weapons that were scarce across the colonies. In 1775, Tash was elected to the provincial House of Representatives, and due to his previous military experience, was a natural candidate to lead American troops into battle against the British. On September 24, 1776, the regiments of Tash and Nahum Baldwin totaling 1000 men began their march across New England towards New York with orders "to march...forward with all possible speed." Documents that have survived in the New Hampshire State Papers and the Papers of George Washington provide us with a remarkable insight into what Elisha Thomas' experience was like in the Revolutionary War. Arriving in Hartford on October 8, the New Hampshire troops moved on to Stamford the following day, where Tash reported:

> We had no Camp equipage such as pots, kittles...Neither was it in the power of the State of New Hampshire to procure any as there was no tin – when I arrived at Stamford Colo. Welch was there & bro't me a letter from General Washington directing me to procure quarters for my regmt...he likewise directed to me to furnish our selfs with Camp utencels from the Inhabitants if posable – I applied to the Committee to furnish me with pots...but Colo Baldwin had got their before me & had got almost all to be had, they made out to get me 3 & I sent Rownd for several miles & procured a small number more...[4]

With only a few cooking implements for five hundred men, Elisha Thomas and the rest of his regiment endured these hardships as the nights got colder with each passing day. On October 13, General Washington sent General Orders to his ragtag army:

> As the Enemy seem now to be endeavoring to strike some stroke...the General most earnestly conjures, both Officers and Men, if they have any Love for their Country, and Concern for its Liberties; regard to the safety of their Parents, Wives, Children, and Countrymen; that they will act with Bravery & Spirit, becoming the Cause in which they are engaged; And to encourage, and animate them so to do, there is every Advantage of Ground and Situation, so that if we do not conquer, it must be our own faults – How much better will it be to die honorable, fighting in the field, than to return home, covered with shame and disgrace; even if the cruelty of the Enemy should allow you to return? A brave and gallant behavior for a few days, and patience under some little hardships, may save our Country, and enable us to go into Winter Quarters with safety and honor.[5]

The very day Washington communicated this inspiring message to his troops, he contacted Colonel Tash about sending his New Hampshire regiment north to secure the area around Fishkill on the Hudson River:

> Sir: Since I wrote to you by Lieutt. Colo. Welch upon the Subject of fixing on Quarters for your Troops, I have received from the Committee of Safety for this State, such an account of its

alarming Situation, owing to the Number of Disaffected, together with the little Confidence that can be placed on the militia of some of the Counties, that I find it necessary to order a part of the New Hampshire Troops to their Assistance, and do therefore direct you to march your Regiment with all possible to dispatch to Fish Kills, where you will receive further directions from the Committee. I think it will be proper to send an Officer forward, to give the Committee notice of your coming, that they may assign you the places where it will be most suitable to post your men.[6]

Tash immediately obeyed Washington's order, but when his soldiers arrived at Fishkill, he was informed by local authorities that they only needed two companies of troops. He ordered the remainder of his men, including Elisha Thomas, back to Peekskill, where they established guard posts some eight miles along the eastern bank of the Hudson in order to "watch the motion of the Enemy." Colonel Tash closed out his letter to New Hampshire by proudly reporting that his soldiers were "almost all in good health and high spirits."[7] But for Elisha Thomas, that was all about to change.

Sometime during November 1776 (the exact date remains unknown), a terrible accident changed Elisha's life forever while he was stationed at Verplancks Point on the Hudson. While loading his flintlock musket during an alarm, he discovered the lead ball in the cartridge was too large for the caliber of his weapon and while ramming it down the barrel, the bullet became lodged in the bore. In an attempt to fix this dilemma, Thomas was foolishly ordered by his commander Captain John Gordon to fire his weapon to clear the barrel. As the flint of his musket struck the steel and ignited the gunpowder in the pan, suddenly the entire barrel burst and sent hot iron flying in all directions. In the blink of an eye, Elisha's left hand holding the weapon up was "torn to Pieces...and his Thumb carried away, and his Fingers & hand rendered almost wholly useless." Thomas was immediately brought to the regimental surgeon, and then probably to the larger American military hospital at Peekskill. But there was little the doctors could do for him except to bandage the wound, stop the bleeding, and perhaps administer some wine or opium to dull the excruciating pain. He was quite fortunate not to have developed an infection from his injury, since the quality of healthcare Revolutionary War soldiers received was very poor by today's standards. Elisha Thomas was discharged from Tash's regiment on November 30, 1776, and began making his way across the war-torn landscape back to New Hampshire.[8]

By the early 1780s as the war continued on without him, Elisha and his family had relocated to New Durham in Strafford County, where he was struggling to provide for his growing family. To make ends meet, Thomas served as the constable for the town, notifying townspeople of upcoming meetings and reminding them to pay their taxes. Coincidentally, after the war ended Colonel Tash also moved to New Durham, where he became a town selectman. The evidence suggests that Elisha and his former commander were on good terms after the war.[9] In September 1787 when Elisha applied for a pension from the new American government, Colonel Tash wrote an affidavit certifying that Thomas had served in his regiment and that he had been severely wounded by an unfortunate accident. Elisha's petition to the General Assembly of New Hampshire paints a vivid picture of his life after the Revolutionary War and the suffering he endured:

> Humbly Sheweth Elisha Thomas of New Durham in the County of Strafford, Yeoman, that in the year 1776, he inlisted into Capt. John Gordon's Company, as a private Soldier, in the Regiment under the Command of Col Thomas Tash of this State, in the federal Service, that in the Month of November in the same year, at the Alarm at Planks Point on North River State of New York in Discharging his Gun, his Left hand, was torn to Pieces, by bursting of said Gun...by Means whereof, he suffered the most excruciating Pain for a long Time, & has ever Since been in a great Measure, deprived of the Means of gaining a Subsistence for himself & a numerous Family of Children – Wherefore Your Petitioner most humbly Prays this honorable Assembly to take his Case in their wise and equitable Consideration, and make him such Grant, or Allowance as Justice and Humanity may dictate, for the Relief of himself & a Poor & Indegent Family and as in Duty Bound he will ever Pray – Elisha Thomas[10]

Elisha's desperate plea to the government was heard, and on December 1, 1787, he was granted a pension of twenty-four shillings a month, retroactive to the date he was discharged from the army in 1776. Certainly this welcome news brought hope to Elisha's struggling family as the long winter began, but on a cold winter's day a few months later, the promise of better future would be swept away in a bloody tide of violence and tragedy.

While on his way to Portsmouth on the morning of February 4, 1788, Elisha stopped at the home of Colonel Tash. There he was met by Captain Peter Drowne, who had led a company of foot soldiers in Stephen Peabody's regiment in Rhode Island in 1778. (It is possible that Thomas and Drowne had actually known each other as early as 1774, when they had both signed the petition in Newmarket mentioned earlier.)[11] Nevertheless, the two men had become close friends since moving to New Durham, and on that chilly morning they proceeded to Randall's tavern to enjoy a dram of rum.

They were soon joined by Colonel Tash and Joshua Davis, who had probably also fought in the Revolution. After one glass of rum became several, Davis and Elisha got into a heated argument and soon the men were exchanging blows.

According to one contemporary account, Thomas "having taken a stone into his fist [which considering his wartime injury could only have been his right hand], was dealing his blows with a great deal of avidity, when Captain Drowne, slipped in between them, and taking Thomas at one side of the room, endeavored, by soft words to cool down his resentment, and to dissuade him from persevering in a conduct so alarming." In a drunken rage, Elisha then withdrew a knife concealed in his clothes and suddenly plunged the blade into Peter Drowne's chest. Thomas was chased out of the tavern but managed to escape into the countryside while Drowne died from his wound later that day. Elisha was apprehended on February 6 and brought in irons to the jail in Dover, the seat of Strafford County. On Friday, February 8, Peter Drowne's body was "honorably interred — his body being borne by six militia captains — a great concourse of people attending this solemn procession, deeply affected with the melancholy end of so good a man."[12] But for Elisha and his poor family, the accidental murder of Captain Drowne only marked the beginning of their troubles.

On Sunday, February 24, a distraught Sarah Thomas left New Durham with her youngest child to visit her husband in Dover, leaving her five oldest children including Joseph, eleven, Hannah, nine, Sarah, seven, and five-year-old James home alone. After the youngsters had gone to bed, they were awakened between ten and eleven o'clock by the intense heat and rustling sound of a fire that had quickly engulfed their home. The following heartbreaking account of the inferno appeared in a local newspaper only a few days later:

> *The fire took place by means of the chimney, which, as is usual in the country, was built of stone and slabs; the slabs taking fire at the top communicated itself to the house, which was all in flames before the children were alarmed. The eldest, a son, immediately jumped through a window and escaped destruction; another leaped out of bed, and attempted to follow his brother, but the flames intercepted him — he therefore, with three others, perished in the flames. They were heard to scream for help, but none could be afforded. The house being at some distance from any other, was consumed before any help could be collected to extinguish the flames.*
> *The effect which a scene so tragical must have upon the humane mind can better be imagined than expressed — but, who can paint the mother as she stood! — the impression*

*these woeful tidings made upon beggars description – her heart already torn by affliction,
and her frame tottering under a load of woes, was poorly able to support a shock so
alarming, or taste of a cup, whose contents must petrify imagination itself! Her husband,
it is said, could not support the stroke, but seemed as though his life was going to pay the
forfeit before justice demanded it. Here we must let the curtain fall. What scenes are yet
to be represented as connected with this tragical history, must for the present remain in
the dark. Should the curtain be drawn again, the probability is, that the conclusion will
be equally tragical.*[13]

This inevitable conclusion would come to pass, but not before another harrowing incident had taken place. In early March, a grief-stricken Sarah Thomas was returning from a trip to the Dover jail when her horse was startled and collided with a passing sleigh, causing a piece of timber to strike her with enough force to break three ribs, and "it was with great difficulty she escaped being torn to pieces." While she was recovering from this painful injury, in April Elisha was quickly found guilty of the murder of Captain Drowne, despite the efforts of his attorney Jonathan Rawson, one of the most respected attorneys in the state at the time.[14] He was sentenced to be hanged in Dover a month later on May 22 between ten o'clock and noon, but his lawyer quickly sent off a desperate petition for a reprieve to state leader John Sullivan:

*Your Petitioner might here suggest, that he has an Innocent Wife, & two remaining
Children, whom the hand of public Justice is about to bereave of their only hope of
Support. – for whom he feels the most earnest Sollicitude – & whom he should wish
might be so left, as to be above necessity – or compulsion to depend upon the cold hands
of Charity, – that as he is about to quit the World, he would also wish to do justice to his
fellow Mortals & thereby be enabled to die in peace with all men. – From the Benevolence
Humanity and mercy, which constitute so conspicuous a part of the Characters of your
Excellency & Honors, he is fully sensible, that your Goodness will add a few to the days
of life now allotted him; and while he approaches the throne of Grace and most devoutly
implores the pardon of all his Sins, he shall not cease ardently to pray, that Heaven will
be pleased to bless your Excellency and Honors – with Wisdom Health & long and
uninterrupted happiness, and his latest breath while employed in requesting mercy for
himself will also implore the benediction of Heaven you & your Posterity –
Dover April 28th 1788   Elisha Thomas*[15]

Only two days after signing this humbling document, Elisha did not help his case for clemency. Using a tool covertly slipped into his cell, Elisha removed his iron cuffs and crawled up the chimney and began chipping away through the bricks to create an escape hatch. But "by the time he had got a hole through the chimney, he found the morning so far advanced, that it would be needless for him to prosecute his plan any farther...he therefore, with a heavy heart...crept down, sad and slow, to his dreary habitation again."[16] On May 16, the condemned man submitted yet another desperate plea to the authorities desiring to obtain "a short respite from the dreadful sentence pronounced against him...a small addition to the few number of days allotted him upon the stage of existence." The citizens of Dover were apparently sympathetic to his case, and on May 19, only three days before the day appointed for Elisha's execution, two more petitions were sent to the governor. One bore the signatures of over forty gentlemen, and notably, a separate document signed by many "ladies of the town of Dover" eloquently expressed a desire to have their own voice in public affairs:

> *That while the Public Concerns of the State have convened your Excellency & Honors together, a Request from the tender Sex, while it may appear unexpected, cannot when the Principles of it are thoroughly examined, appear improper or extraordinary. There are most certainly Times & Seasons when to be silent would betray a want of the Sensibility, so often attributed to the Sex; and not to speak, would discover a total disregard, to Sympathy, Communication, & the finest Feelings of Humanity – this therefore being not only a suitable Time, but a proper Season to call forth those Affections. – The Subscribers most earnestly, & ardently, would plead with your Excellency & Honors, in Favor of the unhappy Convict, under sentence of Death in Prison at Dover, and entreat a small Respite from the Execution of the awful Sentence pronounced against him.*

Upon reading these pleas for mercy, John Sullivan and his advisors decided to postpone the execution until Tuesday, June 3. That morning, after embracing Sarah for the last time, with the help of his lawyer, the grief stricken Revolutionary War veteran composed his own compelling narrative titled *The Last Words and Dying Speech of Elisha Thomas*, which was printed as a broadside and sold to the public on the streets of Dover and Portsmouth. It has been transcribed exactly as it appeared in 1788:

> I, Elisha Thomas, now in the Prison in *Dover*, under sentence of Death, upon the charge of murdering Captain *Peter Drowne*, on the fourth of February last; — willing and desirous to confess to the world, what I recollect of that unhappy event— as a man just launching into the eternal and invisible world, being all I

recollect of that unfortunate day. On the morning of that day being bound to *Portsmouth*, I stopped at the house of Col. *Thomas Tash*, where Captain Drowne lived, and after some conversation, we agreed to go to Mr. *Randall's*, about half a mile distant, in order to procure a dram; we went and drank as near as I can recollect, one pint and a half of Rum, and was about to separate with all that friendship that had subsisted between us for five years, which…was very intimate; as we were ready to set out we saw a company consisting of Col. *Tash*, *Joshua Davis*, with Col. Tash's two sons, coming up to the house; we had immediately something more to drink; after a little while we began to pull up from the floor, and unluckily *Davis* and I had some words; and soon after my heels were knocked up, and I was thrown upon the floor; I was immediately shoved behind the door, and as Capt. *Drowne* came to speak to me, his heels were somehow or other tripped up;— the witnesses against me swore, that *Drowne* immediately pulled off his coat, and that I went out of the door, and *Drowne* followed; I solemnly declare, I know not in what manner I got out, not where I was till nearly one rod from the door, I then turned round and saw Capt. *Drowne* standing in the entry, and saw him stagger; at the time I turned round and saw Capt. *Drowne, Thomas Tash* had taken hold of my shoulder, and I cut his fingers; I supposed *Drowne*'s staggering was owing to liquor;— I immediately heard somebody call out, "*Drowne is killed, Thomas has killed him.*" I should have returned to the door, had not Col. *Tash* exclaimed, "*then I'll kill him*" and immediately pursued me with an ax, but was stopt by Mr. *Randall*; I run to avoid being killed a little way down the road, and then returned and went home; the next morning I surrendered myself to justice.

I solemnly declare I had no enmity against Capt. *Drowne,* nor do I know how it happened, unless it was done it the scuffle getting me out of doors; nor could I have harboured a thought of killing my intimate friend, companion, and benefactor; and I most sincerely believe had not the company before mentioned ever came to the house, that Capt. *Drowne* would still have been living, and that I should not have been under the sentence soon to be executed upon me; to their violent proceedings I am afraid is to be attributed the loss of both our lives.

The stories that have been propagated round the country, that I confessed that Mr. *Kenniston* and myself had formerly murdered a man, are void of foundation, and as a dying man I declare, nothing of that kind ever happened. Other stories told about myself alone are equally false.

The Court, Council, and Jury I firmly believe determined according to the law and evidence given to them, and I lay nothing against them. The witnesses own consciences will best determine, whether from prejudice, they did not in some parts of their testimony injure me; but I leave them to that God in whose presence I must soon, and they ere long appear.

I solemnly declare that whatever the world may say of me, that I never had any intention of taking the life of any fellow mortal, whatever: — but alas! I am now called off the stage of existence, at the age of forty-two for a crime that I should as soon thought of perpetrating upon my wife and children, as upon Capt. *Drowne*. I hope most sincerely, that my untimely end, may prove a warning to all, more especially to the rising generation, to avoid bad company, intemperance, and giving way to unruly passions, which I confess have proved my ruin.

I most sincerely thank the Reverend Clergy in the vicinity, for their attention and kindness to me, as well before as since my conviction, for their kind cautions and wholesome instructions, from time to time given to me. To the Rev. Mr. *Gray* in particular, I cannot neglect returning the unfeigned thanks of gratitude, for his pious warnings and admonitions, as well in private as from the desk, the few crimes I times I have had the opportunity to hear him, and for his consolations from time to time offered.

I cannot forget to return my thanks to the Gentlemen and Ladies of the town of *Dover*, who so humanely petitioned his Excellency and council, for a short respite of my execution— may they enjoy long and uninterrupted happiness here, and may the best of Heaven's blessings await them hereafter. — Nor must I neglect the same testimonials of gratitude, to Mr. Footman and family for the many kindnesses I have received from them during my confinement.

I now recommend my soul to the all-merciful Creator of all Worlds and all Creatures, most ardently imploring forgiveness, of my manifold transgressions, and that the redeemer would most graciously receive me to the arms of his everlasting mercy, when I leave the world.

       ELISHA THOMAS.

Dover Prison, June 3, 1788.
Signed in presence of
Jonathan Rawson

On June 3, Elisha made his final march to the gallows at the foot of Swazey's Hill near the Cocheco River (now in the vicinity of Henry Law Park in Dover.) In Portsmouth on that very morning, George Osborne, printer of the *New-Hampshire Spy*, observed: "Prayers have been used in the several churches and congregations in this vicinity...for the unfortunate Mr. *Elisha Thomas*, who is to be executed this day." Within a few hours, perhaps 6,000 spectators had assembled to watch the hanging, closely monitored by a local militia regiment to prevent any unrest. The crowd watched as Elisha Thomas shook hands with the Sheriff and was then "launched into eternity!" After his body had swung from the gallows for a time, his body was placed in a simple pine coffin, and then taken up the road to the Pine Hill burial ground overlooking the community which had so passionately appealed on his behalf. Even the timing of Elisha's execution had an aspect of cruel irony. He would never have the chance to witness the ratification of the legal document which sought to preserve the ideals he had fought for during the Revolution. On June 21, 1788 in nearby Exeter, delegates narrowly voted to make New Hampshire the ninth and final state needed to ratify the new Constitution, forever changing the course of history.

Less than a month after Elisha had been executed, disturbing new details concerning his case soon came to light. On June 10, the *New-Hampshire Spy* revealed to its readers that Thomas had long been "suspected of setting fire to a Mr. Davis's barn, of Newdurham-gore, some time before his perpetrating the horrid act for which he was executed...the barn, in which was a quantity of hay, and several head of cattle, was entirely consumed." Published with this revelation was a short, but profound note Elisha had sent to Eleazar Davis, the local tax collector, shortly before his execution:

Sir,

Being about to appear before the Omniscient GOD – and being willing to obtain his forgiveness, and knowing that the only way is to confess not only to GOD, but also to the injured.

I have now to confess to you, that your opinion of my burning your barn too true. Alas it is now too late to make you any satisfaction, but by requesting your forgiveness most sincerely, with a sensible contrition of the Crime; – I have requested a merciful God to forgive the offence, but could obtain no rest, until I had made this to you.– I commend your and my own soul to that being who alone is able to save.

    Farewell forever,
    ELISHA THOMAS

This document offers a new perspective on the events which led to Peter Drowne's murder. Joshua Davis was a relative of Eleazar, and that winter morning in February 1788 at Randall's tavern, he may have accused Thomas of setting the barn on fire, which perhaps instigated the deadly drunken brawl. For Elisha's widow, the publication of this humiliating letter must have stung like salt water on a festering wound. In just a few months, Sarah Thomas had endured the destruction of her home and the deaths of four children, her husband's public execution, and had nearly been killed herself in an sleigh accident. The Thomas family had truly been, as one newspaper commented, "marked out by fate, as the peculiar objects of destruction."[17] Now the daunting task of continuing her life in the wake of such devastating tragedy had begun.

More than a half century later, on July 3, 1843, an elderly woman appeared before the probate judge of York County, Maine with a remarkable tale to tell. Her surname was now Moulton, but as a young woman she had been known as Sarah Thomas. At the age of eighty-eight, she had applied for aid from the federal government, after Congress had passed legislation allowing pensions for the remaining widows of Revolutionary War soldiers. Her application provides a unique glimpse into her life before and after the tragic events of 1788. When the first federal census was recorded two years later in 1790, Sarah Thomas was one of the very few single women living in New Durham, somehow supporting her three surviving children, including toddler James, who had been born only a few months after Elisha's execution. This must have a very difficult period for Sarah, but it is certainly a testament to her perseverance and strength. Five years later, she married George Bickford of what is now Parsonsfield, Maine, on March 21, 1795 and left the painful memories of New Hampshire behind.

For the next forty years, Sarah was an active member of the Baptist Church in Parsonsfield. After her second husband George died on June 21, 1820, Sarah married the elderly Samuel Moulton some nine years later. She was widowed for the third and last time on December 25, 1837. In 1843, in order to corroborate her story and provide further evidence of her relationship to Elisha Thomas, Sarah obtained affidavits from some of his elderly comrades-in-arms from New Hampshire that had served with him during the Revolution, including Noah Wedgewood and Eleazar Bennett. Ebenezer Bickford, her second husband's nephew, even came to her aid, recalling that as a young boy during the 1780s, "his father had lived in New Durham near the house of Elisha Thomas and knew him and his wife and children." Looking back across the vast expanse of time she had survived, Sarah's love for her first husband and her long-lost children had not faded. She admittedly "had no records or means of stating the...date of her first marriage with said Elisha Thomas," but did fondly recall that "she was nineteen years old when she married him." Perhaps Sarah shed tears when she thought of the happy, innocent days of her youth before tragedy struck.

Fortunately for Sarah, she was awarded a substantial pension and a retroactive sum totaling more than $700 that must have improved her quality of life during her final years. It remains unclear, however, when Sarah's long, harrowing journey came to an end, but the exact date of her death is irrelevant in comparison to her resilience in the face of overwhelming tragedy and hardship. During the mid-twentieth century, the crude slate slab marking Elisha's grave at Pine Hill cemetery in Dover was replaced by the Daughters of the American Revolution with an official government headstone in recognition of his military service during the American Revolution, and not the awful circumstances of his final days.[18]

Endnotes: Chapter Three

1. *Roll of The Soldiers in the Revolutionary War 1775, to May 1777*, Isaac Hammond ed. (Concord: 1885) 107, 135, 191. *The Diary of Matthew Patten of Bedford, N.H. from 1754 to 1788*, (Camden, Maine: Picton Press, 1993), 342.

2. *The Diary of Matthew Patten*, 352; *Rolls and Documents Relating to Soldiers in the Revolutionary War*, Isaac Hammond ed. (Manchester: 1889) 6.

3. *New Hampshire State Papers, Volume XIV* (Concord:) 399-400, *New Hampshire State Papers, Volume VI*, 609, *New Hampshire State Papers, Volume XI* (Concord: 1882) 582, and *New England Historical Genealogical Register*, 1907 (61) 360-371.

4. *The Papers of George Washington, Volume 6* (Charlottsville: University Press of Virginia, 1994) 387, and *Documents and Records relating to the State of New Hampshire From 1776 to 1783*, Nathaniel Bouton ed. (Concord: 1874) 387.

5. *The Papers of George Washington, Volume 6*, 552-553.

6. *The Papers of George Washington, Volume 6*, 558-559.

7. *Documents and Records relating to the State of New Hampshire From 1776 to 1783*, 388.

8. *New Hampshire State Papers, Volume XII*, Isaac Hammond ed. (Concord: 1883) 703, and *New Hampshire State Papers, Volume XVI*, Isaac Hammond ed. (Manchester: 1887) 327, 329, 473-474. For medical care during the Revolution, see Mary C. Gillet, *The Army Medical Department 1775-1818* (Washington, D.C.: 1981) 16-18, 72-74.

9. *New-Hampshire Gazette*, September 22, 1787, and also *The Town Papers of New Durham, New Hampshire* (On microfilm at the New England Historic Genealogical Society, Boston, MA)

10. *New Hampshire State Papers, Volume XII*, 703-704.

11. *New Hampshire State Papers, Volume XIV*, 462, 468.

12. *New-Hampshire Spy*, February 8, 1788, *Massachusetts Gazette*, February 29, 1788, and *The Last Words, and Dying Speech of Elisha Thomas* (Portsmouth: 1788).

13. *New-Hampshire Spy*, February 29, 1788, and Records of the First Free-Will Baptist Church, New Durham, NH, transcribed copy available at the Dover Public Library, Dover, NH.

14. *New-Hampshire Gazette*, March 12, 1788, and *New-Hampshire Spy*, April 22, 1788.

15. The original petitions are at the New Hampshire State Archives, Concord, NH.

16. *New-Hampshire Spy*, May 6, 1788.

17. *New-Hampshire Spy*, June 7, 1788, and *The Last Words, and Dying Speech of Elisha Thomas* (Portsmouth: 1788).

18. Elisha Thomas Pension File (W26277), National Archives, Washington, D.C.

Chapter Four

"My hellish design"
Rape, Race, and the Death Penalty

On a winter evening in December 1795, a young woman named Sally Messer was returning on horseback to her parent's home in New London, New Hampshire, just a few miles south of Lebanon. Suddenly, a man jumped out of the shadows in front of the horse, wrenched Sally from the saddle, and violently raped her. After the man left her alone in the night, Sally somehow found her way her home and told her distraught parents about the incident. She would eventually summon the courage to face her attacker and carry on with her life. In addition to being a tale of one woman's struggle for justice and redemption, the story of Sally Messer's rape also illuminates the topics of race and criminal justice in New Hampshire at the twilight of the eighteenth century. [1]

The young man who assaulted Sally Messer that night would soon be identified as Thomas Powers, and what is known about him primarily comes from his remarkably candid *Narrative and Confession*, one of the few autobiographical narratives penned by a person of African descent in eighteenth-century America:

> *I Thomas Powers, was born in Wallingford, Connecticut, September 15th, 17[7]6. My father's name is Thomas Powers; and my mother before her marriage was Prudy Waterman. I was the second and youngest Son of my father, with whom I lived, till I was two years old. He then put me out to live with Mr. Moses Tharp, of Norwich...where I resided one year and then returned me to my father, who, being a very pious man, endeavored to instruct me in my several duties, to God, my parents, and to all mankind, as far as my young and tender mind was capable of receiving any virtuous impressions. But I was naturally to much inclined to vice, to profit by his precepts or example; for I was very apt to pilfer and tell lies, if I thought there was any occasion.*
> *When I was nine years old, I was put out to live with Isaac Johnson, of Lebanon, (Conn.), where I lived two years, and very early began the practice of debauchery. It was here I began my career in the gratification of that corrupt and lawless passion, which has now brought me to the threshold of eternity, before my years were half numbered. Being one Sunday at home from meeting, with nobody but a young Negro woman, who lived in the house, she, enticing me to her bed...soon taught me the practice of that awful sin...for which together with disobedience to my master, and many other villaneous tricks which I*

44

used to play upon him, he often corrected me, but to so little purpose that he dismissed me from his service.

Then I returned home once more to my father, where I lived for a few months, till he, not liking my behavior, bound me out to Mr. Oliver Hyde, of Norwich, (Conn.) During my residence with him, who was a pretty kind master, I was taught to read and write a tolerable good hand; but being naturally vicious I improved my talents...to very bad purposes. I used to make a point of pilfering whenever I could; for when I saw an opportunity, the devil, or some other evil spirit, always gave me a strong inclination...

In the year 1789, I broke open a store in Norwich...took a few articles of goods and fifteen dollars in Cash. In the next place, knowing my present master, Oliver Lathrop, to have on hand a large sum of money, I supposed that I might take about twenty dollars and neither of us fare the worse. I, however, soon repented of this bargain; for being discovered, I was forced to return the money, and rake a few stripes on my back; but if I had received my just deserts I might possibly have escaped the fate, which now awaits me.

In the year 1793, I moved with my master from Norwich, in Connecticut, to Lebanon, in New Hampshire, where I soon run the length of my chain, and compleated my villainy, committing a number of crimes, which black as I am, I should blush to repeat.

Before I removed from Norwich...I attempted to ravish a young girl, who was visiting in the neighborhood. For this purpose, I took an old sword, and went into the woods where I supposed she would return, and concealed myself in the bushes, where I waited till 12 o'clock; but as providence ordered it, she did not go home that night, and so escaped the snare I had laid for her.

Thomas Powers' chilling plot to assault a young woman in Connecticut in 1793 was fortunately dashed because she unknowingly changed her plans; Sally Messer would not be so lucky. The similarities between this foiled attempt and the brutal rape of December 1795 are uncanny:

On the 7th day of Dec. 1795, being at work with Mr. Gordon Lathrop, I agreed to meet him in the evening, at Thomas Rowels, to wrestle. Accordingly a little after sun down I sat out, without any evil intentions. I overtook a young woman, whom I knew to be − − I passed on by her, a pretty good jog, till after a little querying with myself, and finding nothing to oppose, but rather the devil to assist me, I determined to make an attempt on her virgin chastity. − So I waylaid her, and as she came up, seized her with one hand, and her horse's bridle with the other, she ask'd me what I wanted? − I told her to dismount and I would tell her. At the same time taking her from her horse, I threw her on the ground, and in spite of her cries and entreaties, succeeded in my hellish design. Then left her, and went to the place proposed, where I found my antagonist; but the evening being far spent, I returned to my master's house and sat down, as usual, to play chequers with the children.

It was not long before I heard people round the house, and was afterwards informed they were after me; but seeing me so lively at play, says the Esq. "It can't be Tom" — so they went away. I soon went to bed...but in about two hours, I was awaked from sleep by a number of people who entered my room, and called me their "prisoner." I was confined, when I had my trial before Esq. Hough, who sentenced me to prison; accordingly I was immediately secured in Haverhill gaol, on the 10th day of Dec. As we were passing by the place, where the crime was committed, I was questioned concerning the fact...but I, like a hardened villain...denied every syllable of the truth, and had but little sense of my situation, till the key of the prison was turned upon me, when my feelings were such as no pen or tongue, can describe. [2]

Since the seventeenth century, rape was considered a capital crime in New Hampshire. In 1791, state authorities passed updated legislation that ordered "if any Man shall ravish and carnally know any Woman...by force against her Will or if any Man shall...or carnally know and abuse any Woman Child under the age of ten Years every person so offending on Conviction shall suffer Death." While Powers may have been ignorant of New Hampshire law, the deep depression which descended over him in prison were surely inspire by the fear that he might pay for his deeds with his life.

Ironically, thanks to his own narrative, much more is known about Thomas Powers' personal history than is known about his unfortunate victim. But here's what we do know: Sally was the eighth child of Samuel and Sarah Messer, born in October 1772 in Methuen, Massachusetts before her parents moved north to help establish the town of New London, New Hampshire in 1779.[3] As a child growing up in rural New England, nothing could have prepared Sarah for the brutal attack she suffered. In the days that followed, she undoubtedly endured severe emotional and physical trauma, just as sexual assault victims do today.[4] Soon afterwards, one local newspaper painfully noted that Sally's "lips were much bruised by his endeavoring to stop her screaming. She was also bruised in other parts."[5]

In addition to recovering from this traumatic encounter, making the decision to press legal charges against her rapist must have been a very difficult experience for Sally, as it can be for even women today. Just like modern rape victims, women of the past were often reluctant and ashamed to tell their families about what happened to them and were even more "embarrassed at the thought of telling intimate sexual details to male court officials or jury members. But the criminal prosecution of a sexual attack required more than individual courage. The decision to prosecute a sexual assault was a personal, legal, and, perhaps most importantly, social decision."[6] The fact that Sally's father was a town selectman and justice of the peace most certainly played a role in the apprehension of Thomas Powers the same night his daughter was assaulted, but this speedy turn of events also indicated Sally's own determination to prosecute her attacker.

Thomas Powers was equally determined to elude the hands of justice. On the morning of April 4, 1796, Powers and three of his fellow inmates at the Grafton County jail in Haverhill escaped stole a boat, and paddled three miles down the Connecticut River before setting it adrift to throw off the authorities on their trail. According to Powers,

From thence, we went to Capt. Frye Baley's in Newbury, where we stole a horse, and went fifteen miles to Ryegate [Vermont]. On Sunday evening, we arrived at St. Johnsbury, & took up lodgings in a barn. At twelve we took up our line of march, and returned to Barnet, where I parted with my companions; It being my object to go to Portland, and ship myself aboard a vessel. I, however, missed my road and came back to Littleton where I enquired for Lake Champlain, and as I was going quite the other way, I was suspected of being a rogue, and I confess they had some grounds for their suspicion, as one of them was acquainted with me. I was of consequence, immediately returned to my old lodgings in Haverhill. Here I was now hand-cuffed, and my arms pinioned; and put into the upper loft of the Prison; but on Sunday, the 4th day after my last commitment, I sawed off my pinions across the grates of the prison; and with the help of a knife, got a piece of board, with which I pryed off the grate. I then went to work to cut up my blanket, into strips, and tying them together. From the grate, I descended from the upper loft...and I ran as fast as I could, after being almost spent with fatigue, in getting my liberty...but I made my escape into the river road, and at break of day, I found myself at Capt. John Mann's in Orford. I then thought it prudent, to avoid discovery, to go back into the woods, where I lay till night. I then proceeded on to Lyme, and broke into a blacksmith shop, to rid myself of my Hand cuffs which in my travels, I found rather uncomfortable companions...However I could not succeed; so I went on to Gould's Tavern, and took a horse, which I rode about three miles; but not being able to get him any farther, I attempted to drown him to get my revenge; but could not easily succeed and I left him...When I got to the edge of Lebanon, it was day light; so I wandered about in the woods till evening, when I went to Mr.

Quimbe's shop in Lebanon, and sawed, and twisted my hand-cuffs about two hours, and gave out being quite overcome for want of food.

I then went to my master's house, looked in at the window, but guilt being my companion, I dared not enter. I then retired some distance from the house and sawed my cuffs against a rock, till by the help of a file, I liberated my hands, and went to Mr. T. Rowel's, whom I supposed to be a friend; But he, like most friends...forsook me, and turned my enemy. For upon seeing how cold and hungry I was, he seemed to pity me, and told me to go to a certain barn, and he would bring me some refreshment; but instead of victuals, he mustered all the force he could to take me. Being however, aware of his treachery, when day light appeared, I fled to the woods, and lay there, where I suffered extremely from the cold. Upon seeing them come into the woods I lay down under a log, and as they passed along one of the trod on me, but did not perceive me. I then thought best to shift my course...and one of them saw me, as I ascended a little rise of ground, and hailed me. I pointed to a barn at some distance, and said "He has just gone by the barn." – which turned the attention of the whole that way; he then supposed me to be one of their party, as it was between day light and dark.

This gave me a little breath again, and I thought of trying to get some refreshment by milk, from a cow of my master's, as I had not eat or drank for nigh 4 days, but could not find her, where I expected. I however found some raw potatoes and eat of them freely. At last I took up a resolution to use my hand-cuff bolt, for me defence, and to go into the house; which I did, but found none but children round the tea-table, who were exceedingly frightened, and run away, all but a boy, who told me to take what I wanted, if I was hungry. I seized half a cheese, and half a loaf of bread, which was on the table, and ran off. I soon met a Mr. Colburn, who knew me, and told me to go with him, and nobody should hurt me adding that I should have any refreshment I wanted. I followed him home, and no sooner had we got there, then he sent to inform my pursuers. I stept to the door, and saw them coming over the hill – I started to run and Colburn struck at me, but I escaped and ran till I fainted and fell. His dog followed me, however, and barked till they came up and took me, as their prisoner.[7]

Despite having escaped twice from prison, Powers trial before the Grafton County Superior Court in Plymouth for committing the "most barbarous rape" of Sally Messer finally began in May 1796. While a transcript of these proceedings unfortunately cannot be found in the surviving court records at the New Hampshire State Archives, one eyewitness commented the trial was "conducted with the greatest propriety and good order—and notwithstanding the delicate nature of such trials, not a word was uttered during the whole, that could offend the most delicate ear." Sally's testimony was crucial to the case and one reporter poignantly commented that the "unfortunate Girl, told her story with great presence of mind— Truth seemed to flow from her lips, while injured innocence hovered over her cheeks."[8]

After hearing the gut-wrenching testimony from his victim, the jury quickly convicted Thomas Powers and the court sentenced him to hang on July 7, although his execution was ultimately delayed until Thursday, July 28, 1796. Powers remained defiant and on July 14, his legal counsel sent a desperate plea for mercy and a powerful argument against the death penalty in general, to Governor John Gilman:

In the utmost distress and Agony, not only on Account of the deplorable and most lamentable state in which by his own folly and ignorance of the Laws he now stands, as an apparent candidate for the world of Spirits and into which he at this time has a prospect to enter and explore on the 28th instant; and which, without your interposition, he enivatably must; but also on Account of the irreparable injury which the public, but more especially Miss Sally Messer and her particular friends and relatives have sustained, by means of the commission of a crime by this supplicant more black than he is; most humbly sheweth, Tom Powars, a poor and unfortunate prisoner in the Gaol in Haverhill in this State; which place of confinement, though to those more fortunate might seem unpleasant, to him appears a Paradise when compared to that situation which...appears shortly to await him...If to take the life of Tom Powers could in the least remove the injury sustained...the greatest satisfaction might be taken in his Execution; but if it cannot, you will be pleased to consider, whether to punish for the sake of punishing, is Characteristic of goodness and a temper of mind which is virtuous.

If Tom Powers who is an infant, and not in strictness a Man as is mentioned on your Laws could declare to all the world in as strong and unequivocal terms as Language is capable of describing, that if his life could be spared, he would never again commit a Crime of the kind which for which he has been condemned to Death; and of which Crime...he acknowledges himself Guilty...and like the Burnt child who fears and dreads the fire, he would be most likely to, and in all probability would avoid...running into an error of that nature, which would to himself work the greatest of injuries; that is to say, if his Life is worth living. Tom Powars has not asked seventy times seven to be forgiven, but takes encouragement from the goodness of the Governor and the people...to pray with all fervent prayer and supplication to be once pardoned. — What honor or happiness can accrue to the people by causing the ground of New Hampshire to be stained with the Blood of black Tom Powers?

While this argument certainly had some merit, his impassioned plea for mercy fell on deaf ears as New Hampshire leaders did nothing more to halt the scheduled execution.

When the day of his execution, Thursday, July 28, arrived a broadside, or large poster, titled "The Last Words and Dying Speech of Thomas Powers" was printed by the dozens in Haverhill and was sold to thousands of spectators gathered to watch him die. This document professed its authenticity by telling readers it was "written by his own Hand, and published at his request." One of the few surviving copies is preserved at the Tuck Library of the New Hampshire Historical Society today. Included with Powers' biographical account of his short, violent life was a fascinating letter written by Lucy Wright, a free black woman who lived just across the Connecticut River in Fairlee, Vermont. "My Poor Unhappy Countryman", she began, "You may think it strange when you receive these lines, for I am an entire to you; but I am a black woman, and a mother of children. I have lived in Norwich some years, have some acquaintance with your parents; all of which seem to give me liberty to write to you." Lucy was free since slavery was illegal in Vermont, but she must have felt empathy for Thomas not only as young, black man, but also as a misguided soul who now was going to pay the ultimate price for his earthly deeds. "I have thought much about you since you was put in prison, and much more since I hear you was condemned." She urged him to repent: "Oh! Poor Thomas, you may trifle with me, and all those who may speak to you, but you cannot trifle with your Maker." Eventually Powers did feel remorse for his deeds, and "desired to see the young Lady, whom I had injured. This she refused, but said she, would receive any message I wished to send to her. I then set down and wrote a confession of my crime, and of the justness of my punishment. I begged pardon, most sincerely for the injury, I had done her." Despite Sally Messer's evident desire to see Powers punished for raping her, she did ultimately find it in her heart to tell Thomas in writing hat "she could forgive me, and hoped that God would do the same."[9]

A few hours before his execution on Thursday, July 28, Thomas Powers and a "numerous concourse of spectators" were addressed by Noah Worcester, a highly respected minister from Thornton, New Hampshire. Like other sermons composed for executions across New England, Worcester's speech was filled with both theological and pragmatic themes, first discussing the spiritual fate of the condemned man's soul and depicting Powers' trial in the afterlife in familiar legal terms, but of infinitely more consequence:

> *Unhappy Fellow Mortal.*
>
> *At your request I speak on the present occasion. You will therefore suffer me, to address you as one on the borders of eternity; hearing the gospel for the last time; and this day to give account how you hear. The great GOD, who brought you into this world, gave you a rational soul, and placed you in a land blessed with gospel light. You have proved yourself to be by nature, a child of wrath, by being a child of disobedience. You have been a lover of pleasure more than a lover of God; by yielding to the temptations of Satan, and indulging your own vicious inclination , you have paved a way to an infamous death...You are soon to appear before another tribunal, at which the fate of your soul is to be decided for eternity. Before the setting of the sun, your soul is to appear at the bar of God, and from his mouth you must hear a sentence never to be revoked, a sentence which will fill your soul with joy unutterable, or anguish insupportable. If you are...now possessed of a broken heart, and a contrite spirit, and from such feelings are disposed to cry, God be merciful to me as a sinner: You may freely apply the gracious promise of Christ to yourself, today shalt thou be with me in Paradise. And the gallows will be to you as the last step to heaven. But if you are now possessed of the temper of that impenitent wretch, who could spend his last moments in railing rather than praying, how perilous is your situation! Should you continue in such a temper but a few minutes more, you are undone! Forever undone!*

Reverend Worcester then turned his attention to the crowd who has assembled to watch this grim spectacle:

> *The occasion on which we are convened has had no precedent in this county, and but very few in the State. And it is devoutly to be desired that this event, may have such a happy influence upon all classes of people, that a similar occasion for convening, shall never be needful. As the rising generation are deeply interested in the events of this day, I shall close with an address to them...Here you see one, in the bloom of youth, to be this day cut off from the land of the living, by the judgement of men, and the righteousness of God. The course of wickedness he has pursued, has led him into the snares of death; soon he must bid adieu to earthly objects, and what will become of his precious soul is known to God. And think ye this unhappy creature is a sinner above all the young people in the land, because he suffers such things? — I tell you nay, but except ye repent, ye shall all*

likewise perish. You may, perhaps, continue impenitent, and escape the county prison and gallows, but you cannot continue long in impenitency, and finally escape the prison of despair. This event is a solemn call to you, to flee youthful lusts, to shun vicious courses, to repent, and make your peace with God; and if you make a right improvement of the event, it will mean an everlasting benefit to your souls.[10]

The terrible moment had finally arrived as Thomas Powers "was suspended between the heavens and the earth till life departed his body."[11] This eerie description confirms the fact that most hangings in early America were particularly horrific to watch, as the condemned person often struggled for a few minutes, dangling in the air as they were slowly strangled to death instead of having their necks broken mercifully quick.[12]

What became of Thomas Powers' soul is beyond the realm of historical inquiry, but the fate of his body is rather disconcerting. In June 1796, Powers noted in his *Narrative and Confession,* "a number of Doctors made application to me for my Body, for Dissection, after my execution." This practice may seem a bit grotesque, but as early as the 1640s, Massachusetts lawmakers had authorized medical authorities to "anatomize" the bodies of dead criminals. This practice became common throughout New England, and by the late 1790s, when the medical school at Dartmouth was in its infancy, the study of human anatomy and physiology was flourishing in America and the demand for human cadavers soared.

Coincidentally, the same year that Thomas Powers was executed, the New Hampshire legislature conveniently authorized doctors to perform autopsies on the bodies of executed criminals, as long as they had "purchased the same of said criminal for the purpose of dissection having a Certificate from a Justice of such county."[13] This is precisely what happened in Thomas Powers' case, because he "readily consented" to sell his dead body to Dr. Daniel Peterson of Boscawen and Dr. Moses Long of Hopkinton, "for the small sum of ten dollars, thinking it might afford me a comfortable subsistence while here, and my bones be of service to mankind after the separation of soul and body."[14]

Some eighteenth-century criminals feared the dissection of their bodies after death more than being hanged. When Whiting Sweeting of Albany, New York was sentenced to death in 1792, he admitted that upon "receiving the sentence of death I was not terrified, yet to hear of the Dissection of my body, seemed disagreeable to nature." Sweeting's body was picked up by a surgeon after his execution, but he reluctantly delivered it back to the family untouched for a decent burial.[15] Thomas Powers' body, however, was not spared from the scalpel. According to local folklore, the two doctors dissected Powers' corpse, then "had the skin tanned, and a pair of boots made from it." This was an especially gruesome example of the desire of affluent whites to maintain their dominance over the bodies of black people in early America, and perhaps a post-mortem punishment since Powers had corrupted the body a young white woman.[16]

Remarkably, Sally Messer seems to have found some happiness in the wake of her traumatic experience. During the late 1790s, she was courted by Jacob Messer, a militia officer and distant cousin from Methuen, Massachusetts, and the couple were married in Massachusetts on November 28, 1799.[17] Hopefully the rest of Sally's life was pleasant, but she probably never erased the dark memory of her encounter with Thomas Powers on a cold winter's eve in 1796.

Endnotes: Chapter Four

1. *New-Hampshire Gazette*, June 11, 1796.
2. *The Narrative and Confession of Thomas Powers, a Negro, formerly of Norwich in Connecticut, who was in the 20th year of his age...*(Norwich, CT: John Trumbull, 1796).
3. *A History of the Town of New London, New Hampshire 1779-1899* (Concord: Rumford Press, 1899) 126-127.
4. Information concerning the trauma of rape victims was found at www.rainn.org, the website of the Rape, Abuse & Incest National Network.
5. *New-Hampshire Gazette*, June 11, 1796.
6. Sharon Block, "Bringing Rapes to Court", Common-place. org The Interactive Journal of Early American Life, April 2003. For more on the prosecution of rape in eighteenth-century New England, see *Laurel Thatcher Ulrich, A Midwive's Tale: The Life of Martha Ballard, Based on Her Diary 1785-1812* (New York: Vintage Books, 1991) 115-126.
7. *The Narrative and Confession of Thomas Powers*, 7-11.
8. *New-Hampshire Gazette*, June 11, 1796.
9. Power's complete petition is located in *Miscellaneous Provincial and State Papers of New Hampshire, 1725–1800, Volume XVIII* (Manchester: 1890), 881-885, and The Narrative and Confession of Thomas Powers, 12.
10. *Sermon Delivered at Haverhill, New Hampshire, July 28, 1796, At the Execution of Thomas Powers...by Noah Worcester A.M.* (Haverhill: N. Coverly, 1796) 17-19, 21, 29-30.
11. *Vermont Journal*, August 5, 1796.
12. *Irene Q. Brown and Richard D. Brown, The Hanging of Ephraim Wheeler* (Cambridge: The Belknap Press, 2003) 238, 254-255.
13. *The Laws of New Hampshire 1792-1801*, 335.
14. *The Narrative and Confession of Thomas Powers*, 12.
15. *Michael Sappol, A Traffic of Dead Bodies: Anatomy and Embodied Social Identity in Nineteenth-Century America* (Princeton, New Jersey: Princeton University Press, 2002) 100-105.
16. Charles Carleton Coffin, *The History of Boscawen and Webster, From 1733 to 1878* (Concord: 1878) 478, and also Joanne Pope Melish, *Disowning Slavery: Gradual Emancipation and Race in New England, 1780-1860* (Ithaca: Cornell University Press, 1998) 140-150, 185-187.
17. *A History of the Town of New London, New Hampshire 1779-1899*, 127, and *Vital Records of Methuen, Massachusetts to 1850*.

Chapter Five

"An outcast from humanity"
The Life and Death of Josiah Burnham

While Josiah Burnham's "atrocious deed" would become infamous in New Hampshire folklore, little attention has been paid to his long, strange life that began during the mid-eighteenth century.[1] It is a tragic story that began with great promise but ended in bitterness, financial ruin, and astounding violence. Josiah Burnham was born into a distinguished family in Farmington, Connecticut on August 12, 1743. His paternal grandfather was William Burnham who graduated from Harvard in 1702, married Hannah Wolcott two years later, and became the minister of Farmington in December 1707. By the time of his death in 1750 at the age of sixty-six, Reverend Burnham had become one of the most prominent clergymen and affluent citizens in colonial Connecticut.[2] Perhaps due to his grandfather's influence and social status, Josiah received a decent early education and "acquired some knowledge of the Latin language" but apparently never attended college. In 1758, the Seven Years' War between the French and British empires was entering its third year, and the colony of Connecticut organized four regiments of men to join the conflict. According to Josiah, that same year at the age of fifteen, "I left my studies and enlisted into the French war, as it was called...though under Great-Britain and the American colonies...where I continued three seasons, undergoing many hardships and difficulties in defence of my infant country." Records indicate that Burnham probably served as a drummer in the First Connecticut Regiment, which fought at the brief but bloody skirmish of Bernetz Brook in New York on July 6, 1758 and then at the decisive battle of Carillon near Fort Ticonderoga two days later.[3]

After his military service, at the age of eighteen Josiah began working in a local store, for a period of three years, during which time his mother Ruth sadly passed away on June 28, 1762 at the age of thirty-nine.[4] There is nothing to indicate of how deeply this loss affected Burnham, but during his early twenties, Josiah left his family behind in Connecticut, and moved to New Jersey, where he "was there engaged as a teacher in an English school for six years, without any remarkable occurrence happening." Perhaps a bit restless after this experience, in 1769 he decided to become a sailor and explore the world beyond New England. Decades later, Josiah recalled:

On my return to Connecticut, I had an inclination to try the Whale-fishery; accordingly the summer following, at the age of 26, I went to Nantucket, in Massachusetts, where I engaged in the business of my inclination. Soon after I was employed, we fitted and set sail, proceeded on our expedition, passed to the banks of Newfoundland, where we made a stand for a few days, refitted and recreated ourselves by fishing, which was really an amusement, as fish were very plenty around these banks. We then continued on our voyage to the Islands of Zoar [known today as the Canary Islands], making very successful attacks on whales, which were the principal objects of our pursuit. After having satisfactory success we returned, being on our voyage five months and fifteen days. On the winter following, I resumed my former occupation of school-keeping, in my native town and district, where I again became one of my father's family. In March following, having become acquainted of the compass and the theory of surveying, I was determined to reduce it to practice...accordingly, I received recommendations from three gentlemen, who were well known to the President of Dartmouth College (Mr. Wheelock) to whom they recommended me. I immediately set out for Hanover, and on my arrival there, the President received me very politely, and offered me two rights of land lying in Landaff, if I would superintend a settlement there.[5]

For a young man who only a short time before had been enjoying life as a sailor on a whaling ship, to be welcomed by someone as accomplished and well-connected as Eleazar Wheelock was incredibly fortuitous. But Burnham inexplicably turned down Wheelock's generous offer, and continued across the Connecticut River to Newbury, Vermont, where he entered business for himself, including surveying the entire town of Warren. Now over thirty and "being tired of the single life" as he phrased it, sometime before 1776 Josiah married Betsey Chase, "a supposed widow." With a touch of dour sarcasm, Burnham admitted that "immediately after my marriage we heard from her former husband, but he being married again, the news gave me satisfaction."

Around 1777, as the American Revolution raged to the south and west, Burnham and his wife moved back into northern New Hampshire, where he built the first homestead in the newly incorporated town of Coventry, so named because its first residents hailed from Connecticut.[6] Josiah would live there for nearly twenty years, but during this period he was certainly not one of the more popular residents in town, or the entire state of New Hampshire for that matter.

When exactly Burnham first came into conflict with his neighbors is unclear, but by the early 1780s he had entered into a long-running feud with Samuel Atkinson of Boscawen, whom Josiah claimed he had once "thought a friend to me." According to his side of the story, "Samuel Atkinson...found I had taken bonds for a large quantity of wild lands, came and told me that he should see the proprietors in a few days, and he would take the bonds, and get the deeds from them for me." Burnham must have soon regretted trusting Atkinson with this crucial financial transaction, for Atkinson utterly deceived him and "made the proprietors believe that he had bought the bonds of me, and had the deeds running to him, and recorded in his own name, which immediately broke our friendship."[7]

While Josiah Burnham eventually recovered his property, he was now out to even the score against Atkinson or anyone else who crossed him. Throughout the 1780s, Burnham and Atkinson made numerous appearances in the Grafton County court, turning a simple land dispute into a vicious personal vendetta. In November 1784, Josiah was the defendant in a case of trespassing (or agricultural sabotage) brought against him by Atkinson, who accused Burnham of cutting down five acres of hay on his farm and also using a team of horses and a sled to "tread down cut up & destroy, one...acre of grass" worth three pounds.[8] Two years later, Atkinson had Josiah arrested again for destroying a portion of his hay, and apparently won a judgment of fifty pounds against Burnham, which he apparently refused to pay. These legal battles continued for over a decade, which Josiah considered to be "vexatious suits against me" that "shamefully abused my character, and finally, reduced both of our properties to very low ebb." Burnham did apparently have the last laugh, for Atkinson was eventually committed to prison for the inability to pay his own debts, and died there as a pauper in October 1796.[9]

Samuel Atkinson, however, was far from the only person who Josiah Burnham had trouble with during the late eighteenth century. In November 1784, the same month he was battling Atkinson, Chase Whittier of Coventry accused Josiah of taking "a certain iron gun charged with powder and ball" and shooting an ox belonging to him. What Burnham's grudge against Whittier was remains unknown, but the deposition of Joseph Flanders, who claimed to have heard "Josiah Burnham say that he went and shot an ox standing by a stump, which I supposed to be Chase Whittier's" was difficult to refute.[10] While these charges certainly ruined Burnham's local reputation, he ran into more serious legal problems when his debts began to accumulate.

Beginning in the seventeenth century, when a lawsuit for debt was filed in New Hampshire's courts, the local magistrate usually ordered the sheriff or his deputy to take either cash or possessions of the debtor equivalent to the value of the damages claimed by the plaintiff. If the debtor had the misfortune of not having sufficient money or property to pay the debt, the enforcer of the law was required to physically take the body of the debtor into custody until the debt was paid, which could drag on for months, or even years. In 1782, for example, a suit was filed against Josiah Burnham in the Rockingham County Court by Jonathan Blake for a debt, and the court eventually ruled in 1783 that Burnham had to pay Blake eleven pounds and fourteen shillings. Josiah appealed the decision, and after cleverly forging a receipt from Blake, in 1784 he somehow convinced the same judges to award him sixteen shillings and six pence, which sent Jonathan Blake to jail himself and plunged him further into financial ruin. In early 1791, this suit was still unresolved and Blake, now determined to send Burnham to prison, submitted a petition to the New Hampshire General Assembly, who ordered both parties to appear before the Grafton Superior Court in May.[12]

Another lawsuit was brought against him in 1785 in Grafton County by Jonathan Hale of Framingham, Massachusetts for the sum of fifteen pounds, because he had never paid Hale back for a loan made in February 1784. Josiah was arrested in September 1785 and committed to the local jail, the first of what would be many visits during his lifetime.[13] In 1789, another suit was filed against him by Nathaniel Merrill, who challenged Burnham's ownership of some land in Landaff, and Merrill eventually won the judgment in this case in 1794. Then a personal misfortune during the late 1790s made life even more difficult for Josiah, when his house in Coventry caught fire and was destroyed with most of his worldly possessions.[14] Out of necessity, Burnham and his wife then moved to Haverhill, New Hampshire, where he would miserably spend the last few years of his life.

Burnham's legal troubles reached a crisis in 1795 when he lost no less than seven suits for outstanding debts to various individuals in the New Hampshire courts. Virtually destitute at this point, he had no way of paying up, and spent large parts of the next few years in debtor's prison. By this time, because of his lengthy legal battles and reputation for treachery, the aging Josiah had become a rather despised member of the local community. In November 1795, Burnham filed a complaint with the local authorities after one Josiah Magoon threatened his life and then proceeded to beat him severely. Magoon was eventually brought to court in March 1796 to answer the charges, but because Josiah failed to show up, the charges were dropped and Magoon was sent on his way.[15] One winter evening a few years later, Burnham stopped at the store of John Montgomery in Haverhill where some of the locals liked to gather and chat. That particular night, according to Josiah, he began talking with "some of the towns-people, who did not perfectly agree in sentiment with me, some small dispute arose, and after considerable debate, anger ensued, and one man....took a knife and cut my clothes in many places." His journey home after this intimidating encounter was even more humiliating:

> *From this circumstance I left the store, and took my way towards home. Before I had gone far I was tripped up by a rope being laid across the road and very much hurt, and shouts of laughter were heard around me; however I got up again, and went on, but before long I was again headed, and used in the same manner, at which they redoubled their snickers. From this abuse, I was not able to perform any business for about eighteen months. – Who will not judge this an abuse? After being stunned by two heavy falls on the ice – dragged by my heels some distance, and then soused into a cold pond of water and there left senseless. Is this not abuse? O shame! I now forgive you all; but remember your guilt! – This I record as a fact, which actually happened to me in February, 1803.[16]*

A year later, Burnham was most likely back in prison in New Hampshire for debt, because he gave his wife a power of attorney to handle his legal affairs in Massachusetts, where he also owed people money.[17] To add insult to injury, around 1805 Burnham's wife Betsy deserted him after nearly thirty-two years of marriage due to "some trifling dispute, concerning property, which fell to her by one of her connexions, which she refused to let me share any advantage from." Given Josiah's deepening financial crisis, her refusal to help him pay his debts with her inheritance must have obliterated any remaining affection they had for each other.

In the fall of 1805, the animosity between Burnham and the local populace reached a new level of ferocity, when one night a mob assembled outside his dwelling in Haverhill and demanded Burnham step outside. Understandably concerned by what they might do to him, he refused, but watched in disbelief as the group of "evil minded persons" climbed to the top of the house and began to pry the boards off the timber frame. According to Burnham, "many were on the ground using their faculties there, and in a short time the house was laid principally on the ground. The mob then retired with a huzza!"[18]

Now that his residence had been ravaged, by December 1805, Josiah Burnham was back in the Haverhill prison for debts he could not pay, and had become a bitter and disgruntled soul. He was confined in the same cell with two other local men who had stumbled upon financial troubles and sadly, two of these three unfortunate men would not make it out alive.

Unlike Josiah Burnham, who it seems was universally disliked by his neighbors, Russell Freeman was one of the more respected and successful citizens in northern New Hampshire before financial problems led to his downfall. Born in Mansfield, Connecticut in 1750, Russell's father Edmund played an integral role in the incorporation of Hanover, New Hampshire, and his older brother built the first house in town before much of the Freeman family relocated there. During the spring and summer of 1777, Russell served as a private in Colonel Jonathan Chase's regiment sent to reinforce the American forces at Fort Ticonderoga.[19] By 1784, Russell had become one of the most prominent residents of Hanover. For several years he represented the town in the state legislature, and during the mid-1790s became Speaker of the New Hampshire House of Representatives.[20] In 1800, Freeman and others successfully petitioned the state government to form a corporation to build the Fourth New Hampshire Turnpike from Boscawen west to the banks of Connecticut River in Lebanon to increase trade and improve travel in that region of the state. By 1804, the construction of the controversial toll road had been completed, but at a far greater cost than originally anticipated, sending Freeman deep into debt and unable to pay his creditors.[21]

The plight of debtors had long been a troubling issue in New Hampshire, and various reform efforts were made with little success. In 1782, for example, the legislature passed "An Act for the Ease & Relief of Prisoners for Debt" which admitted that "detaining Prisoners for Debt in Gaol, who have no visible means, or rational prospect of discharging their debts...is a great damage to the Creditors as well as the Prisoners and their Families, and when they are capable of labor, their detention becomes a public loss." A similar law went into effect in 1791, but a decade later the plight of imprisoned debtors in New Hampshire had barely improved.

On November 1, 1800, the *United States Oracle of the Day*, published in Portsmouth, printed a scathing editorial titled "On Debt Prisoners" which related the pitiful story of a helpless debtor locked up in a local jail. The man was a traveler from the South who suffered from a serious illness, and when he could not pay for his medical care, the doctor took his patient to court and succeeded in having him thrown in a squalid cell with only a bed of straw, "very scanty fill'd, one course blanket, and a log of wood" as a pillow. The editorial concluded, "though true it is that the murderer and plundering thief are often times suspended from the gallows, when the debtor's punishment is confinement only, but that confinement, when the means of subsistence is deny'd, is by the far the greatest punishment, so the greatest tortures that can possibly be inflicted on the most atrocious villain, is the harmless debtor's fate, but (for sake of humanity) I hope it cannot be attributed to any other cause than want of sufficient knowledge of the affair, that our wise Legislators have not made provision for them. I should be sorry to find it intentional neglect."

Despite pressure to change this inhumane system, it seems that a few years later the situation for debtors in New Hampshire was grim as ever. In mid-1804, Russell Freeman sent a desperate petition from prison to the state government he had once lead, "setting forth that he was destitute of property and confined by creditor's advancing money, and praying relief."[22] By 1805, however, the aging Freeman saw no chance of being able to pay of his debts and gain his liberty, so he wrote the following gut-wrenching letter to his family from prison, excerpted here:

Dear Children,

In my state of long confinement, and under the prospect that it may not probably come to an end till death shall put a period to it, my mind has been occupied with much concern on your behalf; and it has been with painful regret to call to my remembrance that at this age of my life and yours a separation should take place between us in the manner as has come to pass. All of you, and especially my sons, are, and have been, of such an age that you have stood in most need of a father's instruction, care and advice; but you have been deprived of this privilege for more than two years past, and whether we shall have the opportunity to see each other again is to me quite uncertain. Should this be the place of my exit, your minds will undoubtedly be much affected and agitated for a season at the solemn event, and your own reflections will call back to your remembrance the time of your having had a father to assist, a tender mother in nourishing and taking care of you by night and by day in your infancy and childhood...

And now my dear ones, let me enjoin it upon you to be dutiful and kind to your honored mother in her advanced age of life. She is your own parent, and has undergone more for you in bringing you into the world than was possible for me to do. She has dandled you upon her knees and supported you at her breasts; and her care and attention to you has been that of a kind and faithful parent...She has been an ornament in her family, and a cordial friend and companion to me for more than twenty nine years. For virtue, chastity, good economy, and faithfulness in her family, none could go before her; and for her sake and mine...do all you can to comfort her broken heart, and to keep her from sinking down under the weight of her trials...and in this way may you obtain divine blessing, and be considered as an ornament to your parents when they shall be no more! Receive these broken pieces of advice and instruction, as coming from your affectionate father and true friend, in prison.

RUSSELL FREEMAN.[23]

When Freeman arrived at the prison in Haverhill, Josiah Burnham was already there, and he commented that at "my first acquaintance with Mr. Freeman, he appeared to be a very sensible man, and agreeable in conversation."[24] Had only these two despondent old men commiserated on their misfortunes in life, perhaps the tragedy to come could have been averted. "I had no great difficulty with him," claimed Burnham, "until Mr. Starkweather was committed," causing the dynamic between the prisoners to change dramatically for the worse. Joseph Starkweather was also a resident of Haverhill, but little else is known about him. According to Burnham, Freeman and Starkweather had "a particular fondness for each other...and... I was different in many sentiments from them, which kept a continual bubble of dispute on all our arguments, and often my temper would rise to that degree, that I found it ungovernable." In December 1805, Josiah's belligerence towards his fellow prisoners boiled over with deadly consequences:

On the 17th of December, about 11 o'clock in the forenoon, a very severe contest arose, about some uncivil conversation, from which we went from words to blows; – the contest became so hot, and feelings myself very much abused, I called to Mr. Corliss, the gaoler, for some assistance, who soon came, commanded us to be peaceable, and withdrew from the door, in expectation we should not quarrel any more, as he left us less noisy than he found us; but in a few minutes I had occasion to call further assistance from Mr. Corliss...however, the contest increased instead of abating, and continued until about 8 o'clock in the evening; and, my anger being raised above my senses, I wreaked my vengeance upon them, which put an end to their existence![25]

Contemporary newspapers offered more gruesome details about what transpired in the jail in Haverhill on that winter night in 1805. According to one, "while...Freeman was seated at a stool, near and in front of the stove which warmed the room, and his...fellow prisoner, Starkweather, was in the closet...between the hours of 8 and 9...this monster came up behind the former and with a large knife with two edges, which he had worn concealed under his arm during his confinement and many previous months, stabbed

Mr. Freeman in the body below the ribs with a repeated and mortal stroke."[26] When the Starkweather heard the cries of his companion and rushed back into the room, Burnham lunged forward and thrust the blade fashioned from an old scythe into his side and then tried to slit Starkweather's throat. Burnham "then alternately cut and mangled them in other parts of their bodies, in a most brutal manner."[27] When the guard Corliss heard the bloodcurdling screams, he found the two men bleeding to death all over the floor, and Burnham attempting to commit suicide.

Starkweather died within a few hours, and Russell Freeman lingered in unimaginable agony until the following morning, after having seen his wife and children for the last time. While Freeman and Starkweather and Burnham were all victimized by the same legal system, their lives were taken by Burnham in retribution for all the misfortunes and humiliations he could tolerate no longer. But there was no sympathy for Josiah Burnham, and his contemporaries only harshly hoped that "the avenging arm of justice" would "rid the world of such an outcast from humanity."[28]

A few weeks later, Burnham was indicted for murder of Freeman and Starkweather, and languished for a few months in prison awaiting his trial. During this period, Burnham claimed to have had two premonitions, one of "a bright circle...wherein I beheld three faces of the fairest features and complexion" which he believed to be the Holy Trinity, and another night appeared a reddish globe which he concluded was a vision of Hell. On Monday, June 2, 1806, he finally appeared before the Superior Court of Grafton County in Plymouth to learn his fate. Because Josiah had no means to hire his own counsel, the court appointed two lawyers to defend him; Alden Sprague of Haverhill, and an inexperienced but promising young lawyer named Daniel Webster, who had only graduated from Dartmouth in 1801. Nearly fifty years later, after he had become one the most famous lawyers and politicians in American history, Webster made the following comments about his role during this sensational trial:

> Burnham had no witnesses. He could not bring past good character to his aid, nor could we urge the plea of insanity on his behalf. At this stage of the case, Mr. Sprague, the senior counsel, declined to argue in defence of Burnham, and proposed to submit his cause to the tender mercies of the court. I interfered with this proposition, and claimed the privilege to present my views of the case. I made my first and only solitary argument of my whole life against capital punishment, and the proper time for a lawyer to urge this defence is, when he is young, and has no matters of fact or law upon which he can found a better defence.[29]

One eyewitness noted that the "counsel for the prisoner managed his defence with great ingenuity" but because "the evidence was too clear and explicit to admit of doubts," the jury took only fifteen minutes to find Josiah Burnham guilty. The next day, Chief Justice Jeremiah Smith sentenced him to pay the ultimate penalty for his crimes on July 15, 1806.[30] A few weeks later, however, Burnham petitioned Governor John Langdon and succeeded in obtaining a reprieve, which delayed the execution until August 12, 1806, which by an amazing coincidence would be Burnham's sixty-third birthday.

During his final days, Josiah wrote an anguished yet eloquent biographical essay which brought readers intimately close to the mind of a condemned man pondering his life and impending death. "When I reflect back, upon what I have seen, heard and done," Burnham confessed, "I can hardly persuade myself that all the bustle and pleasure of the world had any reality. Shall I tell you that I bear my dreadful situation with fortitude and resignation? No, I bear it because I must bear it, whether I will or no. I have spent almost sixty-three years in sin and rebellion against God...and I feel not forgiven!"[31]

Between ten and eleven o'clock on the morning of August 12, Josiah Burnham was marched with a noose around his neck to the west side of Powderhouse Hill in Haverhill, where perhaps 10,000 people from both Vermont and New Hampshire had congregated to watch him die. Like Elisha Thomas eighteen years earlier, the prisoner was escorted from the prison by the county sheriff and a company of local militia to enforce civil order. Eyewitnesses reported that Burnham "kept step with the music as accurately as any soldier" and also "marched forward with the appearance of dignity and firmness."[32] The military spectacle perhaps reminded Josiah of his youth and cast his mind back decades earlier to the French and Indian War.

Once the condemned man was standing on the gallows, a powerful sermon was given by Reverend David Sutherland of Bath. "His discourse was animated and affecting," reported one newspaper, and "his address to the criminal was such as would have moved the stoutest heart."[33] Below is an excerpt of what Sutherland said to Burnham and the vast sea of people before him:

> *Unhappy fellow creature, you are now an old man. In the course of your long life you have experienced many painful seasons of adversity, but this is the most trying of them all. You are now exhibited as a spectacle of horror to this immense concourse of your fellow men. Already you are pinioned, the fatal cord is wreathed about your neck, the terrible gibbet is*

erected over your head, and your grave is open beneath your feet. A few minutes more and you shall be in eternity! Whilst this company is dispersing...and reaching their respective homes, you shall have received an irreversible sentence, from the mouth of the Judge of the whole earth...The crime for which you suffer is of the deepest dye. What degree of provocation you received is unknown to us; but whatever it was, surely it did not warrant the atrocity of your revenge. Besides the crime for which you suffer, it is generally believed that you have indulged yourself much in some of the most scandalous vices, such as lewdness, profanity, and passion... During several months after the commission of the deed, you attempted to justify your conduct in very profane and blasphemous language, by which you added greatly to the enormity of your guilt. At last you professed a change of principles and feelings...still, however, pious people who have conversed with you have observed a lamentable want of humility, tenderness, and contrition; and indeed, to this hour, they have no evidence of that radical change of heart, without which you cannot enter into the kingdom of heaven.[34]

With "intrinsic force and spirit," Sutherland then made a deep and lasting impression on the crowd by pointing out, "the transactions of this day are calculated to produce deep humiliation of the mind...Here we have a striking display of the total depravity of that nature we possess, and of what we would all be, were it not for the restraining grave of God. Whilst you are the spectators of this scene, and when you depart from this place, be entreated to preserve the deepest solemnity of spirit. With the agonizing struggles of a man strangled to death, fresh in your view, surely none of you can be so brutish as to regale yourselves with the intoxicating cup, join vain company, or participate in the carnal merriment of a ball-room. Let this execution impress the words of the Redeemer on each heart, except ye repent, ye shall all likewise perish."

By this point in the proceedings, many faces in the throng of spectators were soaked with tears, but Burnham was "less affected by his situation then a great part of the spectators around him."[35] Once the sermon concluded, Josiah was offered the chance to address the audience and deliver his final statement before being dispatched from the gallows into the unknown. Josiah must have relished this opportunity, yet "he seemed at first to be considerably embarrassed and difficult in utterance...but afterwards proceeded with much ease...and was frequently at a loss to express himself." Here are some of his last words:

I should wish for the attention of this honorable audience, while I mention something of my situation. I have committed a most horrid crime, to which I was not sufficiently provoked. I was not justified by the laws of God nor man, I look upon myself justly condemned, for it was against the honor of God, it was against mankind, it was against myself. I have prayed God to forgive me, and could with the whole world forgive me. I have been full of trouble in my mind, but could not cry; let me have ever so much trouble, I could not do this. I was carried away with my passions, but I would not excuse myself on that account; I would caution, I would exhort you all not to be governed by your passions. When brought to my trial I meant to plead guilty, but being advised not to, I plead not guilty...this has given me great trouble, for I am sensible I did wrong. I am a wretched spectacle to the world.[36]

Burnham than turned to where various relatives of Freeman and Starkweather were seated and asked for their forgiveness. The noose around his neck was then tied tight to a large beam above his head, and the condemned man was informed he had less than ten minutes to live. The rising tension of the awful proceedings was palpable, and "the sensibility of the spectator was wrought to up to the highest pitch." Before a hooded cap was placed over his face to shield the crowd from seeing it distorted by the agonies of death, Josiah was allowed to take a large gulp of some liquor, perhaps rum. It was most certainly a grand symbolic gesture, his final toast to the world, and perhaps an attempt to dull the unimaginable pain he would suffer moments later. His haunting last words were, "Lord Jesus, have mercy on my soul!" A moment later, the rope which supported the plank of wood on which Burnham stood was severed by the very blade which he had used to end the lives of Russell Freeman and Joseph Starkweather. His tortured life was finally over.

Like Thomas Powers a decade earlier, Josiah Burnham was concerned about would happen to his body after the execution. On July 3, he signed a document bequeathing "my Mortal body, after its execution, to my well beloved friends, Nathan McKinistry, of Newbury...in Vermont, and Ezra Bartlett, of Warren...New Hampshire, Physicians, to be by them decently buried, and if Said McKinistry should think it will be beneficial to mankind, I hereby give liberty to him to take up my said Body, and in a decent manner, to perform on my...body all the most Capital operations in surgery and afterwards that said body may be committed to its mother earth."[37] Only a few hours after his burial, Burnham's fresh corpse was soon "dug up by the doctors who took it into their possession, having previously purchased it, and conveyed it away."

For many decades after his execution, according to one later New Hampshire writer, Josiah Burnham's shocking story was "told by every mother in the long winter evenings to her children about the family hearth, and the narrator never failed to relate that before death he sold his body to the surgeons for the purpose of dissection...that he took his pay in rum, and was choked into the other world drunk."[38] According to one local historian, Burnham's body was taken across the Connecticut River into Newbury, Vermont, where doctors McKinstry and Bartlett summarily dissected it in a barn, but they never buried Burnham's body as he requested. As late as 1902, Josiah Burnham's skeleton and the murder weapon were alleged to be on display in the anatomical museum at Dartmouth College. Today, however, all traces of these macabre relics from the sixth execution in New Hampshire's history have mysteriously vanished, perhaps waiting to be rediscovered.[39]

Endnotes: Chapter Five

1. Edwin Sanborn, *History of New Hampshire From Its First Discovery to The Year 1830...* (Manchester, NH: 1875) 261.

2. Catharine North, *History of Berlin, Connecticut* (New Haven: Tuttle, Morehouse, & Taylor, 1916) 158-161.

3. *An Analysis or Outline of The Life and Character of Josiah Burnham* (Hanover, NH: 1806) 2. On page eight of the *Rolls of Connecticut Men in the French and Indian War 1755-1762* (Hartford: 1905), a Jesse Burnham (possibly a nickname for Josiah) appears on the payroll as a drummer, a possible position for a teenager, in the Second Company of the First Connecticut Regiment, having enlisted on April 22, 1758 and discharged on September 2. This same Jesse Burnham re-enlisted in April 1759 in the same company and regiment. For this regiment's role in the war, see Ruth Sheppard, *Empires Collide: The French and Indian War 1755-63* (Osprey Publishing, 2006) 134-135.

4. North, *History of Berlin, Connecticut*, 161.

5. *The Life and Character of Josiah Burnham*, 2-3. Eleazar Wheelock was a native of Connecticut, a Yale graduate, and a well-known Congregational minister who was responsible for founding Dartmouth College in 1769, thanks to a royal charter issued by King George the Third. He served as the college's first president until his death in 1779, and may have needed a surveyor like Burnham since much of the college's land grants was wilderness during the 1770s.

6. Coventry is known today as Benton, New Hampshire.

7. *The Life and Character of Josiah Burnham*, 5.

8. Records of the Grafton County Court of Common Pleas, New Hampshire State Archives, Concord, New Hampshire.

9. *The Life and Character of Josiah Burnham*, 5, and *Courier of New Hampshire*, November 1, 1796.

10. Records of the Grafton County Court, New Hampshire State Archives.

11. For more on debt collection and imprisonment in early New Hampshire, see *The Laws of New Hampshire, Province Period* (Manchester: 1904) 22, and *Daniel Webster, Legal Papers, Volume 1 The New Hampshire Practice*, Alfred S. Konefsky and Andrew J. King, editors (Hanover: Dartmouth College Press, 1982) 84-87.

12. *The Laws of New Hampshire, Volume 5, 1784-1792* (Concord: Rumford Press, 1916) 572-573.

13. Records of the Grafton County Court, New Hampshire State Archives.

14. *The Life and Character of Josiah Burnham*, 4.

15. Manuscript 795653.1, Rauner Special Collections Library, Dartmouth College, Hanover, NH.

16. *The Life and Character of Josiah Burnham*, 6.

17. *American State Trials, A Collection of the Important and Interesting Criminal Trials which have taken place in the United States...Volume VIII*, John D. Lawson, editor (St. Louis, Missouri: 1917) 3.

18. *The Life and Character of Josiah Burnham*, 6.

19. *New Hampshire State Papers, Volume XV*, Isaac Hammond, ed. (Concord: 1886) 17-18, 38.

20. *New Hampshire State Papers, Volume XX*, Albert S. Batchellor, ed. (Manchester: 1891) 61, and *New-Hampshire Gazette*, June 4, 1796.

21. John J. Dearborn, *The History of Salisbury, New Hampshire...* (Manchester: 1891) 300-315, and John Shirley, "The Fourth New Hampshire Turnpike-No. 4," *Granite State Monthly* (July 1881), 428-430.

22. *New-Hampshire Sentinel*, June 16, 1804.

23. This moving letter was published posthumously as *A Father's Legacy to his Children* (Hanover: 1806).

24. *The Life and Character of Josiah Burnham*, 6-7.

25. *The Life and Character of Josiah Burnham*, 7.

26. *Farmer's Cabinet*, December 31, 1805.

27. *Columbian Centinel*, January 8, 1806.

28. *Political Observatory*, January 3, 1806.

29. "Reminisces of Daniel Webster-No. 3," *Granite State Monthly* (December 1880) 121-122.

30. *Salem Register*, June 12, 1806.

31. *The Life and Character of Josiah Burnham*, 9.

32. *New-England Palladium*, August 22, 1806 and *The Reporter*, August 23, 1806.

33. *The Reporter*, August 23, 1806.

34. *American State Trials, Volume VIII*, 19-20.

35. *Vermont Centinel*, September 3, 1806.

36. *Vermont Centinel*, September 3, 1806. Subsequent details about the hanging come from this source.

37. *Independent Statesmen*, August 13, 1876.

38. Shirley, "The Fourth New Hampshire Turnpike-No. 4," 428.

39. Frederic P. Wells, *History of Newbury, Vermont, From the Discovery of Coos County to the Present Time* (St. Johnsbury: 1902) 128, and personal communication on December 21, 2007 with Sarah Hartwell, Rauner Special Collections Library, Dartmouth College, Hanover, New Hampshire.

Chapter Six

"Strange and Unaccountable"
The Vanishing of David Starrett

On the morning of Tuesday, March 24, 1812, David Starrett left his home in Hillsborough, New Hampshire and traveled across the countryside on his way to Boston. Starrett was leading what appeared to be a very successful professional and personal life. Born in Francestown in 1774, he graduated from Dartmouth in 1798, became a lawyer, and was soon admitted to the bar of the Supreme Judicial Court of Hillsborough County.[1] In 1802, Starret married eighteen-year old Abigail Ellery Appleton, daughter of the respected Reverend Joseph Appleton and Mary Hook of North Brookfield, Massachusetts. Over the next several years, the couple had three children, their first son Joseph in August 1804, a daughter Emily three years later in January 1807, and finally Albert, born in October 1810.[2] By that time, Starret was reportedly "regarded as a man of scrupulous integrity...successful in his profession, prosperous, and apparently happy."[3] But as Abigail and their children said goodbye to David on that March morning, they certainly never suspected they were gazing upon his face for the last time.

Starrett arrived in Charlestown, Massachusetts on March 25 carrying a large trunk, and obtained lodging at the Indian Chief tavern owned by Samuel Gordon, carrying with him a trunk. The following day, Starrett went over the bridge across the Charles River into Boston and visited the home of Samuel Dana of Boston, but Dana being absent Starrett returned to Charlestown. Late in the afternoon, he left the tavern, telling Gordon he was going back downtown but would return by nine in the evening. The following day, Dana and Samuel Bell, one of Starrett's business associates from New Hampshire, came to the tavern but he had not yet returned. Three days later, Starrett's horse was still in Gordon's stable with no sign of its owner. A few days later, a sensational advertisement appeared in Boston newspapers:

> *"The Subscribers, friends of David Starrett Esq. an Attorney at Law, of Hillsboro', in the State of New-Hampshire, have endeavored to collect all the facts and circumstances relating to his disappearing after he left Gordon's Tavern on Thursday evening the 26th of March last — and from such examination, are fully satisfied, that Mr. STARRET was*

robbed and murdered either in Charlestown or Boston, between the hours of 7 and 9 on
that evening – and that his body may have been thrown from the Charles River Bridge at
that time. – And desires if possible to ascertain that fact, hereby offer a reward of Two
Hundred Dollars, to any person who will produce the body of Mr. Starrett, (if dead) or so
much thereof that his person may be identified. S. Dana, N. Appleton."[4]

Starrett was indeed well-connected; Samuel Dana was an eminent lawyer and
politician, who served many years as a Massachusetts state representative, and in 1812,
was the acting president of the Massachusetts senate. Nathaniel Appleton originally
hailed from New Ipswich, New Hampshire, had also attended Dartmouth and acquired
great wealth with the firm which established the first large-scale American textile
manufacturing facility in Lowell. Samuel Bell was also a well-known New Hampshire
lawyer who graduated from Dartmouth in 1793, and was the President of the
Hillsborough Bank until it went bankrupt in 1809.[5]

On April 4, the Starrett disappearance gained even more notoriety when
Massachusetts governor Elbridge Gerry offered an additional five hundred dollars for
any information concerning his fate. This proclamation divulged that on March 26, the
day following Starrett's arrival in Charlestown, he "went to Boston, and assigned that
evening for meeting there a person at his house, and for making him a payment of
money. And whereas Mr. Starrett returned the same day, (Thursday) to Gordon's
tavern; from whence he departed on foot for Boston, about seven o'clock in the evening
of that day, carrying with him a small Trunk, in which he had put about five hundred
dollars in specie, and seven hundred dollars in bank bills, on the morning of his
departure from Hillsborough. And whereas Mr. Starrett has not been heard of since that
evening, and at nine o'clock thereof the Trunk was found, with its clasp forced...near
the entrance of the great gate of Thayer's Hotel in Charlestown, and robbed of its
contents."[6] This ominous discovery fueled fears that Starrett had been robbed and
murdered as he traveled between Charlestown and Boston.

Despite the fact his corpse had never been found, in early April two men were
arrested to the north in Newburyport "on suspicion of their being concerned in the
murder of Mr. Starrett" but both of them were acquitted.[7] The news of her husband's
sudden disappearance must have been a stunning blow to Abigail Starrett and her
family when it reached their rural home. One local newspaper poignantly commented,
"Mr. Starrett has left an amiable family at Hillsborough and numerous relatives in New
Hampshire, to whom he was endeared as well by the ties of consanguinity as by the

friendly & correct deportment of a life spent in utility; and who now feel the ten-fold pangs of a solemn and awful uncertainty attending his unexpected exit."[8]

To aid in the identification of the body should it come ashore in Boston Harbor, a remarkably detailed description of Starret's appearance was also published: "The said David Starrett, Esq. is about 38 years of age, about 5 feet 6 inches in height, is tolerably well formed, light complexion, light hair, partly balded head, light blue eyes, speaks deliberately, and not loud, good teeth, is supposed to have a scar on the little finger of the left hand, made originally by a cut with sickle. He had on when he disappeared, a light colored Surtout, black Coat, light colored cassimere Pantaloons, a striped worsted Waiscoat, Boots...round Hat, round Hat, half worn, made in Boston...a middle sized, light red Dog, with white under the throat extending up to the ears, with a long tail, was with him."[9]

But not all were convinced that Starrett was dead. On May 23, the *Boston Patriot* argued, "the prevalent opinion is that he has been murdered; and yet this conclusion is attended with many difficulties and some improbabilities. That a man, accompanied by a dog, should be murdered early in the evening, when the moon shone bright, any where in a very public street or on a still more public bridge, has something in it strange; yet it is not so mysterious, as that a man of Mr. Starrett's character, habits, circumstances, and happy situation...should quit all these desirable things, of which an amiable wife and children made a part, and abscond. To suppose he was murdered...in Charlestown or Boston, carried with it nothing that is incredible; but to suppose that such a gentleman as Mr. Starrett, should run away from his family, from his fortune, his lucrative business and unembarrassed circumstances, carries with it such an aspect of improbability that the mind revolts at it."

Outraged by the rumors that he had fled to avoid some sort of scandal, the residents of Hillsborough who had known Starrett for years responded that he was "a man of unblemished moral character, of correct habits, of undoubted integrity; that he possessed the confidence of his neighbors and fellow citizens; that the greatest harmony appeared to exist in his family." They hoped that "the insinuations of his having absconded" would "cause no relaxation in exertions to discover the perpetrators of so horrid a crime, and bring them to justice."[10] Although Starrett's body was never found, his death was virtually accepted as fact in New Hampshire. On May 5, 1812, Abigail Starrett communicated with Clifton Claggett, the probate judge of Hillsborough County, that she was "irresistibly led to the melancholy and most distressing conclusion, that he was robbed and murdered on Thursday the 26th March, between the hours of 7 and 9 in the evening, in Charlestown or Boston. In this view…and in order that justice may be done to his estate, and to those who may have claim against it, she has deemed it her duty to solicit letters of administration." Abigail also requested that lawyer John Burnham be allowed to assist her in settling her husband's estate. Her request was granted, and two years later in April 1814, much of David Starrett's property, including his home in Hillsborough with "an excellent garden, with a small Orchard,"120 acres of land, and even his personal law library was sold at public auction.[11] As the War of 1812 raged across the North American continent, Abigail and her children relocated to the small town of Mont Vernon, with the belief that their dear husband and father was gone forever.

But late in 1814 the puzzling mystery of David Starrett took an astonishing twist. For innkeeper Samuel Gordon, Starrett's disappearance brought nothing but trouble; despite a lack of any evidence, it was widely believed that he was somehow involved in Starrett's suspected murder, and as a result, his business at the tavern suffered greatly. But in December 1814, Gordon must have been stunned when he received a letter from William Starrett, David's elderly father, which read: "Sir…I have received such information that I am convinced my son, David Starrett, voluntarily left Charlestown, in March, 1812, and was not destroyed, as I heretofore supposed. I am truly sorry for his mysterious conduct, which has been the cause of so much trouble to you and others."[12] On November 29, the *Boston Repertory* dropped a bombshell by confirming that Starrett was alive and well, and for unknown reasons, had fought in the bloody Mexican War of Independence against Spain during the summer of 1810.[12]

As early as June 1813, there had been clues that a massive deception had been perpetrated on entire region. One of Starrett's brothers (probably Luther) received letters at the post office in Francestown, "which appeared to the post-master to be…inscribed in the hand writing of Starrett, with which he was well acquainted." Then on November 17, 1814, one of his friends in Boston received a letter from Starrett in Louisiana, who made no attempt to conceal his true identity. Starrett admitted, "I anticipate that you will be much surprised when you learn that I am this place; but I hope that surprise will not be accompanied by resentment. Tho' my conduct has been singular, yet I hope, when you learn all the circumstances you will not condemn it; and until then, I beg you to suspend a judgement on the subject. From Boston I travelled by land to Providence…and then shipped in a packet for New York; remained fifteen days there, and shipped for New Orleans, where I arrived 25th May, 1812."[13]

But supporting the far-flung cause of Mexican independence may not have been Starrett's only motive in escaping his life in New Hampshire; newspapers then exposed that he was deeply in debt to Samuel Bell, who had claimed the substantial sum of $7,000 when Starrett's estate was dissolved. Whatever his motivations were, Starrett's behavior was the source of tremendous perplexity and resentment, a moral and ethical transgression. Upon learning of his actions, the town selectmen of Charlestown declared:

> As to David Starrett, and any others who may been concerned with him in the vile imposition he practiced, it is evident, from the manner in which his trunk was disposed of, that it was part of the plan to establish the belief that he had been robbed and murdered. This circumstance is a great aggravation of their guilt; at the supposed robbery and murder of one traveler, gives needless anxiety and alarm to a thousand others...as the alleged commission of crimes, which were never committed, it is a libel on the community; and as the attempt to excite groundless suspicions must have been made, in this instance with the knowledge that such suspicions must fall on the innocent.[14]

Starrett's actions were also certainly an intensely personal and cruel act of betrayal, one that his wife could never forgive. Abigail must have been bitter beyond words to learn that her husband had abandoned her and their three young children, and forced them to endure so much emotional pain and financial hardship. In October 1816, Abigail Starrett filed for divorce from her estranged husband, and her petition to the Superior Court of Hillsborough County read the following:

> Nabby F. Starrett of Mount Vernon, in said county – that on the 12th days of September A.D. 1802, she was married to David Starrett, since resident in Hillsborough...and she ever conducted herself towards the said David as a faithful & affectionate wife, but the said David regardless of his duties towards her and their children, hath willingly absented himself from your petitioner for more than three years together, to wit, for more than the space of four years last past, without making any provision for her support and maintenance, when it was in her power to do so. Also, that he hath been absent for more than three years together unheard of – wherefore the said Nabby prays that a divorce from the bond of matrimony between her and the said David may be decreed, agreeably to the statute on such case made and provided.
>
> Nabby E. Starrett, by
> her Attornies,

David Starrett was given the opportunity by law to appear before the New Hampshire county court in April 1817 and state why the petition should not be granted, though it seemed clear that would never happen. Even though her petition was published in national newspapers for three weeks, he did not show up and her petition for divorce was granted. Others intimately connected with the Starrett affair were equally angered by his actions; in the spring of 1816, Samuel Gordon moved from Charlestown to Boston, and informed "his friends and the public, that he has taken a house in Union Street, known by the name of "Green Dragon" which he proposes keeping as a Boarding House. The situation is central, a few rods only from market. This circumstance, together with his solemn promise to use every exertion in his power to render the situation of his guests pleasant and agreeable, he hopes will induce his old acquaintance (David Starrett excepted) to call and see him."[16]   Gordon eventually moved north from Boston to Belfast, Maine, where he died at the venerable age of eighty-eight on June 23, 1853. [17]

While Gordon was fully exonerated, Starrett's former business partner in New Hampshire, Samuel Bell, was still widely believed to have been involved in the plot. The *Columbian Centinel* alleged in January 1815 that another letter from Starrett had indicated he had traveled to Cincinnati, Ohio on business for Bell after his "death." It was also common knowledge that Starrett and Bell had been involved in the collapse of the Hillsborough Bank a few years before. But in early 1816, the press in New Hampshire began to retract these allegations. On February 3, the editor of the *Farmer's Cabinet* in Amherst admitted, "evidence has been seen by the editor of this paper, which satisfactorily proves to him that the said Bell had no knowledge of Starrett's intentions to abscond, and that he has not been in said Bell's employment as suggested. – From the same evidence it appears that Starrett proceeded directly to South America, and engaged as an officer in the insurgent army, and after its defeat and dispersion, returned to that part of Lousiana, which adjoins Mexico, where he remained so lately as in the month of March last."

On February 16, the *New-Hampshire Patriot* entered the fray on Bell's behalf, arguing that documents had come to light which proved, "not only that Starrett had never been in Ohio, but that no individual in this quarter of the world, excepting the brother of Starrett now deceased, knew the secret of his departure. Perhaps the character of no man has ever been more unjustly vilified, than that of Samuel Bell...To aid in the goodly work of crying him down, and keeping him down, the story of his connexion with Starrett was hatched and sent out to the world."[18] Later that year, the attempts to salvage Bell's reputation seemed to have been successful, and he was appointed as an associate justice of the New Hampshire Supreme Court. In early 1819, when Bell was nominated as the Republican candidate for governor of the state, his enemies in the Democratic Party unleashed a torrent of abuse in local newspapers. A vicious letter to Bell published in the *Concord Gazette* on February 27 doubted that "a candidate more unprincipled, more wickedly ambitious, and more totally devoid of any conscience in removing opposition could be found than yourself." Whatever his political rivals thought of him, Samuel Bell became the ninth governor of New Hampshire, was re-elected three more times to that office, and then served two terms as a senator in Washington. He died in Chester on December 23, 1850, long after the Starrett scandal had faded into obscurity.

But what ultimately happened to the man at the center of this bizarre tale? David Starret's long, strange journey that began in March 1812 ended over a thousand miles away nearly a decade later. During the summer of 1820, word reached New Hampshire that Starrett had assumed a new identity in an attempt to conceal his past, and then had taken his own life. Samuel Dinsmore, a New Hampshire native acting as an aid to the governor of the Arkansas territory, broke the news:

> *I have accidentally obtained some information relative to the celebrated David Starrett, which will be interesting to those who have any anxiety about his fate. After leaving the Republican Army of Mexico, in which he held the rank of Major, he came into this territory – engaged in trade under the assumed name of William Fischer – married – and in June 1819, terminated his existence by blowing out his brains with a pistol. He killed himself at the house of Stephen R. Wilson, on the Saline Bayou, about six miles from Red river and from the province of Texas. I was there a short time since, and received this information from Mr. Wilson who has possession of his papers and effects. Starrett sustained a very respectable character and had acquired a small property. This last act is as strange and unaccountable as his former conduct – no motive at all can be assigned for it.[19]*

Starrett probably employed the alias "William Fischer" by combining his father's given name with his mother's maiden name, but what might have driven him to commit suicide? According to James Miller, a native of Peterborough appointed by President James Monroe as the first governor of Arkansas in 1819, Starrett was also "engaged in a law-suit which involved his whole property; and in order to save it, it became necessary to send to Boston for evidence. This he found would lead to his true name, and he rather chose to put an end to all, at once."[20] Whatever caused him to commit suicide, this brutal piece of news must have come as another shock to Starret's estranged family. David's father also died under particularly violent circumstances; in August 1829, eighty-two year old William Starrett was "killed by an Ox who gored him in the bowels while feeding it in the yard."

Although Abigail Starrett was only twenty-eight when David deserted her and their three children, the emotional wounds her husband inflicted never healed. Abigail never married again, and when she died in 1858, her terse obituary did not make any mention of the bizarre incident which had marred her life: "In Mont Vernon, May 3d, Mrs. A.E. Starrett, aged 73."[21] Despite their father's disappearance, which must have been traumatic for them also, David and Abigail's children apparently went on to lead normal lives. The oldest son, Joseph, operated the tannery in Mont Vernon, served as the deacon of the Congregational Church from 1836 to 1858, and passed away on May 22, 1894. Emily, their only daughter, married Reverend David Stowell of Townsend, Massachusetts in 1837; David and Abigail's youngest son, Albert, married Mary Stevens in Mont Vernon in 1845, had two children, and died there three years before his mother.[22]

But the memory of David Starrett's bizarre actions loomed in the public consciousness of New Hampshire for decades, regarded with a mix of bewilderment and derision. In 1834, when Jonathan Perkins of Newington disappeared amidst similar circumstances, one local newspaper snidely remarked that it was "no doubt another Starret affair." Decades later, one writer commented, "no cause can be conjectured for his wild escapade, which involved those nearest to him in anxiety, grief, and deep mortification, and cast suspicion upon the innocent, except mental alienation; and in view of the tragical termination of his career, that seems the most charitable and reasonable explanation of it." Even during the 1920s, the historian of Hillsborough pondered David Starret's perplexing life: "What could have induced this unfortunate man in the successful practice of an honorable and lucrative profession, surrounded by friends and an amiable, affectionate family, to forsake all in the height of his ambition, to lead a hapless life and die an untimely death in a strange land is a profound mystery."[23] And so it will always remain.

Endnotes: Chapter Six

1. George Chapman, *Sketches of the Alumni of Dartmouth College...* (Cambridge: Riverside Press, 1867) 94, and *Farmer's Cabinet,* October 16, 1804.

2. Charles James Smith, *History of the Town of Mont Vernon, New Hampshire* (Boston: Blanchard Street Press, 1907) 146.

3. Charles H. Bell, *The Bench and Bar of New Hampshire* (Boston: Houghton, Mifflin, and Company, 1894) 657.

4. *Columbian Centinel,* April 4, 1812.

5. Samuel Adams Drake, *History of Middlesex County, Massachusetts... (Boston: 1880) 467, and Appleton's Cyclopedia of American Biography, Volume I* (New York: 1888) 85, and Chapman, Sketches of the Alumni of Dartmouth College, 67.

6. *Repertory & General Advertiser*, April 7, 1812.

7. *Newburyport Herald,* April 6, 1812 and *Salem Gazette*, June 21, 1816.

8. *New-Hampshire Patriot,* April 14, 1812.

9. *Farmer's Cabinet,* April 27, 1812.

10. *Farmer's Cabinet,* May 18, 1812.

11. *Farmer's Cabinet,* May 18, 1812, April, 26, 1813, and March 21, 1814.

12. *Columbian Centinel,* January 7, 1815.

13. *Farmer's Cabinet,* January 16, 1815.

14. *Columbian Centinel,* January 7, 1815.

15. *Daily National Intelligencer,* October 29, 1816.

16. *Portsmouth Oracle,* May 25, 1816.

17. *The National Cyclopedia of American Biography, Volume XI* (New York: James White & Co., 1901) 125, and Joseph Williamson, *History of the City of Belfast in the State of Maine,* (Portland: 1877) 559.

18. On June 17, 1815, the *Farmer's Cabinet* reported the death in Francestown of "Mr. Luther Starrett, aged, formerly merhcant of Hillsborough." This is probably the brother of David who knew of his disappearance.

19. *Farmer's Cabinet,* July 15, 1820, and *Columbian Centinel,* July 19, 1820.

20. *Concord Observer,* December 4, 1820.

21. *Farmer's Cabinet,* August 8, 1829 and June 2, 1858.

22. Smith, *History of the Town of Mont Vernon, New Hampshire,*146-147.

23. Bell, *The Bench and Bar of New Hampshire,* 657, and George Waldo Browne, *The History of Hillsborough, New Hampshire 1735-1921,* (Manchester: John B. Clarke Company, 1922) 540.

Chapter Seven

Savage Acts
A Shocking Case of Child Abuse

Tragically, children of New Hampshire's past were the victims of violence, and these incidents were no less disturbing to people then as they are today. One particularly gruesome incident occurred in 1771 when sixteen-year old Mary Harford, the daughter of Nicholas Harford of Dover, got into a deadly confrontation with nine-year old William Ward, "a poor Boy belonging to ye Isle of Shoals." Harford and Ward were both boarding in the house of Ebenezer Clements, and on Sunday, March 24, 1771, and the tension between them exploded. While Clements and his wife were gone attending church, Mary grabbed a pair of heavy iron tongs and cut William Ward "in a Barbarous manner in 2 places on ye Skull & would have soon Expired had not Mr. Ephraim Kenny & Wife providentially passed that way." Despite the adult intervention in stopping the furious assault, Ward soon died and was hastily buried, only to be exhumed a few days later. After performing a rather unpleasant autopsy, local authorities had Mary Harford taken into custody and tried for murder. Not surprisingly, the young girl was described by one local diarist as being "depriv'd of Natural Reason" and "disorder'd in her Senses" which suggests she perhaps suffered from mental illness.[1] Mary was spared the noose and after this incident, she vanishes from the historical record.

At the dawn of the nineteenth century, another series of horrific crimes which victimized children shocked residents of the Granite State, yet remarkably none of them resulted in capital punishment. In April 1803, a Mrs. Wright of Stoddard was "suddenly seized with a fit of distraction, from previous depression of spirits" and tried to systematically wipe out her own offspring. After forcing her three children to walk some distance from their home, the woman grabbed her youngest child "by the heels, and put a period to its existence by dashing it against a rock. The other two not being so easily handled, she attempted to dispatch them by beating them on the head with a stone; but fortunately missing her aim, the children escaped, and alarmed the family." When she was found by her husband a short time later, the deranged mother was sitting in a pool of water rocking the dead child in her arms. About a year later, Jonathan Laskey of Lee was arrested because he had "in a fit if insanity, cut off the head of his son."[2] While these cases were certainly extreme, during the 1820s, New

Hampshire would be witness to one of the most insidious cases of child abuse and neglect ever recorded.

In October 1807, Amos and Abigail Furnald of Gilmanton were married, and went on to have several children, including a daughter Harriet in 1809. By 1818, Fernald was doing fairly well as a cobbler and farmer, and had taken in a local teenager, Mary Wadleigh, to work as a servant in his house. Her new master, however, soon made sexual advances on Mary, which apparently she did not, or physically, could not refuse. By early 1819, Wadleigh realized that she was pregnant with Furnald's illegitimate child. In May, she left the Furnald household, probably because she could no longer hide her pregnancy from Amos' wife Abigail, which must have been a very awkward situation indeed. In desperation, Wadleigh went to the local authorities to "swear" the child on Amos Furnald, which meant that if he was recognized as the father, then he was legally obligated to support the child. Mary finally gave birth to a healthy son at the end of June, but on the following day, Furnald showed up and wrenched the newborn from her arms, saying would never see the child again. Furnald apparently named the boy Alfred, and eventually told Mary she could keep the child only for a few months.

When Alfred was eight months old, Amos somehow convinced Mary to come live at his house again, which she soon realized was a poor decision. Shortly afterwards, Furnald threatened that Alfred "should be fed in any other way than they would feed a dog, nor have clothes to enough to cover its nakedness...and if the child died there, it should never be buried."[3] That same night, Mary escaped with young Alfred and took refuge a short distance away at her father's home. Early the next morning, however, Furnald appeared at the door and told her "he would have it, or spill its heart's blood." He then forced his way into the house, and Mary tried to stop him by blocking the door. A vicious struggle ensued, which ended when Furnald bit Mary's hand and made off with his son.

Determined to regain custody of her child and confront the man who had tormented her, Mary Wadleigh snuck into to Furnald's house and was able to escape with the child while he was gone. In March 1821, Amos made another terrifying visit to Mary's residence and claimed that the local authorities had given him rights over their child. Towards the end of May 1821, Mary took Alfred back again but in her words, the child "did not then look like a human being; it appeared to have been frozen on the outside of the thighs and the seat, in large places." Mary nursed her son back to health, but on July 4, Furnald appeared on her doorstep and said that he was taking the child back for good. According to Mary, she "begged him to let her have it, but he said he would not." After battling Amos Furnald for more than two years for the custody of their child, Mary Wadleigh finally submitted to his will. The next day, she meekly made her way to Furnald's home, and left two ginger-bread cakes for Alfred.[4] She would never see her son alive again.

After taking custody of the child, Amos Furnald quickly tired of this responsibility, and paid a local woman named Susan Sanborn ten dollars to take care of Alfred for about a year. During this respite from his sadistic father, Alfred regained much of the weight he had lost and appeared to be a fairly healthy boy. But Furnald returned to claim the child in September 1822, and Ms. Sanborn did not see Amos or the child again until early April 1824, when he told her one day out of the blue that he believed the boy was dying. When Sanborn arrived at Furnald's house, she discovered young Alfred lying in a cradle only wearing a short and very dirty shirt, no shoes, and already dead. To her horror, "there appeared to be nothing but skin upon the bones...very large lice were on the body...very hard washing and soaking were necessary to get the filth off of the body, which appeared to have dried on a day or two."

A local man who had been working for Furnald, James Garmon, informed the local justice of the peace about the disturbing circumstances of the child's death. After an inquest was held on April 9, poor Alfred Furnald was buried in a lonely grave, and one witness noted that his father was noticeably absent at the funeral. Soon after, a warrant for the arrest of Amos and Abigail Furnald was issued, and they managed to escape capture until the morning of April 27, when they were cornered by six men at their home. In September 1824, Furnald and his wife were indicted by a grand jury, who charged them with the murder of Alfred Furnald by physical abuse, starvation and neglect. The indictment also accused them of being "wholly void of tenderness and humanity." When the lurid details of the Furnald's deeds were finally revealed, one local publication branded it "the most shocking and horrid of anything of the kind, ever witnessed in New Hampshire."[5] Furnald's trial would certainly add credence to that claim.

On the morning of Wednesday, February 9, 1825, the trial of Amos Furnald began in Dover, since the crime the defendants were charged with had transpired in Gilmanton in Strafford County. The Furnalds were tried separately, and Amos was chosen first, since the case against him was the strongest. Representing the Furnalds were Stephen Lyford and Jeremiah Mason, a Yale graduate from Portsmouth who had already served as the New Hampshire Attorney General and was recognized as one of the nation's best defense lawyers. The state's case was made by Lyman Walker, the council for Strafford County, and Levi Woodbury, a brilliant young prosecutor who had just finished a two-year term as governor, and who would go on to be a New Hampshire senator and Secretary of the Navy before his death in 1851.[6] Since the Fernald case was recognized to be one of the most controversial trials in the state's history, dozens of newspaper reporters lined the courtroom, eager to document every gruesome detail for a public who was hungry for news. One of them was Richard Ela, and thanks to his diligence, virtually a verbatim record of the trial is available to us today.

Lyman Walker began the trial with a blistering description of the crime. At the Furnald household, he alleged, unfolded a "scene of cruelty more barbarous-of inhumanity more depraved and abandoned...not found upon the record of crime, in this, or any other country." The prosecution then introduced a series of witnesses who helped build a solid case against Furnald. First called to the stand was James Garmon, the carpenter who began hewing a timber frame for Furnald's new workshop on April 1, 1824. Garmon recalled that he had seen a young buy outside, who was "so weak as to put out his hand to support himself by the banking of the house." Garmon also noted that Furnald's three other children were "all very comfortably dressed" with good shoes and stockings while young Alfred was barely clothed at all, and was barefoot. About a week later, on the morning of Thursday, April 8, Furnald came to him in a panic and said he thought the boy was about to die. Garmon rushed into the house and discovered Alfred lying in a cradle, barely alive. He grasped the five-year old's hand and thought he felt a pulse, and then it was gone. Standing awkwardly nearby like nothing was wrong was Abigail Furnald, and Garmon sharply told her to get some warm toddy and try to revive the child. But it was too late. Alfred Furnald's miserable existence had finally, and mercifully, ended.

Later that day, Garmon testified, after a group of workmen had raised the timber frame at Furnald's house, he was asked by a neighbor Jonathan Ladd to go to the local justice of the peace and report the death of the child. He was reluctant to go, but Ladd finally convinced him that a terrible crime had been committed at the Furnald household. According to Garmon, on the day the child died, Amos Furnald "kept about his business as usual" as if nothing unusual had happened. Soon after, the workmen headed to the "a local meeting place, where according to workman Jonathan Taylor, "great inquiries were made...respecting the death of the child."

By the afternoon of February 9, 1825 at the courthouse in downtown Dover, "the number of spectators, their anxiety to hear the trial, and the want of room in the courthouse for their accommodation, induced the court...to adjourn to the meetinghouse."[7] After this change of venue, Dr. Jonathan Prescott was called to the stand. Prescott had been the Furnald's family physician for two years, but he testified that he strangely had "never had been called to see this child — none of the family had ever mentioned its being sick." About twenty-four hours after Alfred's death in on April 8, 1824, he arrived in Gilmanton to examine the corpse, and noted with horror that the body was "very much emaciated....there were a number of sores on the back." Even worse, Prescott discovered that the child's scalp was devoid of hair and virtually a giant scab, and gruesomely noted that "three first toes of the right foot, were gone to the first joint — the other toe had lost their nails. On the left foot, one toe was gone to the first joint, and three nails from the other toes."

While Prescott was unable to determine the final cause of death, it looked as if the child had been starved and exposed to the elements intentionally. Dr. John Durkee, who performed the official autopsy on the body, noted that the "stomach was so filled with air that it appeared round and plump" and that there was no food in the digestive tract. Although they were not aware of it, these early physicians observed classic symptoms of a severe protein deficiency caused by starvation known today as kwashiorkor, a term which originates from coastal Ghana in Africa and translated into English means "rejected-one."[8] This is tragically symbolic of the brutally short life of Alfred Furnald.

Jonathan Davis, who worked at the Furnald household during the winter of 1822-23, commented that one day he "saw deceased picking up crumbs of bread from the hearth, and potato peelings from ashes and eating them. On another day, deceased took the shavings of leather soaked it in the shop tub and eat it — said he was hungry." David Sanborn, who was Abigail Furnald's father and lived only a short distance away, sadly reported that he had seen Alfred "at the door barefooted, in the winter" and that the treatment of poor Alfred by his daughter and son-in-law deeply bothered him. Abigail probably hated the child as well, because he was a constant reminder of her husband's infidelity. Additional witnesses called by the prosecution revealed that Alfred not only suffered from malnutrition but he that was physically abused as well.

Nathaniel Ladd of Gilmanton testified that during the spring of 1823, he had seen Amos Furnald "throw the deceased into a puddle of water, before his house. It was early in the spring; cool weather. Prisoner said, 'Lay there, you little devil, and wash yourself.'" Josiah Davis also recalled that in December 1823, when he cutting firewood for the family, he witnessed even more brutal treatment of the child. One day, upon some minor provocation, Furnald struck the child four separate times. After Alfred went outside to escape his tormentor, Davis swore he saw Amos knock Alfred down "with a snow ball, and said, if was not for consequences, he would cut his head off." After Alfred had gone off to do a chore and attempt to escape his father's wrath, Davis testified he saw Amos Furnald beat the defenseless child "severely with a raw hide whip." Joseph Swazey, another hired hand that lived for a few months at the Furnald home, was then called to the stand. He stated that "the deceased was not treated so well as the rest of the family...during the whole time, did not see the child eat either bread or meat. The deceased was never permitted to come to the table...he was kept very dirty." Furthermore, during his time at the Furnald's, Swazey "never saw deceased have any food but potatoes to eat, except twice, when he had porridge." In addition to being forced to eat a diet with virtually no protein, Swazey swore that he witnessed Amos Furnald "strike the deceased, who was then quite small...has seen the other children strike him with a stick."

The abuse Alfred suffered from the other children became almost deadly on one occasion when Swazey was working on a leather harness. Two of other Furnald boys took a piece of leather and proceeded to put it around Alfred's neck and told him he must act like a horse. Although this might have seemed fairly innocent play at first, Swazey became alarmed when the young boy collapsed to the floor, and the two other boys "dragged him round the room by the neck, until he became purple in the face, from being choaked." When cross-examined by Jeremiah Mason, Swazey said he did not raise his concerns with the townsfolk because "he did not wish to breed a disturbance."[9] Had he only done so, he might have saved the boy's life.

Others in the vicinity, however, had heard rumors of the abuse and wished to find out for themselves what was really going on. One day in February 1823, John Burleigh made a stop at the Furnald household because he "heard of the hard usage" of the child. When he arrived there, Amos was gone, and he discovered that the rumors were indeed true; Burleigh took the young boy on his knee, who was only wearing "a very dirty shirt, half way down its back, a petticoat, halfway down its legs, and a slip of factory cloth— no shows or stockings." Burleigh also noticed to his dismay that one of the child's feet was bleeding, and told Mrs. Furnald to do something about it. Overall, Burleigh thought the "child did not look as though it was well dealt by— it was very dirty— its head all a scab." Several weeks later, Burleigh ran into Amos, and told him "he must do better with the child." Furnald warned him: "Do you want to go to my house again and inspect my family— you had better keep at home about your own business."

Benjamin Libbey, a tailor who made clothes for the Furnalds, added weight to the suspicion that the entire family was doing fine financially, but treated Alfred savagely for no apparent reason. In January 1824, while Libbey was working there, he overheard Amos ask his wife where Alfred was. Abigail replied that he was lying down, and had soiled the bed. Mr. Furnald then became agitated, and told her, "G—d d—m it, go and get him up, for by and by he will die, and they will lay it out to our starving him to death." These words, of course, would prove eerily prophetic for poor Alfred and Amos Furnald himself.

When the prosecution had finished calling its overwhelming arsenal of witnesses, the primary witness introduced by the defense was sixteen-year old Harriet Furnald, who was used by Jeremiah Mason show that the other Furnald children were treated decently and humanely. Harriet claimed that Alfred was treated as well as the other children, but during the cross-examination Levi Woodbury exposed some inconsistencies in her testimony:

Q. Was it ever sick enough to have a doctor?

A. It never had any doctor's medicine, but mother gave him herb drink.

Q. Has the child ever been sick more than once?

A. Yes.

Q. How many times?

A. I cannot tell how often.

Q. You said your mother brought the child down — why did he not come down himself— was he not able to walk?

A. I cannot tell why he was not brought down?

Q. Was not your brother of the same age out of doors every day?

A. Yes.

Q. Why was not this child out with him?

A. I cannot tell.

Q. Can you give no reason why this child did not go out to play with the other children?

A. I suppose he did not go out, because he was not strong enough.

Q. Was he sick all winter?

A. He was never very well.

Q. Was he not well when he came from Mrs. Sanborn's to your house?

There was a palpable tension in the room as Woodbury waited for a reply from Harriet Furnald. But none came. According to reporter Richard Ela, "to this and several other questions asked of the witness, she returned no answer, and was passed by for the next witness." This was Amos Furnald's oldest daughter Lucinda, who had spent three years, off and on, living at Benjamin Libbey's as a household servant. When she was home for a three-month period, she had to share a bed with Alfred, and she remembered "he looked very pale, and was very small for his age...he wet the bed very much." Lucinda recalled that the boy "was not dressed like her brother of the same age — brother wore jacket and trowsers, stockings and boots — this child wore a slip and stockings, but no shoes or boots." After her sister was dismissed, Harriet Furnald, was once again called to the stand by Levi Woodbury. The question remained, if Alfred was so healthy, why could he not walk or move on his own power around the house?

> Q. Who brought the child downstairs generally?
> A. Mother brought him down.
> Q. Why did she bring him down — was it because he was too feeble to come down himself?
> A. I don't whether that was the reason or not.
> Q. Did anybody say the child was sick?
> A. Father and mother said he was not very well.
> Q. Was the child worse while Garmon worked at your father's than he had been before?
> A. I don't remember that he was — he appeared to be weaker.
> Q. Was any medicine given to the child?
> A. No.
> Q. Was there any thing said about sending for the doctor to see him?
> A. I don't remember that there was.

At this juncture in the questioning, Harriet Furnald lost her composure, and "betrayed great hesitation and incoherence in her answers, and finally became silent, and answered nothing." The teenager had evidently mixed feelings about what had happened to her half-brother, but possibly said nothing because she feared retaliation from her father. The judge, C.J. Richardson, decided to adjourn the court after an exhausting a day of disturbing testimony.

The questioning of Harriet Furnald resumed on the morning of Thursday, February 10, and did not reveal much more, except that she had spent a few minutes with Alfred the morning he died and could do nothing to save him. Over the next two days, Jeremiah Mason called several other residents of Gilmanton to the stand, including Jacob Rundlet, Daniel Tucker, and James Elkins, whom he used in an attempt to discredit the testimony Garmon, Swazey, and Jonathan Davis. In his closing remarks, excerpted here, Mason reminded the jury of twelve men:

> *A duty more solemn and important, can never devolve upon you in life, than that which you are now called upon to discharge. Men can never be placed in a situation more deeply responsible. You are required to exercise the last and highest act of power, which is claimed by society – to pass in judgement upon the life of citizen...I have no doubt of your intentions toIscharge that duty agreeably to your oaths...But...I feel it may be my duty to remind you that you confine your attention solely to the legal evidence in this case.*
> *In a case of an ordinary nature, I should not make a suggestion of this sort to an intelligent jury. But this is a case, which, from its nature, is calculated to make a deep impression on every mind – the bare reading of the narration in the indictment excites feelings in every heart in every breast that cannot be suppressed. The public papers have contained exaggerated statements of this transaction; and gentlemen, you were told by the counsel who opened this case on the part of the State, that a great excitement prevailed in the country in relation to it.*

Obviously, Mason was deeply concerned that the jury would be influenced by the "great excitement" and Amos Furnald would not receive a fair trial due to the tidal wave of indignation that had swept across New Hampshire. While the prosecution wanted the jury to sympathize with the poor, defenseless victim, Jeremiah Mason, on the other hand, drew the jury's attention to Harriet Furnald:

> *I never saw a person in a more unfortunate situation – which was to be most envied, she or her father, I know not. If you can conceive a situation of deeper anguish than hers...you must be gifted with uncommon power of imagination. Distinct marks of intense feelings never were exhibited than when she came before you. Was this acting? If it was, it was surely great acting. These were grounds for the deepest alarm in her mind. She thought her answers might affect the life of her father. Had she come with a story well conned before hand, would she not have been ready as far as the story went? I do not complain of the extent to which this witness was pressed. The counsel on behalf of the State, had a right thus to press the witness – but surely her peculiar – her afflicting situation entitles her to some charity...I admit that her account of some portion of the facts is very*

imperfect...Her account, though imperfect, is perhaps as little as so could be expected from her situation.

Mason asserted that the expert testimony and the autopsy, in his opinion, did not conclusively prove the child had died due to starvation and abuse. He argued that since none of the doctors who testified had seen the body of someone who had starved to death, therefore it could not be proved what the child had died from. "That the human body must be sustained by food, everybody knows," Mason concluded, "but whether after death for want of sufficient sustenance, that appearances here stated by Durkee...would present themselves, is a mere matter of opinion. None of the physicians ever had the means of knowing practically and with certainty. This evidence will afford...no satisfaction to your minds, that the deceased came to his death by starving, since other causes of death...would account for the same appearances."

While the defense attorney pitied Harriet Furnald, he had not a shred of sympathy for Mary Wadleigh. Though his client had probably raped and tormented her for years, Mason tried to convince the jury to totally disregard Wadleigh's testimony, reflecting his own moral beliefs and opinions about "fallen" women in American society:

> *What is her account of herself? That she is twenty-four years old — that she was never married and that she is the mother of four children [the other three died in infancy]. A profligate abandoned woman is capable of anything. This woman, thus early — thus continually profligate, is entitled to no credit. When a woman loses her virtue, and with it her standing in society, she loses all moral restraint and decency. Where a woman like this, testifies on the stand to such a course of abandoned baseness, no man's life shall depend on her testimony...Why rely upon the evidence of a being so profligate and abandoned? As other evidence of the facts stated by her, exists...I place her testimony out of the case I consider it as entitled to no credit — and trust you will unite with me in that opinion.*

In his closing argument, Mason warned the jury, "gentlemen, the life of the defendant, and of his wife, the parents of seven children, is in your hands. All their prospects in this world, and perhaps in another, depend on your finding...you must either acquit the defendant, I find him guilty of wilful and deliberate murder."

Levi Woodbury gave the closing argument for the prosecution, and he charged that Amos Furnald had certainly committed premeditated murder, but in a form that was far more cunning and cruel than any seen before. His remarks lasted more than three hours, a portion of which appears below:

The prisoner, doubtless, deemed the child a constant reproach and eyesore, as well as an expense imposed against his will, by the rigor of the law. To destroy it at once by poison or by blows, would have exposed him to detection, immediate and certain. He therefore resorted to means less palpable, but equally sure. He evinced, by his passionate threats, an intention to break down its health and spirits, by a relentless system of cruelty. He persisted in a course to brutalize its mind, by ignorance the most deplorable; to destroy its social feelings by driving it from the table, and the society of children his own age; to make it feed like his swine, without spoon or knife; to lodge it in cold and solitude; to clothe it in rags and filth – and if its nature could not thus alter and undergo the life of a dog...he knew the child must ere long perish and thus relieve him from the detested burthen of its maintenance, and put far away such a standing memento of his profligacy...

Go home, then, gentlemen of the jury if you can, after this evidence, acquit the prisoner – go home and tell the friendless and the poor how they may be threatened, scourged, frozen and starved...without punishment on their oppressors, in a country boasting of its humanity, its equal laws and its impartial justice. Send home again, also, to his former neighborhood, the heartless wretch before you, where his return will carry dismay like the approach of pestilence, and encourage him to repeat these enormities on his other illegitimate offspring, who may chance to fall within his merciless power...The tender years and barbarous treatment of this child cannot be concealed – his utter desertedness at his utmost need – his protracted sufferings – his forlorn and agonized hours...cannot be forgotten – his mutilated and fleshless corpse, haunts the imagination, and seems to swell the cry for justice, which went forth long since, from the recesses of his grave.

After this emotionally draining discourse, the jury took two hours to deliberate and then made their way back into the makeshift courtroom filled with anticipation at about midnight on Saturday, February 12. Isaac Lord, the foreman of the jury, handed the judge a small scrap of paper, which he then read aloud. In the end, the jury ignored the advice of the both attorneys; they did not acquit Amos Furnald, nor did they convict him of capital murder. Instead, he was found guilty of manslaughter.

On the following Monday, Jeremiah Mason sought to have a mistrial declared, and the court decided to postpone a decision (and Abigail Furnald's trial) until the next term of the Strafford County Court in September 1825. Amos, due to his pending conviction, was held in prison, and therefore his family was left without any means to support themselves, and legally became paupers. In March 1825, however, an announcement appeared in local newspapers that Nathaniel Wilson, of Gilmanton, had generously agreed to "make suitable provision for...Harriet Fernald...three children of Amos Furnald and Abigail Fernald, wife."[10] By September, however, Furnald's counsel had withdrawn their request for a new trial. At the age of thirty-nine, he was sentenced to thirty days of solitary confinement and five years of hard labor in the New Hampshire State Prison in Concord, but considering the shocking nature of his crime, Furnald was lucky to have escaped the hangman's noose. No record of Abigail Fernald's trial has been found, but it seems that she was acquitted because her name does not appear anywhere in the Register of Convicts at the New Hampshire State Prison preserved at the State Archives in Concord.

When Amos Furnald arrived at the state prison on September 13, 1825, it was fifteen years old. The building was constructed primarily from locally quarried granite and was surrounded by a granite wall fourteen feet high. The cells were only 10 feet square and were supposed to house four to six men, which must have been rather interesting. Certain prisoners were also placed in solitary confinement for a few days as an extra punishment. The convicts were required to split and cut stone for ten to twelve hours per day, rising at 4:30 in the morning, getting time for lunch and dinner, and then work until seven in the evening. Each of their movements during the day was dictated by the ringing of a bell. On Sundays, prisoners were required to attend religious services, which was hoped would help them reform their evil ways.

In order to perform hundreds of hours of manual labor, their daily diet often consisted of corn meal, large quantities of potatoes, bread, and salt pork or beef, and even beans, coffee, and milk on occasion. While the prison by-laws created in 1812 dictated the facility to be as clean and sanitary as possible, that wasn't always the case. In 1819, one visitor to the New Hampshire State Prison commented with disgust that yard was "filled with filth and rubbish." The cells could not have been much better.[11]

It was amidst these surroundings that Amos Furnald spent five years until his release on October 13, 1830, as winter was fast approaching. It is probable that given his dark past, Amos Fernald was certainly not welcome in Gilmanton or many other communities. While the exact date of his death remains uncertain, during the late nineteenth century, one New Hampshire historian reported with poetic justice that Furnald starved to death after developing an illness (possibly throat cancer) which prevented him from eating. "His body was buried...in what is now Tilton, about a mile from the village, but between the fence and the travelled part of the road" as a posthumous dishonor. The ultimate fate of the woman he victimized, Mary Wadleigh, who had lost both her son and all of her respectability in local society, remains a mystery but surely she must have been psychologically scarred for the rest of her life. The inhumane fate of Alfred Furnald quickly became notorious in the annals of American criminal history. In 1836, one compilation of infamous American crimes categorized Alfred Furnald's death as "the most savagely atrocious homicide committed in a Christian land."[12]

Endnotes: Chapter Seven

1. "The Diary of Master Joseph Tate of Somersworth, New Hampshire," The New England Historic and Genealogical Register 74 (1920): 130, and also *New-Hampshire Gazette,* April 5, 1771.

2. *New-Hampshire Sentinel,* April 2, 1803, *The Reporter and Farmer's Museum,* June 9, 1804.

3. *Trial of Amos Furnald for the Murder of Alfred Furnald: Before the Superior Court of Judicature, Holden at Dover, Within and for the County of Strafford and the State of New Hampshire...* (Concord, NH: 1825) 33-35.

4. *Trial of Amos Furnald for the Murder of Alfred Furnald, 36.*

5. *New-Hampshire Statesman,* January 31, 1825.

6. See http://www.nh.gov/nhdhr/publications/justices/mason.html and http://www.encyclopedia.com/doc/1E1-WoodbryLv.html.

7. *New-Hampshire Patriot,* February 21, 1825.

8. See http://www.righthealth.com/Health/Kwashiorkor/

9. *Trial of Amos Furnald for the Murder of Alfred Furnald,* 40-41.

10. *New-Hampshire Patriot & State Gazette,* March 28, 1825.

11. Milli S. Knudsen, *Hard Time in Concord New Hampshire: The Crimes, the Victims and the Lives of the State Prison Inmates 1812-1883,* (Westminster, Maryland: Heritage Books, 2005) 1-16.

12. "The Register of Convicts at the New Hampshire State Prison, 1812-1883", manuscript at the New Hampshire State Archives, Concord, New Hampshire; John M. Shirley, Esq., *The Early Jurisprudence of New Hampshire,* (Concord: New Hampshire Historical Society, 1885) 5; and *P.R. Hamblin, United States Criminal History: Being a True Account of the Most Horrid Murders...*(Fayetteville, NC: 1836) 178.

Chapter Eight

Mayhem at the Muster
The Rise and Fall of the New Hampshire Militia

Between the end of the American Revolution and the outbreak of the Civil War in 1861, among the largest and most flamboyant events that occurred in communities across New Hampshire was the annual militia muster. As local men donned colorful uniforms while thousands of civilians turned out to watch, the climax of these activities was the afternoon "sham" battle, when regiments imitated the maneuvers of combat with an enemy force. These events usually occurred in the autumn, so open fields could be trampled by the troops after the crops had been harvested. In 1822, a poem titled "The Sham Action" appeared in New Hampshire newspapers which celebrated this annual martial spectacle:

> 'Twas Autumn and the day was bright –
> Well arm'd the soldiers were and brave,
> With powder furnish'd for a fight –
> If noise and smoke such name may have,
> A sham fight call'd throughout the land
> by men the highest in command!
>
> Now, the battle rages hot,
> Shrill bugles scream – sharp sabres clash,
> Some victim trembles ever'y shot,
> And soldiers quake at every flash!
> For who till now did ever see
> Such fighting and such rivalry![1]

The tradition of militia musters in New Hampshire can be traced back to seventeenth century, when French and Indian attacks were a serious threat, and in 1680, the first law regulating the militia of the New Hampshire colony went into effect.[2] Beginning around 1720, all males in New Hampshire between the ages 16 and 60, unless they were physically unable, were required by law to own a firearm and participate in local militia drills. These organizations of citizen-soldiers were called upon frequently during the eighteenth century, including Queen Anne's War, the raid of Louisburg in 1745, and the French and Indian War during the 1750s. In 1773, the last Royal Governor of New Hampshire, John Wentworth reorganized the colonial militia into twelve regiments, unaware of course, that only a year later many of these citizen soldiers would turn against the Crown during the raid on Fort William & Mary in December 1774, and inflict heavy casualties on the British regulars six months later at Bunker Hill. Immediately after the American Revolution, the New Hampshire militia was expanded into more than twenty regiments spread across the state, and these troops played an important role maintaining the peace during those tempestuous times.

On the afternoon of September 20, 1786, as the members of the New Hampshire legislature were meeting in Exeter, about two hundred armed men surrounded the building, angry that the politicians had done little to ease the severe economic crisis which swept across New Hampshire. The fact that a violent uprising known as Shay's Rebellion had recently been quelled in western Massachusetts only heightened the tensions. When Moses French of Hampstead gave orders to his ragtag force to load their muskets and block the doors of the hall where the lawmakers were gathered, it seemed that bloodshed might be unavoidable. After sunset, the leader of New Hampshire and Revolutionary War hero, John Sullivan, attempted to reason with the disgruntled citizens. They eventually allowed Sullivan and his colleagues to exit the building unharmed.

At eleven o'clock that evening, Sullivan sent out riders to assemble the state militia and by morning a large force of infantry and cavalry totaling about 2,000 men had arrived in Exeter to prevent any further disturbance. They quickly surrounded French's small force, and according to one newspaper, "the whole affair was conducted with much coolness and moderation...and though orders were...given by some of the officers of the insurgents to fire on their assailants, there was happily no blood spilt on either side."[3]

That this potentially explosive incident did not dissolve into civil war was indeed a critical and yet forgotten moment in New Hampshire's history. Later that autumn, after regimental musters were staged across the state from Portsmouth to the White Mountains, Sullivan offered "his most cordial thanks to the officers and soldiers of the respective regiments...for their soldierly, spirited and regular conduct. The advances they have made in uniforming themselves, the great proficiency they have made in the military exercises...cannot fail to secure this state against the attempts of foreign and domestic enemies."[4]

Several years later in 1795, the legislature passed another militia reform act, which required that "every free, able bodies white male citizen of this state...of the age of 16 years and under forty years...shall be enrolled in the militia."[5] The next few decades would be the "golden age" of militia musters in New Hampshire. Glowing depictions of these events can be found throughout newspapers in the Granite State during this period. For example, at a muster near Concord in October 1795, the *New-Hampshire Gazette* reported that the 11th Regiment "made a brilliant appearance both in dress and in exercise. In the evening, the Field and Staff officers of the regiment...with a number of the citizens of the town, partook of an elegant supper at Stickney's Hall." During this dinner, over ten toasts were made to celebrities of the day, including President Washington and the Marquis De Lafayette.[6]

Indeed, these gatherings were as much about socializing as they were concerned with military discipline. At the homestead of Matthew Harvey in Sutton, officers of the local regiment were invited to dance in the impressive ball room on the second floor of Harvey's home after every muster on the family farm. For those not privileged enough to attend these sumptuous parties, New Hampshire's citizens still had every reason to be proud of their militia. When the 21st Regiment mustered on September 17, 1798 on a prominent hill in Boscawen, one eyewitness declared "the day was charmingly serene and pleasant...and the spectators beheld with the most pleasing astonishment, those military evolutions...which would not have disgraced continental soldiers."[7] But the future of the New Hampshire militia in the coming decades, however, would be anything but pleasant and orderly.

While many members of the militia took pride in their duty, evidence suggests that some less well-to-do men were resentful that state law compelled them to attend musters where they were treated like inferiors by arrogant, wealthy officers. As early as 1804, an anonymous editorial in one publication urged civilians to be "divested of all prejudice against the profession of a soldier, and be made sensible that it is not a state of degrading servitude, but of honorable exertion for distinction and glory."[8] More than a decade later, after the War of 1812, a vigorous debate about the usefulness of the militia was waged in New Hampshire newspapers. In 1819, an openly critical piece on the entire militia system declared that it was a "useless burden on the people" because of the heavy taxes which were necessary to pay for the massive quantities of food and alcoholic beverages consumed at musters. The consumption of alcohol at the musters and its side effects would become a particularly thorny issue as time passed.

The general lack of discipline and firearms safety amongst the militia was also a serious concern; when another militia reform law was passed which fined soldiers two dollars for firing their weapons without the specific orders of their officers, one newspaper editor noted, "this excellent section is violated on every muster day to the great annoyance of the public."[9] A few years later, one militia solider from Mont Vernon returning home from a muster who "feeling the spirit of the occasion...charged his musket very heavily, which on his discharging it, burst, and completely tore off one of his hands at the wrist, scattering it in atoms in all directions." This shocking disfigurement was far from being an isolated incident.[10]

Supporters of the militia argued that rowdy segments of the public were the ones that undermined the military discipline and distracted civilian soldiers from their duty. In 1825, an anonymous soldier in the Thirtieth Regiment based in the Lake Sunapee region wrote that the citizens could not "too highly appreciate the spirit of improvement which actuates the officers and soldiers of the N.H. militia." He argued that there was "one evil that attends our present system, that ought to be, and *must* be remedied. At every training or muster, groups of *able bodied* men are seen about the parade, dancing, wrestling, swearing and getting drunk. Ask one of them why he does not perform military duty, his reply is, *I have a certificate from the Surgeon!*" According to this soldier, fraudulent medical ailments enabled almost one fourth of his regiment to be excused from duty. Another proponent of the militia asked "why this system is answerable for the appearance of the spectators on the field, or for their vices. They are not ordered there...and the militia law does not compel them to get drunk."[11] As the nineteenth century wore on, the debate whether musters and even the entire militia systems should be scrapped raged as lively as a sham battle on a crisp autumn day.

Though the War of 1812 was in the recent past, the threat of invasion by an enemy nation was far-fetched to some, and thus the need for an active militia was questioned. "What is it to guard against?" sarcastically asked one opponent. "Who is there to invade us? We have nothing to fear from Vermont, for they have wisely reduced their peace establishment to one training a year. Are we in danger from Canada? Why, they must pass through Vermont before they get to New Hampshire...Then, sir, for what purpose is all this expense? Is it for a few dandies to show themselves to the multitude on muster days?" Another writer in Concord argued that the entire militia should not be disbanded because "the militia is the only sure and safe defence of a republican government...our people are secure in the enjoyment of their rights; their present situation is pleasant, and their prospects flattering. But human nature is unchanged...We have no security that peace which we enjoy will never be disturbed. We have no right to expect it." [12] While this political battle was waged in many of New Hampshire's newspapers, some of the annual musters were becoming quite violent. During the fall of the 1829, the muster day in Effingham served as a backdrop for a murderous plot. Amidst the gunfire and smoky chaos of the sham battle, "two persons followed another from the field and discharged a musket at him, loaded with buck shot, one of which entered his head near the ear." The unidentified man nearly died, and the shooter apparently fled the state to avoid capture.[13]

The heyday of the militia musters across New England was paralleled by the rise of the temperance movement in America, which sought to curtail or even totally ban the consumption of alcohol, which it supporters firmly believed to be the cause of violent crimes and the moral decay of society. By 1830, the New Hampshire Society for the Promotion of Temperance had been organized, and that same year similar groups were established in Cheshire, Merrimack, Sullivan, and Rockingham counties.[14] Soon the annual musters became one of temperance movement's primary targets and they used local newspapers to wage their own war of words.

An eyewitness at the muster in Walpole in 1830, where a few thousand spectators had gathered, reported with disdain that he "saw more people intoxicated than I had seen for ten years before." Three years later at the muster of the 5th Regiment in Dunstable, "the usual concomitants of the muster field were present in abundance – men, women, children, peddlers, auctioneers, gamblers, grog-booths, and grog-drinkers! These in fact were the most conspicuous part of the parade – and their maneuvers attracted more attention than did those of the military." However, it seems that despite the popularity of the musters, the temperance societies made some progress towards their goal; at the gathering of the 32nd Regiment in Lisbon in 1830, the sale of alcohol was banned entirely by the colonel to avoid the perennial firearms accidents and fist-fights. A decade later, when the muster of the Fifth Regiment was held in Amherst, one spectator reported, "on the whole, this military jubilee passed off with as little of the usual disorder, vice and profligacy, as could be expected from such an incongruous assemble...the rumsellers and gamblers made their appearance as usual but by the vigilance of the Selectmen, aided by commanders of the regiment, they were required to removed their stands from the field." [15]

In late September 1839, however, the muster in Goffstown dissolved into a huge drunken brawl. According to one source, the trouble began when a fight broke out between some gamblers who had been drinking heavily; another source claims the soldiers themselves sought to drive the pesky gamblers off the field. Whatever their motive, when the Manchester Rifle Company intervened, they were attacked with great ferocity by the drunken crowd and "got into a regular knock down." When one of the gamblers, Elbridge Ford, was struck by the musket of one of the soldiers, Jeremiah Johnson, Ford retaliated by striking Johnson on the head with a wooden club. Johnson initially appeared to be fine but within a week he died at the age of thirty-four, leaving a wife and four children. Ford was apprehended and charged with manslaughter. Nearly a year later, his first trial had ended in a hung jury, conflicted over whether Ford had acted in self-defense. Ultimately, Elbridge Ford was found guilty and sentenced to five years of hard labor in the state prison in Concord.[16] By the time Ford was a free man again, however, the twilight of New Hampshire's muster days was on the horizon.

Despite the stubborn efforts of temperance movement, the widespread consumption of alcohol at militia musters remained the norm during the 1840s. At the muster of the 25th Regiment in Barrington in September 1841, an eyewitness commented that it was "remarkable...the day passed off without any quarrelling or fighting among the soldiers or spectators...although ardent spirits were sold on the field during the day, which is saying more than could have been said formerly on similar occasions." In Dover the following year, the editors of the *Dover Gazette* reported "we witnessed a very great and unusual amount of drunkenness and gambling at our late muster in consequence of liquor being allowed to be sold near the premises." In 1843, when the 9th Regiment assembled in Goffstown, "the sham fight in the afternoon was done in good shape...but the quantity of rum sold on the field during the day was immense. A long range of those traveling grog-shops which are a pest and nuisance wherever they go held their place unmolested by any civil authority."

But the temperance lobby succeeded in having a bill to abolish fall musters pass through the New Hampshire House of Representatives in 1844, only to be voted down by the Senate. In 1845, a similar law was vetoed by the governor but the editor of the *New-Hampshire Statesman* was defiant that in 1846 the reform law would pass "in spite...of the entire tribe of new-rum vendors...nine of out every ten of whom favor the Muster System because it brings grist to their mills. This is a matter the delay in which the patience of the people will no longer tolerate."[17]

This was indeed a major shift in public sentiment. At the dawn of the nineteenth century, the militia and muster days were a source of pride in New Hampshire, but in less than fifty years, they had become a target of derision and disgust. "Indeed, the time has arrived", snickered the *New-Hampshire Statesman*, "when a respectable man, if seen upon the muster field as a spectator, is almost under the necessity of making an apology, if he would keep his reputation unspotted with men whose good opinions are worth seeking and retaining." Another pro-temperance writer scathingly described the muster of the 11th Regiment in 1845, "as among the last places a moral man will visit, except by compulsion, and from which he will pluck his children as from devouring fire."[18]

In 1846, the state government abolished militia musters indefinitely, but the following year that ban was rescinded after lobbying by powerful supporters of the old militia system. Over the next few years, the musters remained as chaotic as usual while public outcry against them grew ever louder. In September 1848 at the muster in Epping, John Thorn pulled out a knife and stabbed Stephen Thomas, who fortunately survived the vicious attack. The annual muster in Barrington was described "as one of the most immoral assemblages that ever disgraced a country town of New England" until September 1849, when irate residents confronted the "Rumsellers and Rowdies" and forced them to leave. During the muster of the 5th, 9th, and 22nd Regiments at Amherst in 1850, residents were embarrassed by the "motley mixture of mad, militia, music, and misery— such a mixture as we pray may never again mar the usual comfort of our peaceful and quiet village."[19]

In July 1851, New Hampshire abolished the compulsory annual militia musters permanently: "The militia of this State shall be subject to no active duty, except in case of war, invasion, insurrection, riot." Some communities continued to maintain independent volunteer militia units, such as the Strafford Guards in Dover and the Abbott Guards in Manchester, but when the Civil War broke out a decade later, the vast majority of troops who enlisted had little or no military experience which would have been useful. Ironically, the first few regiments organized in the state in 1861 were issued old smoothbore muskets and gray militia uniforms from the state armory before they were clothed in Federal blue. Meanwhile, the riotous militia musters that were a ritual in New Hampshire for more than half a century were replaced by annual fairs that are still popular today. At Amherst in October 1851, the local publication *Farmer's Cabinet* celebrated the end of one tradition and the dawn of a new one: "Training is gone, muster is gone, and we are glad of it; but Cattle Show, may it live forever!"[20]

Endnotes: Chapter Eight

1. *New-Hampshire Sentinel,* November 2, 1822.

2. Jack Noon, *Muster Days at Musterfield Farm,* (Portsmouth: Peter Randall Publishers, 2000) 5-10.

3. *New-Hampshire Mercury,* September 27, 1786.

4. *New-Hampshire Spy,* December 1, 1786.

5. *Federal Mirror,* June 26, 1795.

6. *New-Hampshire Gazette,* November 3, 1795.

7. *Muster Days at Musterfield Farm,* 60-61 and the *Mirror,* September 25, 1798.

8. *New-Hampshire Sentinel,* June 2, 1804.

9. *New-Hampshire Sentinel,* September 30 and October 20, 1819.

10. *New-Hampshire Statesman,* October 17, 1825.

11. *New-Hampshire Patriot,* October 10, 1825 and *New-Hampshire Sentinel,* October 6, 1819.

12. *New-Hampshire Sentinel,* October 1, 1830, and *New-Hampshire Statesman,* August 27, 1831.

13. *New-Hampshire Sentinel,* October 23, 1829.

14. *New-Hampshire Sentinel,* January 1 and 29, 1830, *New-Hampshire Patriot,* April 12, 1830, *New-Hampshire Gazette,* April 13, 1830, and *Portsmouth Journal,* June 12, 1830.

15. *New-Hampshire Sentinel,* October 1, 1830, *New-Hampshire* Statesman, October 2, 1830, Farmers *Cabinet,* September 27, 1833, *Farmers Cabinet,* October 3, 1844.

16. *New-Hampshire Patriot,* October 7, 1839, *Dover Gazette,* October 15, 1839, *Portsmouth Journal,* September 12, 1840, and *New-Hampshire Statesman,* September 12, 1840.

17. *Dover Gazette & Strafford Advertiser,* September 28, 1841 and September 24, 1842, and *New-Hampshire Statesman,* September 15, 1843 and July 11, 1845.

18. *New-Hampshire Statesman,* September 19, 1845.

19. *Dover Gazette,* October 7, 1848, and September 29, 1849; *Farmer's Cabinet,* October 3, 1850, July 17, 1851, and October 1, 1851.

Chapter Nine

Hellish Times in Hopkinton
Murder and Mental Illness in the Granite State

During the 1830s, politics, popular sentiment, and a new wave of heinous crimes spurred the growing controversy over capital punishment in New Hampshire. As we have seen previously, it was common for ministers to sanction sentences of capital punishment pronounced by civil authorities. But as the nineteenth century progressed, philosophical and political differences between clerics and state authorities over the death penalty became more pronounced. On August 9, 1835, Reverend Arthur Caverno of Great Falls (now Somersworth) became one of the first ministers in New Hampshire to openly question the morality of the death penalty and the authority of secular government to execute fellow human beings. Caverno began by telling his parishioners, "that act which terminates the mortal and probationary existence of man…is an act of awful moment. If it rest with men to say how and when this act shall take place, it certainly should rest upon the clearest authority. But as I do not find such authority, I take the liberty to invite your attention to a candid and prayerful examination of the subject." Caverno's sermon so impressed his listeners that they eventually raised funds to have it published. Aside from suggesting that the death penalty was ineffective in preventing future crime, at the core of his argument was that civil authorities were essentially playing God and placing their own souls at risk. Caverno asked his contemporaries:

> *Will it be said, that although it is true that as God gave life he alone had the right to take it, yet, he has a right, if he please, to delegate the authority contended for by the advocates of capital punishment? But the question is, has God delegated it to us? If he has, give me the proofs, and I say no more. If he has not, than wo be to the man that spills his brother's blood, whether maliciously or under penal sanction. Are not the legislator, the judge and jury, the executioner, and even the assenting spectator, all alike the guilty? How will they answer in that solemn day when the Judge of all, shall make "inquisition for blood"?*[1]

Within a few years of Caverno's sermon, many of New Hampshire's politicians were indeed beginning to think hard about their positions on certain aspects of capital punishment. In 1837, while the efforts to abolish of the death penalty failed, for the first time, New Hampshire law classified first degree murder, which had to be premeditated or committed during a rape or robbery, as virtually the only crime punishable by death. Criminals convicted of second degree murder would instead receive a life sentence and up to six months of solitary confinement. Also, any future executions in New Hampshire were mandated to take place inside the walls of the prison of the county where the crime occurred, and attended only by a small group of officials and family members instead of the massive public gatherings and carnival atmosphere that had long been the popular tradition.

But even after this law changed, the public were evidently more reluctant to give up their time-honored practice of turning out to watch a hanging. For example, in July 1846, Andrew Howard was executed at the Strafford County prison yard in Dover for the first degree murder of Phoebe Hanson, whom he shot dead when he robbed her home in Rochester. According to eyewitnesses, "a mob of several thousands gathered about the prison and threatened to tear down the walls, unless they were allowed to gaze on the spectacle, and that the sheriff felt obliged to yield to their violence so far as to remove the canvas form the of the wall, thus exposing the platform to view. The body was allowed to hang for 35 minutes, and then was confined and given to his friends."[2] As with previous executed criminals in New Hampshire, Howard's body was apparently subjected to an autopsy, and contemporary reports of this examination reflect the rise of one of "quack" sciences of the nineteenth century, the study of phrenology. At this time, many Americans, including those in New Hampshire, believed that the size and contours of one's skull and brain were indicators of a person's character. On July 18, 1846, the *Dover Gazette* included "remarks on the development of Andrew Howard's head…for many of our readers who take a great interest in the subject of Phrenology, as an infallible index in rightly estimating the truth of character." The observations made by the unidentified expert phrenologist were intriguing to say the least: "Much has been said and believed publicly, respecting Howard's mental incapacity…it was considered useless to attempt any education…or to make endeavors to elevate his feelings on higher, moral grounds. The general glance at his cranial development would bring a Phrenologist to a different conclusion…this was not speaking phrenologically a murderer's head."

While the shape of murderer's skull was apparently a matter of interpretation during the nineteenth century, the nature of insanity and determining whether a person had no control over their behavior due to mental illness was also a subject of tremendous debate. Two highly controversial cases with entirely different outcomes in the Granite State during the 1830s forced New Hampshire residents to reconsider their views of the connection between insanity, criminality, and the death penalty.

On the afternoon of April 7, 1837, a fire suddenly broke out in the cooper's shop at Contoocook village in Hopkinton, a few miles northwest of Concord off Interstate 89 today. Since the shop was full of valuable dry lumber, "the citizens rushed towards the burning building in considerable numbers, and when they reached it, found the door shut." John Titcomb, one of the young men employed there, was inside trying to save the wooden staves from the growing flames. The concerned townsfolk shouted they wanted to enter the building, but Titcomb answered that he thought a draft of fresh air would only fan the flames, and convinced them their only option was to save the valuable lumber from destruction. As a board was torn off the side of the structure, however, a particularly gruesome discovery was made. Under a pile of burning rubble and wooden shavings was the severely burnt body of a man, which was "immediately snatched from the devouring element, but so blackened and disfigured as scarcely to be recognized. With the exception of a portion of the shirt and vest on the bosom...the clothes were entirely consumed...and...skin was burned to a crisp."[3] But who was this unfortunate person, and had his horrific death been a tragic accident or something far more sinister?

As the timbers lay smoldering, cooper John Titcomb proposed to the stunned bystanders to go into the village to learn who the dead man was, but they immediately began to suspect that he had ignited the fire, or even worse. Titcomb was soon taken into custody and placed in the local jail. The following day, an inquest was held and the body was identified as Israel Russell, a twenty-eight year old native of Hillsborough who had been working in the cooper's shop with Titcomb. At the house of Albert Crowell, where John Titcomb had been living, authorities also discovered a pair of bloody pantaloons in his room. Titcomb was arraigned for murder at the Merrimack County Court in September, and pleaded not guilty.[4] The remarkable trial a month or so later would delve deep into Titcomb's troubled past, and in the process, help forever change the treatment of the mentally ill in New Hampshire.

Although it was nestled in the rural heart of the Granite State, Hopkinton experienced more than its fair share of violent crime and unrest during the 1830s. It all began on January 6, 1833, when Abraham Prescott, a laborer who lodged in the household of Chauncey and Sally Cochran, attacked the couple with an ax in their sleep, wounding but not killing them. Oddly enough, according to an article in the *New-*

Hampshire Patriot on January 9, the assault was not considered criminal, but a case of "somnambulism" or sleepwalking, and the Cochrans never pursued any charges against Prescott. However, about six months later in June, Prescott was accused of beating Sally Cochran to death in a strawberry patch after she had refused to acquiesce to his sexual advances. Abraham Prescott's lawyers sought an insanity defense, and even called in witnesses to testify that there was a history of insanity in his family. The Prescott case dragged on for three long years, and despite his claims of insanity, he was finally sentenced to hang on December 23, 1835. At the last minute, however, Governor Isaac Hill issued an order postponing the execution, which caused a great deal of consternation in Hopkinton. One eyewitness recalled what happened next:

> *The reprieve of Prescott was not generally known...and on the first day appointed for his execution many people from Pembroke and the adjoining towns congregated at Hopkinton village to witness the public execution. When the news was broken to the large assemblage...that the governor had reprieved Prescott for fourteen days, it created great indignation with a large majority. After dark, the more determined portion of the indignant people...collected in vicinity of the jail and demanded of Mr. Leach [keeper of the jail] the keys of the cell of the condemned man, but he wisely refused to comply with their request. At this time, Mrs. Clarissa Chase [Leach's daughter] was confined in bed with an infant son two days old. She said, − "Father, never give up Prescott to that cruel mob till we are all dead." The violent demonstrations of the people without, however, had a powerful effect on her weak...system, and a few minutes after she spoke to her father she went into convulsions. At this crisis, a mother's appeal came to the rescue. Mrs. Leach unbarred the outside door...and there she stood, a frail and helpless woman, before an infuriated mass of men crazed for blood and revenge. At her appearance with only a lighted candle in her hand, the crowd were hushed to silence in a moment. Mrs. Leach's supplication had its desired effect, and the mob quietly left the jail and repaired to Perkin's hotel, where they hung Prescott in effigy on the limb of a large elm tree in the front of the house.*[5]

In the wake of this public display of anger, on January 6, 1836, an immense throng of people gathered in an open field to witness Prescott's execution. But in the wake of this turmoil, the jail keeper's daughter, Clarissa Leach, died after giving birth on December 26, and her youngest daughter Mary died in January. They were buried together in the same grave at the Hopkinton village cemetery. It was only slightly over a year later when the grisly events involving John Titcomb and his colleague Israel Russell once again shocked the town of Hopkinton to its core. At the trial, however, it would be hotly debated how much Russell's murder had been premeditated or was the inexplicable deed of a man who was battling insanity, a debate still heard countless times in courtrooms today.

The Titcomb murder trial began at the Merrimack County Courthouse on Tuesday, October 31, 1837 in downtown Concord.[6] The presiding judge was William Richardson and Charles Gove, the Attorney General, and prosecutor John Whipple presented the state's case, while Ichabod Bartlett and Charles Peaslee served as counsel for the defense. Whipple introduced as his first witness, John Dodge, who had boarded at the Crowell household in Hopkinton. According to Dodge, Israel Russell and John Titcomb were

both coopers, and worked together in Mr. [Reuben] Wyman's shop. Titcomb had been there three weeks and one day...Nothing unusual occurred at breakfast on the morning of the 7th. As was customary, Mrs. Crowell called me to dinner a little before one o'clock; and, as I passed their shop, I called Russell and Titcomb – called twice, when Titcomb came to the door and said they would be along in a few minutes. I went into the house and sat down at the table. Pretty soon Titcomb came in. Mrs. Crowell observed that he didn't look so pale as before. He replied that he had hurt his ankle...when asked where Russell was, he answered that he had left him shaving staves, but he would be in presently. After I had finished eating, I remarked as I rose that I would tell Russell he shouldn't have any dinner, as he had not come in season. I then left the house and repaired to my own shop – heard nothing until an alarm of fire was raised, when I went to Mr. Wyman's shop. The dead body was found in the northwest corner...It lay 10 or 12 feet from the bench where Russell worked – there was blood about the bench.

Next to be called to the stand by the prosecution was Mary Crowell herself, who added some more interesting details. "About a quarter past 12 o'clock that day," according to Mrs. Crowell, "Titcomb came into the house. I told him something was the matter, for he looked pale as death – asked what it was. He said, nothing. He went and washed, and then shaved himself. Upon Dodge's thus out going [after dinner], Titcomb appeared considerably agitated – ate faster than usual – commenced muttering oaths to himself at the table – as he went out of the house, shut the doors hard after him – from his appearance, suspected he might be intoxicated – looked out of the window after him to ascertain whether he walked strait, but noticed no appearance of intoxication in his gait. I saw him go into the shop and shut the door." By this point, the evidence strongly suggested that Israel Russell had already been dead for some time.

John Whipple then interviewed Charles Farnum, another cooper in Hopkinton village, who first discovered Russell's corpse in the smoldering rubble:

A few minutes after dinner on the 7th of April, I was at my cooper's shop...heard an alarm of fire and perceived Wyman's shop to be burning. I immediately started for it, taking a pail with me. When I reached it, two or three were present. Titcomb was throwing back staves from near the door – he said it was no use to attempt saving the shop – best to save the lumber. I took hold and assisted, then help tear down a shoemaker's shop which stood between the cooper's shop and the house...Just then I thought of Russell – where he was – not having seen him. I asked Isaac Bailey is he had seen him – said he had not. I then made the same inquiry of Chase Fowler – he replied he guessed he was in there – that Titcomb kidnapped him and fired the shop. Fowler than asked Titcomb where Russell was – he said he hoped he had gone to Hell with the shop – but said he was not in the shop – would forfeit his life if he was...I pulled off the bottom board and discovered a dead body which I supposed to be that of Russell. I immediately told Mr. Fowler he had better watch Titcomb. Soon after this, Titcomb picked up his shop apron, saying he meant to go the village where he had agreed to meet Russell. Mr. Fowler told him he should stop him, and seized hold of him to prevent his going. Titcomb made some resistance, drew his fists and threatened to strike Mr. Fowler...Fowler then told myself and another man to take him to the tavern and keep him safe. While at the tavern he was questioned as to where Russell was by myself and others...He said Russell stole his staves and his rum and he hoped he had gone to Hell. During the evening appeared a good deal agitated – once sat with his hands on his knees, lips moved, and he said aloud he was sorry. I asked him what he was sorry for? If he was sorry he had killed Russell? – He replied, no – for he hadn't killed him – but he was sorry they made such a fuss about it.

During the afternoon of October 31, Dr. Griswold W. Wheeler, who performed the grisly post-mortem examination of Russell's body, testified that "both legs were broken two or three inches above the knees, and both arms about midway between the wrists and elbows – apparently with violence – and the whole body badly burned. The skull of the forehead was mostly broken...and on the right temple a large piece of skull was broken in...fragments of the bone compressed upon the brain." Whoever murdered Israel Russell had dealt a deadly blow to his head, systematically broken his limbs after death to hide the body, and then set the building on fire in an attempt to conceal the bloody evidence. This suggested that the culprit had certainly planned the crime, or at least thought about how to destroy the body and escape detection. The prosecution wanted the jury to ask themselves, could this gruesome murder and obvious effort to conceal the crime really have been conceived and carried out by someone who did not know the difference between right and wrong?

Titcomb's attorneys fully admitted that their client had indeed murdered Israel Russell, but they sought to convince the jury that Titcomb was not guilty by reason of insanity. Charles Peaslee presented the opening argument for the defense, which lasted more than two hours and "occupied the greater portion of the time in reading, from medical and legal writers, the law of insanity...and expositions and illustrations of the subtle character and almost infinitely varied manifestations of that most insidious disease." Peaslee also employed a large number of witnesses to show that the defendant had once been a kind, friendly, and religious young man whose respectable character had been irrevocably altered by a frightening illness beyond his control.

During the first day of the trial, spectators learned that John Titcomb had spent the early years of his life in Chester, New Hampshire. One character witness called by the defense, a Mr. French, knew Titcomb well from 1819 through 1824. He recalled that John was "mild, amiable and deserving. In 1822 or 1823, at the age of seventeen, he became a member of Rev. Mr. Arnold's church in that place, and sustained an excellent character." William Paine, who was a deacon at the church in Chester, also corroborated that during this period of his life, John Titcomb's character was "unimpeachable and irreproachable." Around 1825, the young man moved to Bangor, Maine, but Paine and Titcomb continued to keep in touch by letter, some of which were produced and read to the jury as evidence of Titcomb's good character before he began to exhibit symptoms of insanity.

When he moved south to Boston in January 1828, John Titcomb was lucky enough to enter the employment of Peleg Churchill, who ran a successful business as a cooper. Within six months, he made Titcomb the foreman of his new shop, and according to Churchill, "the more his character and habits became known...the more were they esteemed and admired." In 1829, however, John was stricken with a severe case of typhoid. After being bedridden for several weeks, and suffering from high fever, delirium, and excruciating stomach pains, Titcomb somehow survived but with serious damage to his health.[5] According to Peleg Churchill, for months Titcomb was far too weak to perform the labor necessary to do his job. In an extremely charitable gesture, Churchill relieved Titcomb of his duties and took him on an all-expenses paid trip across Massachusetts, Connecticut, and Rhode Island, "thinking himself abundantly repaid in the agreeable companionship, instructive intellectual conversation, and pleasant manners" that Titcomb provided. For the next three years, Titcomb was financially supported by Churchill, worked occasionally at the cooper's shop, and also taught at a local Sunday school in a nearby church. During this period, Titcomb showed no signs of the bizarre behavior that he would eventually exhibit.

In 1834, at a union meeting for journeymen coopers, John Titcomb became friendly with another cooper, William Smith, who helped him get a new job in Boston. In January 1836, Titcomb began working alongside Smith, who began to notice that the amiable and intelligent young man he had befriended began to change. One morning, a disheveled Titcomb came into the shop claiming the family he was boarding with had tried to kill him by putting arsenic in his food, so he moved to another home. Smith testified that John became increasingly paranoid, and from January through October 1836, "he frequently accused us all of designing to kill him in a variety of ways, as by cutting off his arms and legs, beating him to death, etc...Sometimes he would be raving— alternately quoting scriptures and talking about being murdered."

James Martin, one of Titcomb's roomates in Boston in 1836, also commented on the stand that John "often conversed about plots against his life—accused an old gentleman, with whom he slept, of attempting...to kill him, who in consequence, and through fear of prisoner left the house." John's deteriorating mental state reached a crisis when he was boarding with Evert Reed in the fall of 1836, and challenged Reed to a duel. When Reed refused, Titcomb "made so much trouble about the house, locking the doors, talking about conspiracies against his life" that he was evicted and cast out onto the streets of Boston. After this disturbing testimony about Titcomb's descent into insanity, the first day of the trial ended early in the evening and was set to resume at nine the following morning.

On the morning of Wednesday, November 1, the witnesses called by the defense further supported their claim that John Titcomb was a disturbed man, and his paranoia had led him to commit murder. Sarah Grant, who ran the boardinghouse in Boston where he lived from January through March 1836, stated that his paranoid rants about people wanting to kill him greatly troubled her other tenants and ultimately she was forced to kick Titcomb out "on account of his language and conduct." Sewall Butterfield, another man who worked as cooper with Titcomb in Boston, stated that one day John refused to work because he accused Butterfield of being a freemason and wanting to murder him. Charles Titcomb, John's brother, asked Butterfield to try to talk to his brother and convince him there was no such plot, but there was no reasoning with John. "I recommended his confinement in a Hospital for the Insane," Butterfield confirmed. But it never happened.

In January 1837, Titcomb finally left Boston after alienating himself with his unpredictable behavior. At the request of his friend Mr. Shattuck, the two men traveled across the wintry landscape to Shattuck's homestead in Sutton, New Hampshire, northwest of Concord. For several weeks, they worked together in the woods cutting lumber, and according to Shattuck, Titcomb "behaved well", so in a kind gesture he proposed they establish a cooper's shop together. But all was not well in John's mind apparently. According to Henry and Joseph Carleton of Warner, Titcomb told them that Shattuck had plotted to kill him with an ax. Hiram Dimond, also of Warner, testified that John had boarded at his home for only a week before he told Titcomb to leave because Dimond's mother and sister "were afraid to have him remain about the house."

Perhaps the most troubling testimony came from Charles Titcomb, who had long recognized that his brother was mentally ill and had tried but failed to get him help. Charles testified that in March 1836 he had actually applied to have his brother admitted to the State Lunatic Hospital in Worcester, Massachusetts. Since it had opened in January 1833, the insane asylum in central Massachusetts had already been recognized as one of the finest such institutions in the United States, if not the world, at that time. Largely responsible for this reputation was the hospital's superintendent, Dr. Samuel Woodward, who in 1844 would be elected by his peers as the first president of the American Psychiatric Association.[7] Although Woodward could not attend the trial in New Hampshire, he wrote a compelling letter in which he stated that John Titcomb could not be admitted in 1836 because his asylum was already overcrowded with patients. It became clear that had Charles been able to have his brother committed to the hospital a year sooner, Israel Russell would still be alive.

In addition to Woodward's letter, Dr. Rufus Wyman, director of the acclaimed McLean Asylum for the Insane in Charlestown, Massachusetts, traveled to New Hampshire for the Titcomb trial. Interestingly, he had testified in the Prescott case a few years earlier. Wyman stated unequivocally that he believed Titcomb was insane, which according to the reporter present, such a bold assertion from "the high character and manifest intelligence of the witness...produced quite a sensation in the courtroom." Ichabod Bartlett delivered the closing argument for the defense, "which he continued with much ability and eloquence for two hours. At about six o'clock in the evening of November 1, the jury retired to the back room of the meetinghouse, and it only took them a few minutes to return and for one of the very first times in New Hampshire legal history, issue a verdict of "Not Guilty, by reason of insanity." The judge then sentenced the prisoner to be confined in an appropriate institution until "their friends gave satisfactory security for their safe keeping and the safety of the community."[8] On Thursday, November 2, 1837, John Titcomb was transported to the State Hospital in Worcester where he should have arrived years earlier.

The Titcomb case only fanned the fiery debate over the care of the mentally ill in New Hampshire. In March 1838, the *New Hampshire Sentinel* in Keene published a series of essays which aspired to "produce a better informed and livelier interest in the Insane, and accelerate the founding of a State Asylum for their benefit." In addition to providing overwhelming statistics of the large number of insane persons in New Hampshire, these pieces remain a prime example of early investigative journalism. The articles explored the inhumane conditions many mentally ill people endured in prisons and poor-houses, where they were forced to live since there was no municipal or state institution built to care for them. In one case, "a deranged female" in New Hampshire was neglected in a prison cell for so long that "during the winter her feet froze, and both required to be amputated." In closing, the author asked readers, "When therefore we see how many are...insane in our State, is it becoming a civilized and Christian community to do nothing to remove or to mitigate so much woe and wretchedness?" Yet another publication in Concord worried that "we cannot believe that we shall be taunted with having hearts as hard as our Granite rocks."[9]

A careful examination of New Hampshire newspapers from this period reveals that a great deal of violence and in some instances, death resulted from the insufficient care for the mentally ill. For example, on July 8, 1831, the *New-Hampshire Sentinel* reported the shocking suicide of a young woman named Lucy Marsh who had slit her own throat as her family helplessly watched. According to her obituary, "the young lady had been for some time out of health, and so much deranged, that it was necessary to watch her movements." In other instances, it was the relatives of mentally ill persons who became the victims, such as John Weeks of Greenland, "one of the most respectable citizens of that town" who was tragically "shot dead by a deranged person living in his family", lamented the *New-Hampshire Patriot* on April 16, 1821.

Only six months after John Titcomb's sensational trial, a group of influential New Hampshire citizens petitioned the New Hampshire government to support the construction of an insane asylum. One newspaper celebrated the event with vivid imagery; "It is a bright sunny relief to the more somber parts of...human nature. It is a brilliant day— sprung after a weary and tempestuous night."[10] In Concord on July 2, 1838, an act to officially incorporate such an institution was approved by the legislature, but many major details, such as where the facility would be located and who would pay for it, had not been determined. In August, the trustees of the new institution met to begin collecting donations and select a building site. This issue eventually caused a divisive political battle that would threaten the entire project.

In August 1839, a committee of prominent New Hampshire physicians and philanthropists assembled at the Worcester State Hospital to get a sense of how such an institution functioned, and determine where the new asylum would be located in New Hampshire. They ultimately decided on Portsmouth, partly because the city had donated more than $20,000 to the cause, more than any other community in the state.[11] However, there was tremendous opposition from other sections of the state to having the hospital built in Portsmouth. The *New-Hampshire Sentinel* in Keene hoped it would be built in there, while the editors of the *New Hampshire Patriot* in Concord left no doubt where they thought the institution should be constructed with a touch of sarcasm:

> *The Portsmouth Journal thinks Concord is not the place for the Insane Asylum, because the centre is thirty miles north of Concord! This of course proves the central position of Portsmouth, which is forty miles south-east of Concord. The centre of population is in fact about eight-miles northwest of Concord, and falls precisely on that healthful and beautiful swell of land in Boscawen known as Courser Hill, and within the limits prescribed by the President of the Board of Trustees. If the Portsmouth people desire the location at the centre, Concord certainly will not object; and...if the Trustees will take that location, there shall never be heard a lisp of complaint, from any citizen of Concord.[12]*

On April 24, 1840, nearly two years after the initial effort to build an institution especially for the mentally ill began in New Hampshire, the *Farmer's Cabinet* of Amherst lamented, "the prospect now is that the efforts to establish an Asylum for the Insane in this State will be abandoned, and the State disgraced thereby." But not all hope was lost. In December 1840, the squabbles between Portsmouth and Concord were ironed out, and the legislature voted to locate the institution in the state capital which was immediately signed into law by Governor John Page. By the autumn of 1841, construction was underway, and the asylum was located "about half a mile southwest from the State House, on a beautiful eminence which commands a view of Concord,

Pembroke, Bow, Hopkinton...the walls of the building are now up and the roof slated."
Even the *Portsmouth Journal* admitted, "notwithstanding our preference for a location in
our own neighborhood, yet we but cannot rejoice that an Asylum for the Insane has
been erected in our state."[13]

In 1845, after the facility had been open for two years, the *New-Hampshire Annual
Register* reported during that time, 220 individuals "in the various grades of mental
derangement, have enjoyed its benefits — of whom 63 have become clothed in their
right minds again, and have gone to their homes."[14] But the exiled John Titcomb would
never regain his sanity or return to New Hampshire. After spending about twelve long
years at the Worcester Insane Asylum, Titcomb contracted cholera, a severe intestinal
infection caused by food or water contaminated with the bacteria vibrio cholerae.
Within five days of being infected, Titcomb likely experienced symptoms that quickly
caused severe dehydration. John Titcomb finally succumbed on August 23, 1849, and
was buried on the hospital grounds.[15] In retrospect, Israel Russell's senseless murder
and John Titcomb's fate in an out-of-state mental institution exposed the severely
inadequate care for the mentally ill in New Hampshire during the nineteenth century,
and served as a catalyst for change.

Endnotes: Chapter Nine

1. Arthur Caverno, *Sermon Delivered at Great-Falls, N.H. Aug. 9, 1835, on the subject of abolishing capital punishment* (Portsmouth: 1836) 3, 19.

2. Quentin Blaine, "Shall Surely Be Put to Death: Capital Punishment in New Hampshire, 1623-1985", *New Hampshire Bar Journal*, Spring 1986; *New Hampshire Patriot & State Gazette*, July 17, 1846;

3. *New-Hampshire Patriot & State Gazette*, April 17, 1837.

4. *New-Hampshire Sentinel*, April 20, 1837.

5. C.C. Lord, *Life and Times in Hopkinton, N.H.*, (Concord, NH: 1890) 131-132.

6. The account of the Titcomb trial is derived from the *New-Hampshire Patriot & State Gazette*, November 6, 1837.

7. Symptoms of typhoid fever were culled from the Center for Disease Control website, http://www.cdc.gov/ncidod/dbmd/diseaseinfo/typhoidfever_g.htm.

8. *New-Hampshire Patriot & State Gazette*, November 5, 1837.

9. Gerald Grob, *The State and the Mentally Ill: A History of Worcester State Hospital in Massachusetts, 1830-1920* (Chapel Hill: University of North Carolina Press, 1966) 43.

10. *New-Hampshire Patriot & State Gazette*, November 5, 1837.

11. *New-Hampshire Sentinel*, March 22, 29, 1838, and *New-Hampshire Patriot & State Gazette*, May 14, 1838.

12. *Portsmouth Journal*, May 5, 1838.

13. *New-Hampshire Sentinel*, October 30, 1839.

14. *New Hampshire Patriot & State Gazette*, May 4, 1840.

15. *Portsmouth Journal*, November 6, 184; G. Parker Lyon, *The New -Hampshire Annual Register and United States Calendar for the year 1845*, (Concord: G. Parker Lyon), 98; Massachusetts Vital Records, 1841-1910, Volume 41, page 364, and the World Health Organization website, http://www.who.int/topics/cholera/en/ accessed on July 2, 2009.

Chapter Ten

"Stolen from the Grave"
Dubious Doctors and the Dead

On June 18, 1824, Sarah Symonds died at the age of thirty and was buried in Bible Hill Cemetery in Hillsborough, New Hampshire. As nearly two centuries passed, her tranquil resting place remained undisturbed until 2007, when it was discovered that her grave had been violated on the night of Halloween to the disgust the people across the Monadnock region.[1] Whether it was a prank by some local teenagers, or perhaps something more sinister, this incident was hardly the first time a grave in New Hampshire had been emptied of its contents; in fact, when Sarah Symonds brief life came to an end during the summer of 1824, burial grounds all over New Hampshire were being robbed of their dead, causing public outrage that forced lawmakers to act against so-called "premature resurrection."[2] Though the act of removing a corpse from a cemetery was certainly a grotesque physical violation of a sacred space, for devout Christians body snatching and denying a person a decent burial was also spiritual sacrilege that prevented the deceased from rising again on Judgement Day, damning their soul for eternity. So how were corpses stolen from New Hampshire cemeteries, who perpetrated these bizarre crimes, and why? The true story behind the body snatching crisis of the nineteenth century remains undoubtedly one of the most bizarre and gruesome phenomena from New Hampshire's past.

By the early nineteenth century, universities across America were buzzing with an influx of medical students, and with them, the study of human anatomy and physiology became all the rage.[3] As a result, demand for cadavers soared across New England, and as discusses in the cases of Thomas Powers and Josiah Burnham earlier in this book, the bodies of executed criminals were often used for dissections. The executions of criminals were so rare, however, that physicians and their students were forced to find a more dependable source of bodies for their anatomical activities: cemeteries. The nasty practice of plundering graveyards often led to violent confrontations between body snatchers and the local populace, who found the exhumation of the dead an affront to their religious beliefs and moral standards.

Probably the most violent reaction to body snatching in American history occurred in April 1788, when a bloody riot raged in New York City for three days after medical students made the mistake of desecrating the grave of a respectable white woman. The incensed populace raided a local hospital where the dissections took place, and before it was over, the local militia was called out to quell the insurgence and six people were killed. As a result, New York became the first state in America to formally legalize medical dissection and simultaneously attempt to protect the graves of the respectable dead.[4]

In New Hampshire, perhaps the first documented body snatching case actually occurred some two years before the New York riot. In August 1786, James O'Neil, described as a "transient person, not having any place of settlement within this, or the United States" arrived at the tavern of Jonas Baker of Charlestown. O'Neil was apparently homeless, broke, and also seriously ill, so out of "pity & humanity" Baker gave him a place to stay, new clothes and food. In December 1786, O'Neil's condition had not improved, so local doctor William Page was called in to care for him, which he did until O'Neil's death and burial in April 1787. This seemingly benign episode would have faded completely into obscurity, was it not for a bizarre entry in the town records about six months later. At the town meeting in September 1787, the "freeholders" of Charlestown voted to form a committee "to make complaint to the state's attorney respecting the digging up and boiling the body of James O'Neil."

More than two centuries later, a great deal of mystery surrounds this perplexing incident. How did the townspeople know his corpse was boiled? Did they find an empty grave and his bones in a cauldron? Who exhumed O'Neil's body and why? The motive for committing such a gruesome act may have had something to do with the cause of O'Neil's death. What illness the poor man suffered from is unknown, but perhaps it tuberculosis or scarlet fever which someone in Charlestown thought might be contagious. For years, historians have searched for more details, but besides the two petitions preserved at the State Archives submitted by Jonas Baker and William Page who sought reimbursement from the state for caring for James O'Neil before he died, no other documents have been unearthed.

Close to a decade later, the unpleasant practice of stealing corpses had infiltrated New Hampshire for good. In March 1796 in Cornish, where Harvard graduate Dr. Nathan Smith was coincidentally teaching human anatomy to local students, the residents of the town authorized the selectmen to punish anyone caught exhuming bodies from the cemetery. Then on May 27, Cornish residents sent an unusual petition to the state government in Exeter, in which they claimed "whereas the dead have been molested & the body of one man removed from a public burying ground...we your petitioners in behalf of the Inhabitants...humbly pray you to take the matter into your wise consideration & pass an act whereby perpetrators may be punished & the dead securly rest." The New Hampshire politicians did not wait long to grant this request. On June 16, they signed into law "An Act to Prevent Persons from Digging Up the Bodies of Dead Peaple."[5] It read:

> *Be it enacted...that if any person or persons shall enter any church yard or any public or private burying place or any place where persons are buried in this State and there dig up or carry away any human body or remains thereof...shall for every such offence on conviction thereof...be fined a sum not exceeding one thousand dollars be publicly whipped not exceeding thirty nine stripes or be imprisoned not exceeding one year as the Court before whom the conviction shall be considering the nature and agravation of the offence may order. Provided nevertheless that this act shall not extend to any persons who may have a licence from any Justice of the peace in the county...authorizing him or them to dig up such dead body when complaints are made and suspicions entertained that the deceased came to his or her death by some unlawful means...*

It is probably no coincidence either that this curious new legislation was created around the same time that lawmakers also heard rumors that Nathan Smith had contacted Dartmouth College about the possibility of establishing a medical school in Hanover. In fact, in 1798 "the board of trustees...made a provision for a medical establishment in the university...and elected Nathan Smith, M.A. Professor of Medicine, who will annually deliver a course of lectures on Anatomy and Surgery; to commence on the first Wednesday in Oct. and to continue ten weeks. The lectures will be accompanied with dissections and experiments under the advantages of a good laboratory and apparatus."[6] As this advertisement illustrates, anatomy courses, and accompanying human dissections, were typically held during the late fall and early spring, when bodies coincidentally disappeared from cemeteries in the vicinity of Dartmouth.

But how did one exactly go about stealing a body from a grave? Lurid descriptions abound in old newspapers which provide macabre insight into how body snatchers conducted their dirty business. First of all, information had to be supplied to doctors or their pupils that a death had occurred nearby, and when the burial had taken place. The obvious goal of any hired body snatcher or medical student was to exhume the body the deed as quietly and neatly as possible without arousing the suspicions of the family or friends. But this was not an easy task. Descending on a cemetery under the cover of darkness, body snatchers required a carriage or wagon of some sort to transport the corpse and also utilized various tools, including a shovel, a crowbar or auger to remove the top of the coffin, a lantern, and a long hook or rope to pull out the body to complete their grisly mission.[7] When the bodies of seven men and women were brazenly exhumed from the cemetery in what is today Essex, Massachusetts between 1812 and 1818, it was believed the bodies were "dragged from their deposits with ropes."[8] Only a hole just large enough to pull out the body was made, because unearthing the entire grave consumed far too much time, and was difficult to conceal. Since embalming was not yet widely practiced in New England at this time, a body had to be exhumed very soon after interment before serious decomposition began, which would make the corpse useless for anatomical study. Weather could also be a factor determining when graves were robbed of their contents, as rain or snow could leave obvious traces that someone had been in a cemetery, and body snatchers had to exhume the dead before the ground had been frozen hard by winter's chill. Often the bodies of indigents or individuals who committed suicide were targeted by grave robbers because it was believed no one would visit or protect their graves.

In May 1824, for instance, the body of a young woman named Jane Benton was found in a river near Hartford, Connecticut and it was believed she "came to her death by drowning herself, in a fit of insanity" and was quickly buried. About a week later, Benton's grave was exhumed by authorities who suspected her body had been stolen. Instead of an empty coffin, they were appalled to find "the remains of the deceased with a rope around her neck. The wretch or wretches, concerned in this hellish affair, had unscrewed the lid of the coffin, and by the aid of the rope, drawn the body from thence...but finding it not a fit subject for the knife of the dissector owing to its decayed state, they rudely tumbled it upon the coffin, and hastily closed the grave."[9] When a body was successfully "resurrected" and placed in a large canvas sack, the grave robbers then made the precarious journey back to the confines of the medical school or doctor's office, hoping no one would notice the grave was empty. While this chapter discusses the perpetrators who were caught and a record of their crime exists, there were certainly many who escaped detection and left behind many empty graves in cemeteries across New Hampshire that will never be discovered. The area surrounding Hanover would be particularly affected by this disturbing practice due to its close proximity to New Hampshire's first medical school.

A decade after its first courses were offered in 1798, the Dartmouth Medical School (then known as the New Hampshire Medical Institution) was gaining respectability and attracting notable lecturers. In the fall of 1808, Dartmouth welcomed Dr. Alexander Ramsay, a famous Scottish physician who spent two months in Hanover presenting "Anatomical demonstrations & doctrines of Physiology, Pathology, etc." and awarded gold medals to the students who produced "the best dissections and demonstrations of the Organs of Vision, Hearing, Brain, and Heart at Dartmouth College."[10] An incident at the college a year later points to where a majority of the "subjects" for these anatomical displays were being supplied. In late November 1809, Dr. Nathan Smith hired one of his medical students, Ruggles Sylvester, to procure a corpse in Boston (where they were much more easily obtained) and bring it back to Dartmouth for dissection. But instead Sylvester made the poor decision to steal the body of a young boy named Horace Bicknell who had recently died in nearby Enfield.[11]

The night Sylvester and his fellow students were conveying the child's corpse back to Dartmouth, their visible nervousness raised the suspicions of a toll house attendant on a local road. The following morning town officials confirmed their suspicions at the cemetery and then immediately set out for the medical school. After an arduous search, the sheriff and a few relatives accidently discovered the boy's mutilated body shoved haphazardly into a closet. According to possibly the only newspaper report of the incident, the searchers "also found two other bodies; one a colored female, about 10 y. the other a child apparently still born; and the bones of a full grown female to appearance lately dissected."[12] One of the outraged men grabbed an ax and threatened to demolish the anatomical display and ravage the entire building. When student Ezekiel Cushing flashed two loaded flintlock pistols concealed in his jacket, the townspeople backed down but promised that any miscreants would be prosecuted. They returned the body of Horace Bicknell to the Enfield cemetery, and their anger and resentment towards the medical school smoldered for years. In May 1810, the residents of Enfield, Plainfield, Lebanon, and Grafton sent a petition to the state government, demanding they stop the "inhuman practice of...digging up the bodies of the dead for the purpose of dissection."[13]

A few weeks later, the state legislature acquiesced by passing another law to stop the interstate "traffic of dead bodies" that existed between Vermont, New Hampshire, and Massachusetts. Anyone caught bringing a corpse from another state would be fined a huge sum "not exceeding two thousand dollars, be publicly whipped not exceeding thirty nine stripes, or be imprisoned not exceeding two years."[14] Ruggles Sylvester was tried at the Grafton Superior Court for his involvement in the Dartmouth grave robbing scandal, but stayed out of jail and eventually received his medical degree in 1811.[15] A few years later, Dr. Nathan Smith ultimately left Dartmouth for Yale, partly because he felt New Hampshire's strict laws severely hampered the operations of the medical school. But nevertheless, body snatching reached epidemic proportions across New Hampshire during the decades before the Civil War.

On September 28, 1820, middle-aged Josiah Prescott succumbed to a severe fever and was hastily buried in the North Road Cemetery in Candia. As autumn gave way to winter, Prescott's widow and four surviving children began to suspect something was amiss. On May 13, 1821, the grave was opened by the family, who were stunned to discover that Josiah's body was long gone. Immediately under suspicion was aptly named Dr. William Graves, a physician in nearby Deerfield who was known to have performed human dissections with local medical students. Graves was brought in for questioning but the charges were soon dropped. But the indignation of the residents of Candia was so deep that one of them, Elijah Smith, composed a vivid poem about the grave robbery:

> But here among the cells of clay,
> An awful scene has been displayed,
> Miscreants bold have stol'n away
> A subject which has here been laid.
> Beneath the covert of the night,
> They did commit this shameful act.
> That none might bring their crime to light,
> Or dare to charge them with fact.
> Yet in the resurrection day,
> When all in judgement shall appear,
> Prescott will then without delay,
> Meet those who stole his body here.
>
> Then hear and tremble at the thought,
> Ye perpetrators of the deed,
> That you in judgement must be brought,
> Then guilty of the crime to plead.

Less than a year later, Dr. Graves was again the prime suspect when Simon Batchelder of Allenstown discovered the body of his infant child had been removed from its coffin in the local cemetery. Coincidentally, only a few weeks after the child's death on July 1, 1820, the corpse of a newborn which had been dissected and chemically preserved was found in a closet in Graves' office. Samuel Morrill of Deerfield testified

119

during the trial that he was taken aback when Dr. Graves showed him "a thing that appeared to be a dried child, which gave him a queer kind of turn." As an expert witness, Graves' lawyers called upon Dr. James Pierrepont, a respected physician from Portsmouth who told the court it would take at least two months for even a skilled anatomist to dissect and varnish the corpse of an infant, and it was "not easy to make a good one at all in the summer months." The presiding judge ultimately dismissed the charges against Graves because "there was no evidence to connect the child of Mr. Batchelder with the preparation in Dr. Graves' office; and on the contrary, there was evidence that it could not be the same, for it was proved that such a preparation could not be made in less than two months, while the one in Graves' possession was seen there in less than three weeks after the death of Mr. Batchelder's child."

But the aptly named Dr. Graves did not stay out of trouble for long. In 1822, the residents of Goffstown discovered the young daughter of William McCole had been snatched from her grave, and although the culprit was never found, it's a possibility that Dr. Graves was behind it. In 1837, after he had relocated to the booming mill city of Lowell, Massachusetts, William Graves was accused of "murder, by mal-practice" after a young pregnant woman, Mary Ann Wilson, died in his house only a few days after undergoing an abortion. Dr. Graves miraculously also managed to be acquitted of this heinous charge, and died at the age of sixty on April 1, 1843.[16]

William Graves, however, was hardly the only doctor with New Hampshire connections to find himself under suspicion of body snatching. In the fall of 1822, Charles Knowlton, a young man from Templeton, Massachusetts, aspired to attend the medical school at Dartmouth but lacked sufficient funds for tuition. When he learned that Dartmouth was paying the generous sum of fifty dollars for each cadaver, he and another student dug up a dead body in Massachusetts and secretly carried it on a wagon on their journey up to Hanover. By the time they arrived at Dartmouth and presented their macabre cargo to one of the medical faculty at the college, the corpse was decomposing rapidly and had to be buried without delay. Knowlton and his companion were still paid twenty dollars for their trouble.[17]

In the fall of 1823, an anonymous letter designed to spook anyone who dared desecrate the dead appeared in New Hampshire newspapers:

Hanover, Oct. 8th, 1823.
A warning to resurrection men, alias quacks.

Among a collection of various kinds of bones, many of which are human, deposited in chests in the cellar of the Medical building in this village, for several nights past, there has been a strange and unusual commotion, accompanied with the most doleful and appalling groans; the chests were overturned and the bones scattered to the four corners of the cellar. Upon immediately visiting the cellar, no vestige of any person or living being whatsoever, could be seen, there being moreover no observable access to the cellar, but what was carefully secured. At first a general panic pervaded those who inhabited the building, some fled affrighted from the haunted spot, at midnight, leaving their daily habiliments behind, and one is said to have fainted and become apparently lifeless. Large numbers, to the amount of a hundred or more, collected on one night, to witness the unaccountable affair, and if possible, to detect the cause. Diligent investigation was made, by some, whose patriotic and manly feelings surmounted their fears, but their efforts proved unsuccessful. We can only say, it is an unaccountable mystery, and hope that the dead may rest in the graves hereafter.[18]

This stunt failed to discourage most medical students, and many of the dead did not rest in their graves for long. In 1823, Charles Knowlton once again raided his hometown cemetery in Massachusetts to bring to Dartmouth, but in August he was caught in the act. In May 1824, when the Supreme Judicial Court convened in Worcester, Knowlton was convicted of stealing a corpse, and was sentenced to spend two months in jail and pay a hefty fine. Despite this personal hardship and embarrassment, he still managed to graduate from Dartmouth in August 1824, and later in life, once again earned notoriety and controversy for his pioneering efforts in support of female birth control.[19]

1824 was a busy year for other body snatchers across New Hampshire. On October 31, Bezaleel Beckwith, the forty-three year old tax collector in rural Acworth died and was laid to rest in the town cemetery, but his body did not remain there for long. Less than a month later, the *New-Hampshire Sentinel* revealed that Beckwith's body had been "stolen from the grave, about 10 days after burial!" In early December, Acworth native James Wilson, and another young man named Carpenter, both medical students at the Vermont Academy of Medicine in Castleton, were charged with stealing a dead body for dissection. Apparently, the young men arrived in the village at "3 o'clock on the morning of the 12th, having in their wagon a large box. They tarried until the following afternoon, when they returned to Acworth and completed their purpose." When the terrible discovery was made a short time later, the townspeople immediately suspected the two young students who had left town in a hurry. Wilson was arrested in Vermont and sent back to New Hampshire in May 1825 but it appears that the charges were eventually dropped, and Beckwith's remains were never found.[20] The residents of Acworth were so distraught by this incident that they raised funds to have a unique headstone carved and placed on the Beckwith's vacant grave.[21] It read:

> *This stone tells the death of*
> *Bezaleel Beckwith*
> *not where his body lies.*
> *He died Oct. 31, 1824, aged 43.*
> *The thirteenth day after, his body*
> *was stolen from the grave.*
> *Now twice bereaved the mourner cries,*
> *My friend is dead, his body gone;*
> *God's act is just, my heart replies,*
> *Forgive, oh God, what man has done.*
> *Erected by the friends of the deceased in*
> *Acworth in place of one destroyed by some*
> *ruthless hand in April, 1825.*

Only a few weeks before Bezaleel Beckwith's body was resurrected, Mary Hilton, a seventy-three year old widow in Andover died on October 12, 1824. Two days later, on a Thursday, her body "was conveyed by her weeping friends to the grave, once a peaceful retreat where the wicked ceased from troubling and the weary were at rest. But it is no longer so...On Saturday night her body was torn from the grave, and conveyed beyond the reach of her anxious friends!"[22] When her family discovered the crime the following Sunday morning, an intense search for the culprit began. On January 14, 1825, Zenas C. Johnson, a local doctor who lived in adjacent Salisbury, was arraigned at the Merrimack County Superior Court for exhuming the corpse of Mary Hilton but he pleaded not guilty. Johnson's trial took place the following August and much of the proceedings of this strange case were documented in local newspapers. Polly Clark, who was Mrs. Hilton's married daughter, told the court that she had an awkward conversation with Dr. Johnson about her mother's death; Dr. Johnson "at first denied having any knowledge of her death or sickness — but afterwards he said he saw her grave."

Even more damning testimony came from Dr. Jesse Merrill, the defendant's brother-in-law and landlord, who testified that Johnson had told him after the old woman's death that "from the singularity of Mrs. Hilton's disorder he thought she would be a good subject for dissection." Joseph Cilley, the church sexton in Andover, added that he actually saw Johnson watching him from a distance while he was digging Mary Hilton's grave. Kendal Peabody of Salisbury, who lived only six miles from where the old woman was buried, testified that the day the body was stolen, Dr. Johnson had rented a yellow wagon from him; two other residents of Andover alleged that they saw the same wagon going in the direction of the graveyard and back again early on the morning of October 17. Johnson's lawyers brought in a few witnesses in an attempt to prove that the doctor had actually hired the wagon to travel some fifty miles to visit relatives in Westmoreland, but with the overwhelming circumstantial evidence the jury found him guilty. Johnson was present during the trial, according to eyewitness accounts, but when he was summoned by the court to hear his sentence, the doctor had somehow slipped out of the courtroom and his bond of $250 was forfeited. What ultimately happened to Zenas Johnson remains a mystery.[23]

Highly publicized cases such as this one created a body snatching hysteria across New Hampshire. One newspaper captured the growing outrage against the medical profession:

> *Is it not enough to chill the blood in our veins to think, that we employ in our families those doctors for the healing and sick, but as soon as the patient dies and is interred, we have... them stolen, perhaps by the same physician that attended them in their last illness and shipped for foreign market. So prevalent has this practice become in some places, that the towns have to make vaults with bolts and bars to preserve their dead from the vultures that speculate in the dead...*
>
> *Previous to the incorporation of those [medical] societies, our dead were undisturbed. But now these societies have established many seminaries for the education of their pupils, and those seminaries...have now become factories, where they carry on the business of manufacturing the dead man's bones into anatomies. So lucrative has the business become...that according to the best information, they bid up a large bounty for the dead bodies of our friends; so much, indeed, that any pupil that can produce the dead body of one of friends, shall have three months tuition free, and so on, for every dead body that can be obtained...whether old or young. And so prevalent has the digging up of the dead become that we must pass sleepless nights to guard the sacred remains of our departed friends, or have them stolen and carried into the factory. So much for civilized and christianized American Doctors. O shame, where is thy blush!!![24]*

The New Hampshire government passed another law in 1825 in a desperate attempt to stop body snatching, but it continued to be a major problem. In early 1826, "great excitement" pulsed through the town of Lyme, New Hampshire, when the body of a young woman was robbed from her grave and the "perpetrators of this horrid sacrilege" remained unknown. But some three years later, Dr. Gilman Kimball, a former cadet of Norwich Academy and an 1827 Dartmouth graduate, was convicted of exhuming the body of Abigail Franklin from the same village burial ground in Lyme, and was sentenced to pay a five hundred dollar fine. Despite this professional embarrassment and serious financial setback, Kimball went on to have an illustrious career as a physician in Lowell, Massachusetts, where he became one of the very first Americans to successfully perform gynecological surgery during the 1850s.[25]

Gilman Kimball was not the only prominent New Hampshire physician to be accused of exhuming corpses; in 1826, Dr. Noah Martin (also a Dartmouth graduate) was embroiled in a controversial body snatching trial. Residents of Deerfield were convinced that Martin had been among a group of medical students who had attempted to steal the body of Jonathan Junkins in 1824. On the night of May 9, two local men hid "themselves behind the wall...of the burying yard lay on their arms from 8 o'clock in the evening to near midnight, when two men came up the road, went into the graveyard, looked about a short time and went back again. Soon after, five men came up-three of whom entered the yard and begun to dig at the grave, whilst the other two, armed with swords, patrolled the street."[26] The guards surprised the grave robbers and opened fire, sending them running for cover and into the night. In the street, the two armed men came to face to face with one of the young students, and "they were both positive that Martin was one of the men who had been walking the street...and had been several years acquainted with him, and were sure they could not be mistaken."

Martin was indeed living in Deerfield at the time, and it was common knowledge that he was studying with the notorious Dr. William Graves. At the trial some two years later, however, Martin was able to produce a number of witnesses who convinced the jury he had been at the home of a patient several miles away that evening, and was "far more agreeably employed, than in seeking dead bodies, or disturbing grave yards." Noah Martin would become one of the most successful physicians and politicians in New Hampshire before the Civil War, and served two terms as governor during the 1850s. Although it makes one wonder, who really was among the group of thugs who unsuccessfully tried to steal a body in Deerfield in 1824?

New London was yet another town caught up in the body snatching panic during the early nineteenth century. In September 1829, Dr. Jonathan Dearborn, the unpopular postmaster, suddenly disappeared. It was reported that two years before "suspicions were excited, that a dead body, then recently interred, had been raised from the grave, and that Dr. Dearborn was the resurrectionist." The rumors of his grave robbing exploits persisted, and the family of the deceased person finally decided to open the grave. To their dismay, they found the coffin empty and the lid split in half. Later that same day, Dearborn vanished, leaving little doubt of his guilt.[27] Then in October 1829, another doctor was arrested for exhuming the body of twenty-six year old Abigail Colcord, who sadly died after the birth of her only child. This medical man, whose identify was concealed by local newspapers, was "discharged in consequence of the insufficiency of the testimony against him."[28]

During the 1830s occurred some of the more unusual body snatching episodes in New Hampshire's history. In November 1830, the selectmen of Roxbury, New Hampshire offered a $300 reward for any information about who exhumed the bodies of three children, and the leaders of Milton offered a similar sum after body snatchers invaded their town the following year. These events led one newspaper editor to proclaim, "the absolute necessity of having subjects for dissection in our Medical Colleges, and the total destitution of all legal means of procuring a supply of them, renders some Legislation on the subject of the most pressing importance."[29]

A few months later, another disturbing find was made in Hopkinton, not far from Concord. On May 1, elderly Joseph Philbrick died and was buried in the new village cemetery. Only a few days later, as she laying dying Philbrick's widow requested to be buried in the same grave with her husband and then passed away. While honoring her wish, the fresh grave was re-opened, revealing that Mr. Philbrick's body had already been snatched! A young physician living in town was suspected to be the culprit, but the corpse was nowhere to be found and the charges were ultimately dropped. About a year later, however, an awful discovery was made: "The dead body of Mr. Joseph Philbrick, that was, on the night of the fifth day of May, 1831...stolen from his grave, was, on the 21st of May last, found in the woods owned by Maj. Weeks, in Hopkinton, and was again interred in the grave appointed him by his friends, to rest, we hope, until the resurrection of all the dead."[30]

In April 1834, the body of Alpheus Brown, described as "a stranger partially deranged", was stolen from his grave in Somersworth and soon after found stuffed into a barrel in the store of Mark E. Marshall.[31] In July, another scandal stormed the pages of newspapers when the dead body of an Irish immigrant was found lying in the barn of Samuel Simpson in Concord. A few days later on July 14, the *New-Hampshire Patriot & State Gazette* printed a description of the man's appearance with the hope he might be identified, and due to the oppressive hot weather, reported that after a brief autopsy, the man's body had been "respectably interred in the common burying ground by the Town Authorities of Concord." This was not, however, the end of the story. A week later, a competing paper alleged that the chairman of the city selectmen, a Colonel Davis, had actually "felt a great desire" to see the unknown man's body dissected, and after two physicians refused to open up the body, "it was done by some young men, medical students, by the side of the fence, in the grave yard, where, naked and mutilated, it was exposed to the view of a throng of little children who had assembled...and then committed to the earth."[32]

In Concord, lawmakers soon made grave robbing a felony, but also tried to ease the shortage of cadavers by making it legal "for the overseers of the Poor, or selectmen in any town in this state, to surrender the dead bodies of such persons...to any regular physician...to be by said Physician used for the advancement of anatomical science, provided...that no such dead body shall...be so surrendered, if within thirty six hours from the time of...death, any one or more persons claiming to be kin, friend or acquaintance of the deceased, shall require to have said dead body inhumed." Even when a dead body was legally supplied to a doctor for "the promotion of anatomical science", the legislators were careful to remind them "that it shall be used for such purpose only...and so as in no event to outrage public feeling, and that after having been so used, the remains thereof shall be decently buried."

In a small victory for the medical profession, the state also legitimized dissection by declaring that "it shall be lawful or any physician...or for any medical student...to have in his possession...human dead bodies....obtained under provisions of this act, for the purposes of anatomical enquiry or instruction."[33] Eventually the study of human anatomy gained limited acceptance from the public. In 1836, for example, Dr. Timothy Haynes advertised his "Anatomical Rooms, on Main-street, Concord N.H. where he will devote a large share of his time in demonstrating anatomy to students, and making anatomical preparations for his museum." Several years later, a Dr. Cutter even offered educational lectures on human anatomy and physiology at the town hall in rural Amherst.[34]

But body snatching continued to be a problem in New Hampshire. On July 4, 1839, the legislature ordered that "if any person shall wilfully destroy, mutilate, deface, injure or remove any tomb, monument, grave-stone...placed in memory of the dead...such person so offending shall be subject to imprisonment for a term not exceeding six months or a fine not exceeding five hundred dollars."[35] During the 1840s, the town of Cornish was the site of what might be described as a case of "domestic" body snatching completely unrelated to the study of anatomy. In 1844, a farmer died and his widow remarried two years later but her "second husband it appeared did not, in the lady's estimation, in all things quite equal the first husband." In June 1846, newspapers reported indignantly that when this heartbroken woman revealed these feelings to her second husband, he "started without a word, went to the barn, put his oxen into cart, proceeded to the graveyard, and actually dug up the remains of the first husband— carried the coffin home, and set it down in the kitchen— declaring *'that if it made such a difference he should be on the farm.'*"[36]

There were also rare instances when public fervor demanded that a corpse be exhumed. For example, when Samuel Wilson of Nashua died in 1841, "rumors of suspected foul play were circulated about town, and some of his friends had him disinterred for examination, without leave of the proper authority." When it was confirmed Wilson had really died of natural causes, his overzealous friends were reminded that "digging up of dead bodies without a license from the selectmen...is an offence, punishable by imprisonment." In June 1847, when Almira Harris died miserably in Troy, New Hampshire after being married less than a year, her father Amasa Fuller asked her husband Stephen Harris to have the body exhumed so the contents of his daughter's stomach could be analyzed. Fuller claimed that local rumor was that Almira had been poisoned. While Harris seemed reluctant to take this drastic step, he begrudgingly hired Dr. Luke Miller of Troy to unearth the grave and perform the gruesome task of removing the intestines and liver from his wife's decomposing body and sealing them inside a glass jar. Testing of these remains allegedly revealed traces of arsenic, and Harris was tried for his wife's murder but acquitted in September 1847.[37]

Dr. Frederick C. Waite, who pioneered research on body snatching during the 1940s, argued that the last decades of the nineteenth century were marked by more effective anatomy laws and dramatic changes in the medical school curriculum which led to the decline of body snatching. But midnight raids on burial grounds did not die out completely. In December 1895, two Dartmouth students were convicted of snatching the body of Joseph Murdock after he hanged himself. As late as February 1897, there was a brazen attempt to steal the body Mrs. Zelotus Stevens from the

Blossom Hill Cemetery in Concord. The *New York Times* reported, "a daughter of Mrs. Stevens...visited her mother's grave and saw enough to satisfy her that an attempt had been made to disturb the body. She notified the police, who opened the grave. The earth had been removed and the cover of the outer box had been broken open, as had also the top of the casket, but the body had not been disturbed. It is supposed that the would-be resurrectionists were frightened off."[38] But perhaps no body snatching case in nineteenth-century New Hampshire would arouse as much outrage as the events surrounding the disappearance of a mill girl in Manchester in 1848.

Endnotes: Chapter Ten

1. *Boston Globe*, November 7, 2007 and the *New Hampshire Union Leader*, November 7, 2007. In January 2008, three teenagers were arrested in connection with this case.

2. Frederick C. Waite, "The Development of Anatomical Laws in the States of New England," *New England Journal of Medicine* (December 1945) 718-719.

3. Michael Sappol, *A Traffic of Dead Bodies: Anatomy and Embodied Social Identity in Nineteenth-Century America* (Princeton, New Jersey: Princeton University Press, 2002) 48-60.

4. Sappol, *A Traffic of Dead Bodies*, 105-109.

5. *New Hampshire State Papers*, Volume XI , Issac Hammond ed. (Concord: 1882) 460, and *The Laws of New Hampshire*, 1792-1801, 335-336.

6. Oliver S. Hayward and Constance E. Putnam, *Improve, Perfect, and Perpetuate: Dr. Nathan Smith and Early American Medical Education* (Hanover: University Press of New England, 1998) 36-37, also *Oracle of the Day*, September 29, 1798.

7. Suzanne M. Shultz, *Body Snatching: The Robbing of Graves for the Education of Physicians in Early Nineteenth Century America* (Jefferson, North Carolina: McFarland & Company, 1992) 26-35.

8. See the author's article, "A Most Daring and Sacrilegious Robbery: The Extraordinary Story of Body Snatching at Chebacco Parish in Ipswich, Massachusetts", *New England Ancestors*, Spring 2005, 31-34.

9. *American Mercury*, May 11 and May 25, 1824.

10. *Portsmouth Oracle*, October 8, 1808.

11. *The Reporter*, January 20, 1810.

12. *The Reporter*, January 20, 1810.

13. *Improve, Perfect, and Perpetuate*, 96-101 and *Enfield, New Hampshire 1761-2000: The History of a Town Influenced by the Shakers*, Nancy Blanchard Sanborn ed. (Portsmouth: Peter Randall Publisher, 2006) 261-262; the petition of May 28, 1810 is preserved today at the New Hampshire State Archives, Concord.

14. *The Laws of New Hampshire*, 1801-1811, 894-895.

15. George Chapman, *Sketches of the Alumni of Dartmouth College...* (Cambridge: Riverside Press, 1867) 141.

16. J. Bailey Moore, *History of the Town of Candia...*(Manchester: George W. Browne, 1893) 107-109, and George Plummer Hadley, *History of the Town of Goffstown*, 1733-1920 (Concord: Rumford Press, 1922) 187. *Portsmouth Journal of Literature & Politics*, March 2, 1822, *New Hampshire Patriot & State Gazette*, October 16, 1837, and December 31, 1838. Charles Cowley, A History of Lowell (Lowell: 1868) 125.

17. Robert E. Riegel, "The American Father of Birth Control", *New England Quarterly*, Vol. 6 (1933) 470-490.

18. *New-Hampshire Statesmen*, November 17, 1823 and *New-Hampshire Gazette*, November 25, 1823.

19. *Farmer's Cabinet*, May 1, 1824, *Salem Gazette*, August 27, 1824, and Riegel, "The American Father of Birth Control", 480-490.

20. *New-Hampshire Sentinel*, November 26 and December 3, 1824, and *Farmer's Cabinet*, November 5, 1825. Also see the *Connecticut Courant*, December 7, 1824.

21. Thomas C. Mann and Janet Greene, *Over Their Dead Bodies: Yankee Epitaphs & History* (Brattleboro Vermont: Stephen Greene Press, 1962) 54.

22. *New Hampshire Patriot & State Gazette*, November 22, 1824.

23. The description of Johnson's trial was taken from the *New-Hampshire Patriot & State Gazette*, August 15, 1825. Merrimack County Superior Court of Judicature, Docket 204, January-August 1825, New Hampshire State Archives, Concord.

24. *Vermont Gazette*, July 26, 1825.

25. *Norwich University 1819-1911, Her History, Her Graduates, Her Roll of Honor, Volume II* (Montpelier, VT: Capital City Press, 1911) 157.

26. *Portsmouth Journal of Literature & Politics*, March 11, 1826.

27. *New-Hampshire Statesman*, October 17, 1829 and *New-Hampshire Sentinel*, November 27, 1829.

28. *Dover Gazette*, October 13, 1829.

29. *Farmer's Cabinet*, January 1, 1831.

30. *Dover Gazette*, May 24, 1831, *New-Hampshire Statesman*, May 28, 1831, and *New-Hampshire Patriot and State Gazette*, June 11, 1832.

31. *Portsmouth Journal of Literature & Politics*, April 26, 1834.

32. *New-Hampshire Statesman & State Journal*, July 19, 1834.

33. *Laws of New Hampshire 1829-1835*, 583-584.

34. *New-Hampshire Patriot & State Gazette*, March 21, 1836, and Farmer's Cabinet, August 12, 1842.

35. *Laws of New-Hampshire Passed June 1839*, 405.

36. *Pittsfield Sun*, June 18, 1846.

37. *Farmer's Cabinet*, April 9, 1841; *New-Hampshire Sentinel*, September 30, 1847.

38. Waite, "The Development of the Anatomical Laws of New England," *New England Journal of Medicine* 233 (1945).

Chapter Eleven

Mayhem in Manchester: Missing & Murderous Mill Girls

In 1809, the first textile mill was built along the Amoskeag falls of the Merrimack River in rural Derryfield, New Hampshire, then the hometown of Revolutionary War hero John Stark. It was a humble beginning, but Stark's community would eventually become an epicenter of a different revolution that had an equally profound impact on American society. Ambitious citizens soon changed Derryfield's name to Manchester, seeking to one day emulate the industrial might of its English rival. By August 1846, Manchester had exploded into a bustling city of more than 10,000 residents, and its industrial capacity seemed limitless.[1] But two years later, a bizarre series of events akin to a gothic horror novel raised concerns about the social consequences of industrialization and exposed dark, troubling aspects of urban life in New Hampshire during the nineteenth century.

During the spring of 1847, twenty-one year old Sarah Furber left her parents, William and Dorcas (Butler) Furber behind in rural Nottingham, New Hampshire, and became one of the 1,400 "mill girls" who produced over thirteen million yards of cloth annually for Manchester's Amoskeag Manufacturing Company.[2] Surviving payroll records at the Manchester Historic Association reveal that Sarah operated a loom at the Number Two mill, and she was paid once a month, determined by the number of "cuts," or lengths of saleable cloth, she produced. At the beginning of her employment, Sarah was paid $6.64 on April 24, but by the end of May 1847, Sarah had quickly become a more skilled weaver, doubling her earnings to $13.75. During the 1840s, this was a substantial sum for a young woman, given that when the Civil War began more than a decade later, U.S. army privates were paid only thirteen dollars a month.[3]

Like thousands of others men and women from rural New England who traveled to Manchester, Sarah Furber was likely attracted to new city by the quality of life it offered. Shops such as the one run by Jackson & Paige along the main thoroughfare, Elm Street, offered "bonnets, ribbons, laces," and at the saloon of S.H. Bowman, Sarah could have her hair done "in the most fashionable manner." Then she could visit the store of C.M. Putney, a "wholesale and retail manufacturer of confectionary," to indulge in "ice creams."[4] But some observers of the Industrial Revolution, such as Reverend Henry Martyn Dexter, expressed concerns about the impact of the new culture of consumption on the bodies and souls of young women without their families to guide them. In a sermon given in Manchester in December 1847, Dexter noted with disdain that "A young girl with money monthly in her purse can hardly walk by our brilliantly illuminated show windows . . . and be expected to resist the temptation to gratify her love of dress." He further believed even the sweets consumed by the mill girls were a moral danger: "Satan tempted Eve with an apple, and it is much to be feared that his hook, in our time, is often baited at the confectioners."[5]

Sarah Furber also went to Frank Brown's "daguerreotype rooms," where she posed for a haunting portrait which survives only as an engraving. Later, Sarah would be described by a contemporary as having a "form . . . of perfect symmetry . . . and . . . dark brown locks which fell upon her neck . . . which added new beauty to a face which otherwise was not destitute of attractions." Sarah began to attract attention. "Her society began to be courted . . . At the dance and social party her hand oftenest solicited." [6] Perhaps at one of these gatherings Sarah met the much-older Gardner Ingalls (b. 1800), a portrait painter who shared a studio with his brother in Manchester. Ingalls was described as a "fine looking man of commanding appearance, high forehead and keen black eye."[7] Although he had a wife and daughter back in Lowell, Massachusetts, Ingalls and Sarah Furber apparently began a torrid affair. But in late May 1848, Sarah suddenly vanished. On June 7, the *Manchester Messenger* reported "no little excitement has been caused in this city for two weeks past, in consequence of the mysterious disappearance of a young lady named Sarah Furber…who boarded at No. 10 Amherst St. Two weeks ago, she left her boarding house . . . since which she has not been heard of in any way." On June 9, the *New Hampshire Statesman* even claimed that Sarah Furber had been found dead in nearby Goffstown "with her throat cut." But macabre developments in Massachusetts would soon reveal the true fate of this Manchester mill girl and shock New England to its core.

On the evening of Monday, May 22, 1848, the famed physician and Harvard professor Oliver Wendell Holmes had an unexpected visitor at his home in Boston. On that spring evening, Holmes was greeted by Dr. John McNab of Manchester, who boldly inquired if Holmes was interested in buying the corpse of a young woman. Holmes had recently published his groundbreaking study *The Contagiousness of Puerpal Fever*, which linked infection to the deaths of many women after childbirth. McNab knew that Holmes needed a supply of female cadavers for his research, and at medical schools across New England during the nineteenth century, an notorious "traffic of dead bodies" became prevalent, as medical personnel raided cemeteries for fresh corpses under the cover of darkness.[8] Seizing the opportunity to obtain a "subject," Holmes hastily gave McNab ten dollars for the body, and sent his servant Ephraim Littlefield to discreetly transport the macabre cargo to Harvard. But prior to this dubious transaction, the residents at the boarding house where McNab had arrived with a large, coffin-shaped crate, were disgusted when the box emitted a foul odor and he rudely refused to divulge its contents. The landlord then wrote a damning letter to authorities in Manchester, alerting them to McNab's suspicious behavior.

After examining the body, Holmes and his colleague Frederick Ainsworth also became alarmed and questioned McNab about the circumstances of the young woman's death. McNab would only admit "he had got into a bad scrape, and he must get out of it the best way he could." McNab then paid Ephraim Littlefield five dollars to dispose of the corpse, but Dr. Ainsworth was "convinced that crime was connected with the body . . . and thought it my duty to keep track of the body and await further developments." Ainsworth then embalmed the young woman's body so she might be identified. On the morning of June 7, Manchester's mayor Jacob James arrived at Harvard, and positively identified the deceased as Sarah Furber. They accompanied the body on a train back to Manchester, and on Saturday, June 10, Sarah's body was brought home to her devastated family to rest in Nottingham forever.

At the Manchester City Hall in June 1848, a sensational grand jury hearing exhumed the disturbing details of Sarah Furber's final days, and charged Dr. John McNab and Gardner Ingalls with causing her death. But what was the motive? A search of Sarah's belongings uncovered a letter dated April 27 from Gardner Ingalls that read: "You need not think I am going to forget you, for I can't if I try ever so much. Walter, my brother, is in Manchester painting in the room back of the one I occupied . . . I wrote to him Monday, and told him to get the Doctor down to his room, and to have you go there and have it decided whether it is the case or not, so as to make suitable arrangements when it is necessary. I am impatient to know certain."[10] Ingalls was apparently desperate to know if Sarah was pregnant, which of course she was.

Sarah's roommate, Sarah Clay, testified that Sarah Furber tried to conceal her pregnancy and had planned to have an abortion: "I suspected she was pregnant . . . she had enlarged her dress . . . made a new waist to one dress. She left the mill Monday at noon . . . before she left she came to my room . . . said she was going to be out of the mill about a week." Boardinghouse keeper Phebe Lufkin recounted the troubling events of Wednesday, May 17, 1848: "On Wednesday morning . . . she complained of being unwell, and said she was sick enough to die . . . then she soon vomited two mouthfuls or more of dark colored matter which smelt like laudanum . . . I told her she had better go upstairs and lay down . . . but she said she was better now, and could go without help."[11]

On the corner of Amherst Street, where Sarah lived, was the shop of "H.G Connor, apothecary and druggist," where she perhaps obtained laudanum — a potent mixture of opium and alcohol — in a nauseating attempt to induce a miscarriage.[12]

Since the laudanum made her very ill and apparently failed to induce an abortion, Sarah was forced to turn Dr. McNab to save her from having a child out of wedlock. Another damning note found in Sarah's belongings read: "Miss Furber: — Do me the favor to call this evening — say 8 o'clock . . . Wednesday evening. P.S. Do not disappoint me." But that night, their plan would all go horribly wrong.

Oliver Wendell Holmes served the dual purpose for the prosecution as a participant in the black market sale of Sarah Furber's body and an unrivalled expert on female anatomy of his time. But even Holmes humbly admitted that after performing an autopsy on Furber, "never in my practice have I seen anything like this . . . hope I never shall again." After the abortion was performed by NcNab, probably with highly unsanitary instruments such as metal hook, Sarah probably developed an abdominal infection known today as peritonitis, which caused severe pain and swelling as the infection spread through her body. The last hours of her life must have been nightmarish as McNab watched her die, and concocted a heinous plan to sell her body. One writer contemplated with a shudder, "none but her murderer is known to have been with her, during those days of deepest agony, to alleviate one pang, or whisper in her ear one kind word. There, with him alone, she died . . . no friend was there to hear her last requests or bear a long farewell to her parental home."[13] Even contemporary Edgar Allan Poe would have found it challenging to pen a fictional tale as horrific as the fate of Sarah Furber.

Sarah Furber's death ignited a debate over whether her own actions were to blame, or that she was a victim of the new industrial, morally corrupt society. Not surprisingly, gender often defined the opposing sides of this controversy. In 1848, journalist George Carroll wrote a pamphlet titled "The Manchester Tragedy," in which he claimed Sarah Furber's "moral training might . . . have been . . . defective. It probably was, or she would not have yielded to the allurements of the deceiver, and sacrificed that virtue which is above price — a woman's honor." In contrast, fellow mill girl Lucy Hall was outraged by the crude medical practices which led to Sarah's death. She wrote and published "Lines Composed on the Abduction and Cruel Murder of Miss Sarah H. Furber," which read in part:

> *In men of art and science,*
> *She thought a sure redress,*
> *For all her grief and sorrow,*
> *In long oblivion rest;*
> *O hellish cruel practice,*
> *Which none but fiends should know,*

Yet in our land of science,
It's practised not by few.[14]

The legal and political impact of the Furber tragedy traveled swiftly up the Merrimack River to the state capital of Concord. In January 1849, almost all abortions in New Hampshire were outlawed, and the state pledged to prosecute "every person who shall administer to any pregnant woman with . . . child, any medicine, drug or substance whatever, with intent to destroy such child, unless the same shall have been necessary to preserve the life of such woman . . . upon conviction, be punished by fine not exceeding one thousand dollars, and by confinement to hard labor not less than one year, nor more than ten years."[15]

What became of the men linked to Sarah Furber's gruesome demise? John McNab and Gardner Ingalls were finally indicted in November 1848, then pleaded not guilty and their trials were postponed until May 1849, when McNab became a fugitive and possibly fled to California to join the Gold Rush.[16] He eventually returned discreetly to New Hampshire in the 1860s, and according to contemporary historian John Quincy Bittinger, McNab "was frequently called in critical cases, especially in surgical operations in which he displayed great daring and skill."[17] McNab died in 1879 at the age of ninety-four. Gardner Ingalls apparently served no jail time, since he does not appear in the nineteenth-century Register of Convicts at the New Hampshire State Prison. He died in obscurity on August 15, 1874, and was buried in Sanbornton, New Hampshire.[18] Oliver Wendell Holmes must have regretted his involvement in the Furber affair, but after retiring from Harvard in 1882, he died a celebrity in 1894, and was buried at the famed Mount Auburn Cemetery.[19]

Sarah Furber's fate brutally confirmed the fears many New Hampshire families and authority figures shared concerning the social and moral consequences of the Industrial Revolution, as thousands of young women ventured out into a world far from the safety of home. And the Furber affair was a harbinger of more tragedies to come. In late 1848, when mill girl Elizabeth Nute died shamefully at a local poorhouse near Dover, New Hampshire and was buried in a pauper's grave, the editor of the *Dover Gazette* demanded "in the name of the…the farmers scattered all over our Granite Hills, whose daughters are continuously flocking to these cotton mills, hot-beds of all vices, as they are…a full and thorough investigation."[20] And the issue of young women falling victim to the dangers of an industrial society went beyond the borders of the Granite State. Only a year later newspapers announced the "Supposed Murder of a Factory Girl" in Saco, Maine. Like Sarah Furber, Canadian native Berengera Caswell had become illegitimately pregnant, and died at the home of a local doctor James Smith after a botched abortion in December 1849. He tied her body to a board, and threw it into a tidal creek, hoping that the current would forever conceal the deed. But her corpse was discovered once the ice melted in April 1850, and Smith went to prison for his crime.[21] While Yankee society had failed to save Sarah Furber and Berengera Caswell from a horrible fate in life, ironically these communities banded together to return them to their families after death. In May 1850, when Berengera Caswell's sister arrived in Saco to claim her belongings, the substantial sum of "one hundred dollars was raised to defray the taking of her sister's remains to her parents in Canada."[22] What a sad homecoming it must have been for the parents of these young women.

But contemporaries of the mill girls were not only concerned what might befall them in the morally decrepit streets of New England's mill cities; the citizens of New Hampshire were also alarmed by the shocking criminal acts these young women were perpetrating, and what their punishment should be. During the 1840s, the debate over the death penalty also continued to rage in New Hampshire, when one local newspaper asked: "When will the principle of humanity…become awakened in our legislator's bosoms? When will this brutal savage thirst for human gore, cease?" The state legislature ultimately decided to let the voters of New Hampshire (all men of course) decide this profound question. In November 1844, a hotly debated referendum to abolish the death penalty in New Hampshire was soundly defeated by over 10,000 votes. [23] Only a few years later, New Hampshire officials would be forced to decide whether a woman should receive the death penalty in the Granite State for the first time in over a century.

In 1849, a young woman named Leticia Blaisdell was convicted of first degree murder for poisoning to death Benjamin Blaisdell, the two year old son of her adoptive family. She had also tried unsuccessfully to poison the entire family with morphine, which she confessed to purchasing at a store in Manchester when she worked in the mills there. The apparent motive was that Blaisdell thought she would inherit the family estate in Goffstown if they all died.[24] Almost immediately after the sentence of death was declared by the judge presiding over the trial, an effort to commute Blaisdell's sentence to life imprisonment was initiated by "nearly all the officers of the court that tried her" and the Blaisdell family, whom she had nearly annihilated. When the petition reached the state legislature, it was hotly debated. Walter Harriman, who would eventually become governor in the 1860s, argued that "except for self-defense, I deny that the individual, or society, has the right to take life. God gave. Let Him, alone, take away…I predict the day is not far distant when choking criminals to death according to law will be unknown in New Hampshire."[25] In the end, Blaisdell's death sentenced was indeed commuted by the state government, and on July 5, 1849, the editors of the *Farmer's Cabinet* of Amherst commented, "we cannot but rejoice that we are to be spared the awful scenes that attend a public execution. We believe the community will not suffer by the change of her sentence, which is the prevailing opinion. If not in this, why in any and every case?"

Only a year or so later, New Hampshire's increasing reluctance to use the death penalty on a woman was again revealed when on November 19, 1851, the *Farmer's Cabinet* announced a "Shocking Case of Infanticide" on its front page. A week earlier, a young woman named Kate Poole had arrived in Nashua with a disturbing tale to tell. She claimed that while riding on the train from Manchester on Monday, November 11, her husband had thrown their infant daughter Marian out the window, and then threatened her "with instant death if she raised the alarm." When the train stopped, she claimed he pushed her out of the railroad car and fled. According to the newspaper report, Poole's "plausible story and distressed appearance, awakened sympathy for her, and search was made for the child was immediately made for the child which was not...found until Wednesday morning, when it was taken up with its skull broken, about a mile below Manchester. Suspicion was raised that she was the murderer of the child, and she was accordingly arrested and taken to Manchester."

After an inquest concluded that the child had certainly died from being thrown from a moving train, Kate Poole admitted she had really been traveling alone. She then appeared at the Manchester Police Court on the morning of Friday, November 15. According to a reporter present at the hearing, "the appearance of the prisoner this morning...was very interesting. She was neatly dressed in mourning...She is a medium sized woman, apparently quite young, with rather agreeable features. Her countenance exhibited deep signs of sorrow, and we thought we could distinctly trace in the eye a sort of wildness." During her interrogation, many of the disturbing details came to light:

> She has remarked to someone that she had not the slightest remembrance of lifting the child up to throw it out of the cars, but that she should never forget seeing it fly through the air – it seemed to go like a feather. As soon as she saw that her babe was gone, she screamed "O God, what have I done?" so loud that she supposed that she might be heard in the cars (being in the ladies saloon) and immediately left the saloon and went into the passenger car and sat down and wept... The prisoner states that she is about 23 years of age, a native of Haverhill, N.H., that she worked at Haverhill in the summer of 1850, and

went to school there the succeeding winter to a man by the name of French. She says that her child was born on the 3d day of September. She went to Lowell last spring, and there worked in some of the factories, and stopped at Lowell...last week, when she went to Haverhill and on the succeeding day to Manchester. It seems that she made several trials to obtain a place of work for her board the coming winter, but did not succeed, and says she thought all were against her, and that she had no friends. In this idea, she undoubtedly went to the cars, and while sitting in the depot...without home and with the care of an infant child devolving upon her, her feelings must have been nearly overpowering. Taking all the circumstances into view, we must look upon it more as a case of desperation then of deliberate intention.

Poole's attorney, William Clark, entered a plea of not guilty and she was taken to the Amherst jail to await trial. On a tragic note, newspapers reported that the "mother selected the clothes for the burial of her child" the day before she was arraigned. The *Manchester Mirror* sympathized with the Poole's plight, and asked, "Who but a mother can imagine that woman's desperate feelings? What mother but one driven to desperation, could be brought to the commission of such an act?" Another publication was far less empathetic: "The citizens of Manchester have had in their day their full share of...crimes and excitements...Within a few days our city has been made the theatre of another and unheard of transaction. One that causes the blood to chill in the veins and the enquiry to arise— *of what is human nature capable!*"[26]

The murder of Kate Poole's newborn daughter seems to have been a much more deliberate crime than the deeds of her colonial predecessors Sarah Simpson, Penelope Kenney, and Ruth Blay. Yet Poole was spared the death penalty and convicted of second degree murder. In April 1852, at the age of twenty-three, she was sentenced to spend the rest of her life at the New Hampshire State Prison, with an additional punishment of twenty days of solitary confinement. But many members of New Hampshire's legislature thought her sentence too harsh. Ultimately, Governor Samuel Dinsmoor, Jr. succumbed to growing political pressure and pardoned Kate Poole in August 1852, after she had spent only a few months incarcerated in more comfortable quarters reserved for female inmates.[27] The circumstances which saved the lives of Letitia Blaisdell and Kate Poole clearly mirrored a paradigm shift in the attitudes concerning capital punishment in New Hampshire between the mid-eighteenth and mid-nineteenth centuries.[27] Had they lived a century earlier, there is little doubt that both women would have met their deaths on the gallows of the Granite State.

138

Endnotes: Chapter Eleven

1. Maurice Clarke, John B. Clarke, *Manchester: A Brief Record of Its Past and A Picture of Its Present*, (Manchester: 1875) 23-32

2. *History of Nottingham, New Hampshire* . . . by Elliott Cogswell, pp. 687-88; *A Business Directory of the City of Manchester* (Manchester: 1848) 80, 153

3. Amoskeag Mfg. Co. Payroll, Factory # 2, Ledger 209 (1846-1848), Manchester Historic Association Research Library, Manchester, New Hampshire.

4. *A Business Directory of the City of Manchester*, 157, 194-95.

5. Henry Martyn Dexter, *The Moral Influence of Manufacturing Towns, Delivered at the Dedication of the Franklin Street Church of Manchester, N.H.* (Andover, Mass: 1848) 13, 15, 18;

6. George L. Carroll, *The Manchester Tragedy: A Sketch of the Life and Death of Miss Sarah H Furber* (Manchester: 1848), 7-9.

7. M.T. Runnels, *The History of Sanbornton, New Hampshire*, (Boston: 1881) 2: 390.

8. Michael Sappol, *A Traffic of Dead Bodies: Anatomy and Embodied Social Identity in Nineteenth-Century America* (Princeton, N.J.: Princeton University Press, 2002), 13-73.

9. *Manchester Democrat*, June 16, 1848.

10. Ibid.

11. Ibid.

12. *Manchester Democrat*, February 11, 1848, and *Directory of the City of Manchester* (1848), 201.

13. Carroll, *The Manchester Tragedy*, 12. The symptoms of perionitis were derived from an actual case described in *The Half-Yearly Abstract of the Medical Sciences* . . . *January-June 1862*, (London: John Churchill, 1862), 218.

14. Lucy Hall, *Some Lines Composed on the Abduction and Cruel Murder of Miss Sarah H. Furber, Late of Nottingham, N.H.* (Manchester: 1848), American Antiquarian Society, Worcester, Massachusetts.

15. *Laws of the State of New Hampshire Passed January Session 1849*, (Concord: 1849), 708-709.

16. *Farmer's Cabinet*, May 3, 1849.

17. Bittinger, *History of Haverhill, New Hampshire*, (Haverhill: 1888), 310.

18. Reverend M.T. Runnels, *The History of Sanbornton, New Hampshire* (Boston: 1881) 390.

19. *The Complete Poetical Works of Oliver Wendell Holmes (Boston:* Houghton, Mifflin and Company, 1895), xi-xxi.

20. Dover Gazette, December 2, 1848.

21. Elizabeth DeWolfe, *The Murder of Mary Bean and Other Stories* (Kent, Ohio: Kent State University Press, 2007) 3-29.

22. *Farmer's Cabinet*, May 16, 1850.

23. *New-Hampshire Patriot*, June 6, 1843; Quentin Blaine, "Shall Surely Be Put to Death: Capital Punishment in New Hampshire, 1623-1985", *New Hampshire Bar Journal*, Spring 1986.

24. *Dover Gazette*, March 17, 1849; *Farmer's Cabinet*, April, 26,1849.

25. Amos Hadley, *The Life of Walter Harriman: With Selections from his Speeches and Writings* (Boston: Houghton & Mifflin, 1888) 40-41.

26. *Manchester Mirror*, November 15, 1851, and *Manchester Granite Farmer*, November 22, 1851.

27. *Nashua Telegraph*, May 1, 1852; *Farmer's Cabinet*, August 5, 1852; and "The Register of Convicts at the New Hampshire State Prison, 1812-1883", manuscript at the New Hampshire State Archives, Concord, New Hampshire.

Chapter Twelve

"Farewell Forever"
The Media and Sensationalizing Suicides

While abortion, body snatching, and the death penalty were certainly among the most taboo subjects in nineteenth century New Hampshire, suicide was not far behind. On the evening of Sunday, August 14, 1853, two mill girls in Manchester opened the door of their boardinghouse and stepped into the warm summer air. As they made their way down the street hand in hand dressed in white, it was a sight that would likely have caught the attention of any young man passing by. But these young women were on a mission that would have chilled any warm heart as cold as the windy peak of Mount Washington. Their deaths were perhaps the most sensational and highly-publicized suicides in New Hampshire during the nineteenth century, though far from the only ones. For our own society, which is still struggling with this tragic phenomenon, the history of suicide is a troubling, but worthwhile, subject of study.

The two women at the center of this tragedy were Clara C. Cochran, a native of New Boston, and Catherine B. Cotton, originally from Pownal, Maine. Clara was only nineteen but had taught school in the village of Fisherville near Concord before moving to Manchester to work at the Amoskeag mills in February 1853. Ms. Cotton was twenty-two and had already worked at the mills in Biddeford, Maine and Lowell, Lawrence, and Lynn, Massachusetts before moving to New Hampshire, where the two young women quickly became close friends while living in the same boardinghouse. The other experience they shared was that they both suffered from unrequited love. Clara had corresponded for years with an old schoolmate John Sherwin, whom she hoped to marry someday. But early in 1853, Sherwin rejected her advances and told Clara not to write again until she heard from him. After several of subsequent her letters went unanswered, she lost all hope that her affections would be reciprocated. Ms. Cotton had been deeply hurt when her fiancé in Biddeford, Cyrus Goodwin, suddenly called off their wedding in June 1852 and in March 1853 married another Biddeford girl, Hannah Kimball. Both Clara and Catherine were devastated by their difficulties in finding a husband and began to openly discuss suicide during the summer of 1853.[1]

On a Sunday in late July, the two women mentioned to one of their roommates, Ms. Davis, that three weeks from that date they were going to die. While Davis found their remarks disconcerting, she had no idea how serious they were in carrying out their bold and horrific plan. Over the next few weeks, suicide was a frequent topic in their conversations but on Sunday, August 14, both Clara and Catherine appeared to be in good spirits as they sipped tea and ate a hearty supper with their fellow mill girls. During the afternoon, however, they began packing their trunks with their belongings and composed a few documents which they requested to be mailed the next day. A few minutes before eight o'clock, both girls descended the stairs of their boardinghouse dressed in white as if it was their wedding day, a sardonic irony they surely planned. According to an eyewitness, "one other lady asked them to go out and walk, thinking that thereby their minds might be diverted from the subject which had become so awful." But Clara and Catherine coldly refused to join them.

Within a few moments, Ms. Davis and two other mill girls rushed outside and caught sight of the two women in white hurrying around a corner towards the nearby Amoskeag canal. Before they could stop them, the witnesses watched in horror as Clara and Catherine momentarily stopped on the edge of the canal and plunged into the tepid water "without a word, or scream or a particle of hesitation." Ms. Cotton's body resurfaced a few seconds later and as she floated down the canal, "a young man, James Hall, boldly jumped in and caught her by the dress as she was sinking again but...he was not able to save her. Boards and rails were thrown to her...and though they came within her reach she made no effort to touch them."[2] Ms. Cochran was not seen again until nearly an hour later, when her body was fished out of the canal devoid of life. As news of the shocking dual suicide spread, their belongings at the boardinghouse were searched in an attempt to discover what drove them to commit such "a sudden, deliberate, and self-possessed act." Carefully placed under the oil lamp in their room was a terse note: "To any one who cares to find the bodies of Catharine Cotton and Clara Cochran: You will find us somewhere in the canal, between the Amoskeag Counting-Room and the next bridge."

Even more troubling were a few letters the two young ladies had written before their deaths. While these documents were incredibly personal and painful for their families, the public was hungry for any details of the tragedy. As the editor of one Manchester newspaper observed, "the recent melancholy suicides have created the most intense excitement in our community, and intense curiosity to ascertain the most minute particulars respecting them." Regarding Ms. Cochran's final communication to her sister Ann, the *Manchester American* mused "that such a letter could have been penned by a young girl 19 years of age, with the full determination to hurry herself into the unseen world, almost surpasses belief."

Clara poignantly wrote to her sister on the last day of her brief life: "As for visiting you, I probably never shall meet you again in life, ere you should receive this, I shall be in the silent realms of the Dead! Start not, dear Annie, shudder not, for what use can there be in dragging out a wearisome life, deprived of all enjoyment? I am only a burden to myself and everyone who interest themselves in my welfare...Bury me in Vermont, by the side of mother, and I have money enough to pay all funeral expenses. If there is anything left of my money...send it together with his letters (which you will find in my pocket) to John H. Sherwin, 14 Fulton Street, New York." In closing the final earthly communication to her sister, Clara wrote "farewell forever."

The practice of publishing suicide notes, which would be considered inappropriate even today in the ruthless media of the digital age, was surprisingly common during the nineteenth century. When Lyman Tenney, a Dartmouth graduate, shot himself in 1811, newspapers across New Hampshire could not resist the temptation to publish a highly personal letter to his family. It appeared in February 23 issue of the *Oracle* in Portsmouth excerpted here: "Why did you thus fondly bring me up to disappoint you and disgrace myself? It pierces me to think I blast the hopes of fond indulgent Parents— But I die. May you be as prosperous and happy in this life as the world can afford, and may you enjoy the blessing of your other children without bemoaning your loss in me, more than a blank which was never filled; and may you teach them virtue from my faults." What the young man did to bring on such overwhelming waves of guilt and depression remains unknown. In 1849, when Abram Haynes of Epsom drowned himself in a nearby river, on August 23 the *New-Hampshire Patriot* published his heartbreaking last words: "It is hard for me to part with my dear wife and little son, but I do not want to live. I want all of my folks to be good to my wife and son, for they have always treated me affectionately. So farewell, dear wife, may heaven protect you."

In Manchester in 1853, newspapers also published a profoundly moving note which Catharine Cotton addressed to her former fiancé: "I know for the last time will attempt to scribble you a few lines, and ere these few lines reach you I shall be sleeping in death. Think not that I shall ever trouble you again with a letter...this is the last. You will receive this with anger perhaps; but, Cyrus, forgive me for troubling you. I have forgiven you long ago, but I have not forgotten. I supposed you are in Biddeford now and contented. I hope you are. As for myself I am not happy, but in a few moments I shall be free from the sorrows of this world and I cannot be more unhappy in another. When you read this, think that I am cold in death and shall one day meet you in another world. So farewell Cyrus, go and be happy."

Ms. Cotton was laid to rest in the Valley Street cemetery in Manchester, while Ms. Cochran's body was transported by her family to Grafton, Vermont to comply with her final wishes. According to the *Manchester American* of August 20, 1853, "her funeral was at the house of the father of J.H. Sherwin, whom she mentions in her letter. We learn also that he was at the funeral." While the paper felt obligated to satisfy their reader's appetite for intimate details of the tragedy, the editor reminded them: "We fear that in our astonishment at the cool deliberation of the act, the train of circumstances which preceded it and the guilt which rests upon all the parties concerned, are overlooked." The editorial mourned the horrible end of these two young women, but also strongly condemned their actions: "Suicide is a crime, repugnant to the interests of society, to the better feelings of our nature, and to human and divine laws." The *Farmer's Cabinet* was also concerned about the ethical implications of publishing suicide notes: "It seems to us neither prudent or safe to exalt the unhappy victims of their own rashness...under even unmerited misfortunes to the position of *martyrs* or *heroines,* or to invest with romantic interest a course of conduct which we should shudder to see imitated...*Suicide is murder,* be its motive what it may."

But the publishers of the *Manchester Mirror* could not resist the temptation to romanticize the tragic affair and make a profit. Available to their readers for twelve and half cents a copy was a pamphlet titled *Disappointed Love! A Story drawn from incidents in the lives of Miss Clara C. Cochran and Miss Catharine B. Cotton.*" This fact-based tale exploited the demise of these two mill girls to great dramatic effect, and was evidently marketed towards other mill girls, illustrated by the advertisement for "Perry's Celebrated Hungarian Balm for restoring, preserving, and beautifying the Hair" printed on the back cover. Again, the editor of the *Farmer's Cabinet* took issue with this publication by asking, "How many 'simple minded girls' will the silly romance, founded on this sad event, now publishing in the Daily Mirror, induce to commit a similar folly and wickedness by thus contributing to their morbid taste?"[3] This debate is eerily reminiscent of the more recent one concerning the impact of violent media on youth today.

During the 1840s, Harriet Farley, the editor of the famed *Lowell Offering,* a magazine written by and for mill girls, reflected upon what led some of her co-workers to kill themselves:

> *But, are the operatives here as happy as females in the prime of life, in the constant intercourse of society, in the enjoyment of all necessaries, and many comforts -- with money at their own command; and the means of gratifying their peculiar tastes in dress, &c. -- are they as happy as they would be, with all this, in some other situations? We sometimes fear they are not. And was there any thing, we ask again, in the situation of these young women which influenced them to this melancholy act? In factory labor it is*

sometimes an advantage, but also sometimes the contrary, that the mind is thrown back upon itself -- it is forced to depend upon its own resources, for a large proportion of the time of the operative. Excepting by sight, the females hold but little companionship with each other. This is why the young girls rush so furiously together when they are set at liberty. This is why the sedate young woman, who loves contemplation, and enjoys her own thoughts better than any other society, prefers this to any other employment. But, when a young woman is naturally of a morbid tone of mind, or when afflictions have created such a state, that employment which forces the thoughts back upon an unceasing reminiscence of its own misery, is not the right one.[4]

Many young women indeed found themselves in the "morbid tone of mind" and lost all hope of a better life. In 1845, twenty-three year old Cordelia Crane of Lisbon, New Hampshire committed suicide at her boardinghouse in Lowell by drinking cedar oil which she had bought at a local apothecary shop. Five years later in Dover, Ms. Almira Pressey who "had been employed in the factories" there, easily purchased two ounces of laudanum and used it to poison herself in her quarters on Second Street. [5] In 1849 and again in 1851, two more mill girls drowned themselves in the canals of Lowell, which were vital to powering the gigantic textile mills but unexpectedly became all too convenient death traps. In June 1854, Alice Jones, a factory worker in Weare, made an unsuccessful attempt at drowning herself and her four-year old daughter, while three months later in Great Falls (now Somersworth), Augusta Lord threw herself into the canal, the cause attributed "to be some disappointment in some love affair." Only three years later, another young mill girl, Eliza Hunt, "committed suicide in Manchester...by jumping into the canal."[6] These tragic deaths, perhaps, reveal the intense socio-economic stress these women were under as they made their way through the Industrial Revolution.

Not surprisingly, when the Civil War began several years later, it took a severe emotional toll on the men who served and the women they left behind. When news reached New Hampshire that John Smith of the 4th New Hampshire Regiment had died of disease in South Carolina in December 1861, his seventeen-year-old fiancée Sarah Watson was so distraught that she threw herself into the freezing waters of another canal in Manchester. A decade later in July 1873, Abbie Rollins drowned herself near the Langdon Mills after she was jilted by her fiancé.[7] But heartbroken mill girls were far from the only people in historical New Hampshire who took their own lives in extraordinarily violent ways, leaving their families and friends haunted by their deeds.

The spring of 1850 was particularly awful one in Nashua when a series of suicides shocked the city. It all started in late May when a young woman testified as a material witness against some friends in court, and afterwards her guilt compelled her to try to drown herself in the Nashua River but she was rescued. A few days later, a man only identified by his last name (Brown) hung himself but perhaps the most horrific event of all was the suicide of Mr. Hart Allen, who killed himself after strangling his own two-year old daughter to death in her bed. The motive for this atrocious crime was unknown, but contemporary newspapers linked it to alcoholism. Only about a month later, yet another suicide occurred in Nashua when Levi Hodge, a respectable harness maker with a large family, slashed his throat with a razor. A local newspaper commented, "Mr. Hodge was a gentleman very much respected for his temperate and industrious habits, and no causes can be assigned for this rash act."[8]

A few years earlier, Nashua was also the scene of what most certainly must rank among the most bizarre suicide cases in American history. On August 16, 1847, twenty-three year old Stephen Atwood made a vicious attempt to take his own life by severing his larynx. While Atwood lost a huge amount of blood, the brutal cuts were sutured by Dr. J.G. Graves, whose almost immediate arrival after the suicide attempt postponed what would have been certain death. A remarkable letter written by the doctor to a medical journal a few weeks afterwards appears below:

> I secured the bleeding vessels, dressed the wound, and left the house, with orders to give the patient brandy and water. After the lapse of two hours, or more, the messenger came again, saying that the patient had roused and wished to see me immediately. On my entering the patient's room, he said, 'Doctor, I have got a darning-needle in my heart.' I inquired how the needle came in his heart. His reply was, that he put the needle into his side previous to using the razor – that he feared the needle was not going to make sure work...He placed his finger upon the spot where he said he put the needle, which was just between the fifth and sixth ribs. He had this time had the appearance of great suffering... his breathing extremely difficult – every breath attended with a screech.[9]

Believing his patient was telling the truth, Dr. Graves made an incision into Atwood's chest, and amazingly he was able to extract a small needle near the patient's heart without killing him; in fact, Atwood's delicate condition slightly improved but an infection set in and on the eighth day after the surgery, he died. Thus this young man was finally successful in taking his own life but it took much longer than he must have anticipated.

While the horrific deaths of Clara Cochran, Catharine Cotton, and Stephen Atwood gave them a bizarre sort of fame, the people of New England had inherited from their ancestors ancient and strong superstitions against those who committed suicide. Beginning in the centuries after the fall of the Roman Empire when Christianity established a permanent foothold across Britain and Ireland, those who committed "the sin of suicide" were denied burial within the sanctified cemeteries and buried in an unmarked grave underneath busy intersections, with the idea that their haunted spirits would not be able to rise and disturb the living. For centuries, a stone was also placed over the face of the suicide victim or a stake was driven through their heart as a gruesome form of posthumous punishment and to prevent their soul from rising to haunt the living.[10]

Centuries later across the Atlantic, many of these harsh beliefs concerning suicide were still prevalent. During the seventeenth-century, the colonial governments of both Massachusetts and New Hampshire passed laws that any person who took their own life "shall be denied the privilege of being buried in the Common Burying place of Christians, but shall be buried in some Common High-way where...such person did inhabit...and a Cart-load of stones laid upon the Grave as a Brand of Infamy, and as a warning to others to beware of the like Damnable practices." The *New-Hampshire Gazette* commented on June 15, 1786 that "it is strange that a reasonable creature can believe, and seriously declare, that a horrible attempt upon one's life is a fine action, and in that be charmed with the beauty of such a proceeding, yet we hear every day of suicide being committed." The editor asked, "for if we hate murderers, because murder is a crime against the laws of God, reason and nature; how much then ought we to detest the murderer and assassinator of himself?"   A decade later in 1806 in Hallowell, Maine, this belief was out into practice when a man who murdered his family with an axe and then killed himself was buried separately from them in a road outside the sacred grounds of the town cemetery.[11]

Despite the fact that many New Englanders condemned suicide as a crime and hoped to discourage "self-murder", its frequency remained troubling. On March 30, 1805, for example, when news was received that Jacob Joy of Madbury had hung himself from a tree, the *New Hampshire Sentinel* of Keene wondered "what led him to perpetrate the unchristianlike deed — being in affluence, and enjoying all the domestic felicity, which a tender wife and dutiful children could afford." A year later, when more suicides caught the attention of local newspapers, the *Farmer's Cabinet* in Amherst, New Hampshire unequivocally stated: "It may be said that it is a manly act for one to kill himself. No— certainly, but a most unmanly one— I should esteem that pilot to be an errant coward, who, out of fear of a storm, should sink his ship of his own accord. Now self murder is a crime most remote from the nature of all animals, and an intense impiety against God...from him it is, that we have received out being and we ought to leave it to his disposal to that being from us."[12]

In some instances, just as it is today, suicide became a last resort in order to escape the hands of justice. On May 13, 1790, in Amherst, New Hampshire, Michael Keefe was sentenced to be severely whipped after writing "traitorous and seditious letters" and burning down the barn of Joshua Atherton. But according to a contemporary newspaper, that night in his jail cell before the punishment could be inflicted, "the hardened wretch put an end to his existence, by cutting his throat with a knife. He was found dead, lying on his face, his windpipe jugular veins cut in two...Keefe has left a wife and children, whom he must have tendered most wretched by his egregious crimes. May his example be dispised and his infamy be an admonitor to others...not to be guilty of like offences."[13] Some twenty years later, another young man found himself confined in the jail in Amherst, this time for attempting to use counterfeit money. According to the local *Farmer's Cabinet* of April 24, 1810, "his case did not appear very heinous, and...the probability was that he would not be convicted of guilt. On Wednesday morning, however, his keepers, on carrying him his breakfast, found him in a most shocking and deplorable situation, wallowing in the dust, with his throat cut and his head dreadfully mangled." In spite of his attempt to kill himself, the man's life was saved by a local doctor and "many spectators viewed the solemn spectacle."

A few decades later, John Davis of Hookset found himself at the New Hampshire State Prison awaiting trial for the charge of domestic abuse against his wife. He had already spent fourteen months at the local jail, but according to the *New-Hampshire Patriot* published on September 16, 1833, it appeared that the charges against him were about to be dropped because no one appeared to testify against him. A few hours later, however, a guard discovered Davis with his throat cut "so effectually...that every vein and muscle from one ear to the other were separated." In March 1836, sixty-five year old Enoch Woods, who had showed numerous signs of mental illness, asphyxiated himself in the jail in Keene with his handkerchief before he could be tried at the Cheshire County Court for the vicious stabbing and murder of George Baker in October 1835. Interestingly, after his death Woods' body was not allowed to be buried in the Sullivan town cemetery, but on his own property; it wasn't until 1904 that his bones were finally moved next to his wife's body who had died in 1821.[14]

During the summer of 1854, two more inmates at the State Prison in Concord killed themselves; Justus Squires died on June 5, after digesting a large of amount of lime which he had brought into the prison hidden in his shoes. On August 15, 1854, inmate Horace Hogdon hanged himself with his own handkerchief nailed to the wall of his cell. A few decades later, David Blodgett used his bed sheet to commit suicide in the jail in Laconia after being sentenced to a thirty year prison sentence for the murder of his young wife. [15] But disturbed convicts who found themselves locked up in prison were far from the only people who took their own lives in historical New Hampshire; indeed, suicide claimed just as many victims from the upper levels of society.

The deaths of upstanding New Hampshire men during the nineteenth-century made it painfully clear that their wealth and social status offered no protection from a descent into depression and thoughts of suicide. This fact was demonstrated on Wednesday, November 3, 1819 in Epsom, when storekeeper James Babb recorded in his diary: "Capt. Isaac Osgood of this town put an end to his existence by cutting his throat with a razor...he had been partially deranged for some time and indulged the idea that poverty would soon overtake him...he was as independent as to property as any farmer in town. He arose in the morning, directed his nephew to go to the barn and find the cattle then...lay himself on the floor, his head on a block, and deliberately as it would be seen, performed the fatal operation and died very soon after. I saw him soon after the deed was performed. This scene was awful and solemn." Osgood was only forty, and left behind his wife Betsy and three young children. Only a month earlier on September 28, Babb had observed in his journal that Captain Osgood had drilled the Epsom militia company in preparation for the annual fall muster; yet only a few weeks later on Thursday, November 4, his body was escorted to the local cemetery by those same soldiers and a crowd of 300 people. At the grave, the local minister gave an "impressive and affecting" elegy from Psalm 77, verse 19 in the Old Testament: "Thy way is in the sea, and thy path in the great waters, and they footsteps are not known."[16]

While the razor blade seemed to be the most common suicide device, individuals found ever more creative ways of taking their own lives. On July 17, 1830, the *New Hampshire Statesman* informed its readers that on the July 4th holiday, Philip Emery of Dover had "put a period to his earthly existence... by shooting himself in the bowels" with a smoothbore musket. Over twenty years later, in April 1843, Captain Ebenezer Swett, "one of the most respectable citizens of Pittsfield" also took his own life. Ironically, Swett had been seriously ill and before his death "desired his friends to send him to the Asylum should he become insane, and cautioned them not to leave him alone." One night he went berserk, however, and when his wife ran upstairs to get assistance, Swett disappeared from the house. After a frantic search was made in the darkness, the captain's body was found at the bottom of his own well.

Others used more violent means to end their lives. On October 10, 1871, the *New Hampshire Patriot* reported in gruesome detail that John Morrill of Milford had thrown himself in front of an oncoming train and his "head was severed and thrown some distance from the track, while the body was carried under the engine and fearfully crushed. The deceased had been sick and despondent and repeatedly threatened to take his own life." On September 23, 1875, the *Independent Statesman* of Concord related with horror how a Mrs. White of Marlborough had remarkably managed to slice open her throat with a scythe, normally used to cut tall grass.

Even more disturbing to their contemporaries were the suicides of respectable ministers and judges, whose deaths shook the very foundations of the society in which it was their duty to promote faith and the rule of law. In September 1848, Reverend Samuel Harris killed himself the age of seventy-four. Harris was ordained as the minister in Windham in 1805 and served that community for twenty-one years until he was dismissed by the town because he lost his powerful speaking voice. For the next few decades, Harris was an itinerant preacher in different New Hampshire towns, and also worked for the American Tract Society, which published assorted religious pamphlets. Eventually, his physical and mental health declined, causing his family to have him admitted to the State Insane Asylum in Concord in 1848; but his condition only worsened and his family took him back home to Windham. One night soon after, Harris eluded the "vigilance of those who had the care of him, and threw himself into a well near the house."[17]

The following year, Walter Blair of Plymouth, who was Judge of the Probate Court of Grafton County, committed suicide by brutally cutting his throat with a straight razor. Judge Blair had been previously elected to serve in the House and Senate in Concord, and his service had rendered him "very popular in his county." Sadly, it was reported that "his wife finding on her return to the house that he had gone out, went in pursuit of him, but he was dead which she reached the spot." The suicide of Judge Luke Woodbury of Antrim also "created a deep sensation upon the public mind" during the late summer of 1851. On the morning of August 27, Woodbury went out for a ride to pick some blackberries and when he returned, disappeared into the barn at his farm. After a few hours, his wife Mary discovered his body swinging from a beam inside, and the news of the judge's suicide "fell like a thunder bolt" on his family and friends. He was an 1820 graduate of Dartmouth, and served in the state legislature before assuming control over the probate court of Hillsborough County during the 1830s. So admired was he that in 1851, Judge Woodbury was nominated to run for Governor of New Hampshire, but declined. Interviews with his family discovered that

Woodbury had recently been "quite low-spirited and...that he wished to be free from the cares of office and remain a private citizen during his life."[18]

When New Hampshire women took their own lives, their contemporaries had difficulty reconciling their duty to their spouses, children, and religious faith with the awful act of suicide, which seemed to shun all those virtues and responsibilities. On a summer morning in June 1836, Mrs. John Spaulding of Wilton hanged herself after breakfast, although she was "a member of the Congregational Church in Mason and...had ever maintained a Christian character." About a year later, twenty-five year old Harriet Stevens of Nashua was found dead by her own hand early one morning, although the night before she had asked her husband Luther to wake her early. The inquest found that "she had ever lived happily with her husband, was warmly attached to her children of whom she has left four...and that nothing had occurred to occasion mental agitation...which could lead to the belief that in a moment of partial insanity she had committed the fatal act." On March 10, 1842 in Lebanon, Mrs. Betsey Downer hanged herself with a clothesline, leaving behind her seven children, including a ten-month old infant. She was only thirty-two and perhaps suffered from post-partum depression. On July 5, 1851, forty-four year old Abigail Bonner, who had been ill for some weeks previously, hung herself with some yarn; she had been married to Captain David Bonner since 1826 and left behind no less than seven children, three of them under the age of ten. On July 13, 1860, the *Dover Gazette* reported that the wife of Samuel Scripture threw herself into the Souhegan River in Milford after learning that he had been arrested for robbery; she could not bear the shame and prospect of having to survive on her own.

Even worse were the rare cases when a parent took the life of their child before destroying their own. Such a tragedy occurred in Weare in May 1877, when a Mr. Hurd returned home to find his ten year old son "nearly severed from the body...the walls and ceiling were splattered with blood, presenting sickening sight." Nearby, the boy's mother had hung herself after killing her son with an axe. According to the contemporary sources, this thirty year old woman had "for the past two months been afflicted with a mild type of insanity, but was not regarded as dangerous, except that she had threatened suicide in moments of extreme depression." There were also instances when suicide claimed multiple members of the same family, lending historic credence to the overwhelming evidence that the predisposition for mental illness can be inherited genetically. During the autumn of 1837, the Dickinson family of Swanzey was devastated in just two weeks. On October 17, twenty-five year old Mary Dickinson, "who was supposed to be deranged", hung herself; Mary's father Aaron disappeared soon after his daughter's funeral, and was found dead by his own hand a few days later. In 1866, Isaac Eaton of Antrim, who had suffered from throat cancer, used his razor to kill himself and in his obituary it was noted that "he was the last of three brothers all of whom have taken their own lives."[19]

Just like today, there were also murders of passion that ended in suicide as the killer could not live with the remorse of having killed the person they claimed to love. One of the most tragic murder-suicides ever in New Hampshire occurred in New Boston during the winter of 1853-54. Twenty-three year old Henry Sargent, an industrious young man who spent his winters splitting firewood, had fallen madly in love with seventeen-year old Sevilla Jones, who did not reciprocate his feelings. The Sargents and Jones' lived in close proximity and apparently Henry eventually decided that if Sevilla would not marry him, then no man would.

On the chilly morning of January 13, 1854 Henry intercepted her on the road near the local schoolhouse. Some children were playing nearby and heard the young woman say "Good morning, Henry"; he said nothing, but quickly came beside Sevilla, drew a pistol from his coat and fired four shots, soaking the virgin white snow red with blood as her body hit the icy ground. Henry then shot himself in the head, but lingered in misery for six more hours. In his pockets were found a razor, another pistol if his first misfired, and also a small diary "in which he had recorded at some length the various circumstances that led to such awful results." However, one contemporary newspaper commented that "it is of a character which forbids our publishing it, and which should have precluded it from the public gaze. He has died an awful death, and the curse which he has prayed might fall upon others will ever rest upon his own memory — an awful warning to all who are tempted to flee from the path of right."[20]

Endnotes: Chapter Twelve

1. *Fact and fiction! disappointed love : a story drawn from incidents in the lives of Miss Clara C. Cochran and Miss Catherine E. Cotton, who committed suicide by drowning, in the canal at Manchester, N.H., August 14, 1853*, (Manchester: 1853), 30-32; *Manchester American & Messenger*, August 20, 1853; *Bangor Whig & Daily Courier*, March 17, 1843.

2. *Manchester Daily Mirror*, August 17, 1853.

3. *Farmer's Cabinet*, September 1, 29, 1853.

4. Harriet Farley, "Editorial: Two Suicides," *Lowell Offering* (Volume IV: 1844).

5. *New-Hampshire Statesman*, May 30, 1845; *New-Hampshire Patriot & State-Gazette*, July 31, 1845 and May 2, 1850.

6. *New-Hampshire Patriot & State-Gazette*, October 11, 1849; *Farmer's Cabinet*, June 5, 1851.

7. *Farmer's Cabinet*, June 1, September 7, 1854, July 30, 1857; January 16, 1862; July 23, 1873.

8. *Farmer's Market*, May 23, July 4, 1850.

9. "Remarkable Case of Suicide, and Extraction of a Needle from the Substance of the Heart," *Buffalo Medical Journal and Monthly Review of Medical and Surgical Science, Volume Three*, (Buffalo: 1848), 418-419; *New Hampshire Patriot*, September 9, 1847.

10. Christine Quigley, *The Corpse: A History*, (Jefferson, North Carolina: MacFarland & Company, 1996) 152-153; Reverend Samuel Phillips, *The Sin of Suicide contrary to nature: a plain discourse, occasioned by the late perpetration of that heinous crime ; viz. on January 7th 1767 ; delivered (the substance of it) on the Lord's-Day next following ; viz. on January 11th and publish'd for a warning to survivors*, (Boston: 1767).

11. *The General Laws and Liberties of the Massachusetts Colony*, (Cambridge: 1672) 137; Laurel Thatcher Ulrich, *A Midwife's Tale: The Life of Martha Ballard, based on her Diary 1785-1812*, (New York: Vintage Books, 1990) 293-296.

12. *Farmer's Cabinet*, August 19, 1806.

13. *Concord Herald*, May 25, 1790.

14. Josiah Lafayette Seward, *A History of the Town of Sullivan, New Hampshire, 1777-1917*, (Keene: J.H. Seward, 1921) 317.

15. "Reports of the Warden, Physician, and Chaplain of the N.H. State Prison, June 1, 1855," *Journals of the Honorable Senate and House of Representatives of the State of New Hampshire*, (Concord: 1855) 50; *Independent Statesman*, April 2, 1874.

16. Diary of James Babb, September 17, 1819-June 30, 1820, MS 104, Milne Special Collections Department, Dimond Library, University of New Hampshire.

17. *New-Hampshire Patriot*, May 11, 1843, June 14, 1849.

18. *Farmer's Cabinet*, September 3, 1851.

19. *New-Hampshire Patriot*, May 1, 1837, July 13, 1848; *Farmer's Cabinet*, July 1, 1836, February 15, 1866; *New-Hampshire* Statesman, March 18, 1842; New-Hampshire *Sentinel*, October 26, November 2, 1837.

20. *New-Hampshire Patriot*, June 8, 1848; *Farmer's Cabinet*, January 19, 1854.

Chapter Thirteen

"The Northwood Murderer"
New Hampshire's First Serial Killer?

To discover that their child has disappeared, or even worse, been murdered is every parent's worst nightmare. This is a tragic storyline that has become all too frequent in modern times; but a series of gruesome murders during the nineteenth century across Maine, Massachusetts, and New Hampshire remind us that children have long been victims of violence. But were these vicious killings in three states perhaps connected? The possibility exists that as many as five children in nineteenth century New England may have all been victims of one of the first documented serial killers/child predators in American history, nearly a century before the term was coined by the Federal Bureau of Investigation. Yet perhaps an equally perplexing mystery is why these gruesome, sensational crimes have almost been completely forgotten.

On August 29, 1850, the U.S. census taker visited the home of thirty-four year old laborer Stephen Mills, his wife Loisa, and their five children in Derry, New Hampshire and recorded their existence for posterity. This documentary snapshot of a young and growing family a decade before the Civil War is haunting in light of what transpired at the Mills household only a few months later. On the evening of October 30, thirty-seven year old Loisa Mills briefly left her four daughters and six year old son, Stephen, alone at home to let him know one of the children was sick. When their mother returned that evening, a four year old daughter, whose name was unfortunately not mentioned in the contemporary newspaper reports, had disappeared from the house. The boy Stephen told an alarming story that a man had entered the house through a window and carried off his defenseless sister into the night. Loisa Mills went to a neighbor's house to look for the child, but by the next morning, there was still no sign of their daughter.

Search parties lead by the selectmen of Derry combed the surrounding woods for days with no luck. By early November, announcements of the child's apparent abduction appeared in local newspapers stating that she had possibly been murdered and offered a $100 reward for any information regarding her fate.[1] As winter arrived, hopes to uncover the fate of the Mills' daughter went cold, though there were many suspicions regarding the disappearance. The child's body was never found, and the incident certainly must have taken a devastating toll on the Mills family. Sadly, the

1860 census shows during the intervening decade, Loisa Mills had died without learning the fate of her daughter and Stephen had remarried. More than a decade would pass before the disappearance of the Mills' child would finally be solved.

Some twelve years later, on the morning of Sunday, September 14, 1862, only a few days before thousands of soldiers clashed at the epic battle of Antietam, Isaac and Susan Libby became alarmed when their nine-year old daughter Laura failed to return home while returning from Sunday school in Maine. The *Bangor Daily Whig* of September 18th reported the horrific discovery which followed: "It being feared that she was lost in the woods, the usual means of search were instituted. A large number of men, with guns to be fired as signals went out. The search was in vain until evening when the body of the child was found not a hundred rods from the house of Mr. L. in the woods. The girl had been killed, her throat being cut from ear to ear. The body was stripped of clothing, and it was evident that the most inhuman outrages had been committed before the murder." Eventually, Lawrence Doyle, an Irish immigrant who worked for Isaac Libby and thus was acquainted with the child, was tried twice for the crime after the first trial resulted in a hung jury, and was ultimately convicted in 1864 for the brutal killing. But Doyle stoutly maintained his innocence until his death from natural causes in the Maine State Prison in 1870.[2]

But while Doyle was in prison, a similar but even more ghastly crime occurred to the south in Massachusetts. For over a century, the beautiful landscape of the Arnold Arboretum owned by Harvard University has offered residents of Boston and surrounding communities a natural refuge from the clamor of the city. Yet many visitors today are ignorant of the fact that it was in those same peaceful environs on Monday, June 12, 1865 that Isabella Joyce and her younger brother John, ages 14 and 12 respectively, came to play during a recess from school. Before leaving their grandmother's home that morning, she expressed concern that John must return to school by two o'clock that afternoon, but his sister said "Don't be afraid, grandma; we'll be back in time for Johnny to go to school."[3] It was the last time she would see them alive.

When the children had not returned by the next morning, their panic-stricken grandmother contacted local police who began to search the surrounding area. Almost a week later after, the awful fate of the Joyce children was revealed in secluded Bussey's woods, today known as Hemlock Hill. Beneath an oak tree, searchers found green leaves, wild flowers, and twigs which had been plucked by children to make wreaths, and one of these creative decorations was found adorning a young girl's hat. There also

155

lay on the ground an unfinished wreath, ominously indicating that something had prevented the maker from completing it. Only a short distance away was found the mutilated body of Isabella Joyce, who was described as being "remarkably well formed...over five feet high, and rather attractive in person, with auburn hair and very clear, bright eyes."[4] Contemporary reports detailed that before being stabbed at least eleven times with a long, sharp knife after death, "she had been outraged in a fearful manner, and from the manner in which her clothing was torn it was apparent that she had violently resisted the assaults upon her until completely overpowered." Another report indicated that Isabella's "mouth was found filled with grass, probably to prevent any outcry" as she was sexually assaulted.

Shortly after his sister was found, John Joyce's corpse was located lying face down near the base of the wooded hill, giving the appearance that he had attempted to escape his attacker but had been stabbed eight times in the back. Based on the appearance of the vicious wounds which in a few instances completely penetrated each child's torso, Dr. Joseph Stedman expressed his opinion at the inquest that the same eight or ten inch blade had been used to kill both children, indicating a single perpetrator had committed "one of the most terrible and revolting crimes which has even occurred in New England." Within days, newspapers across the nation eagerly printed any details related to the Joyce murders. The July 15, 1865 issue of *Frank Leslie's Illustrated Newspaper* even featured lurid sketches of the bloody crime scene which must have raised the eyebrows of their readers.[5]

Despite the brazen sexual assault and gruesome murders in the heart of Boston, the identity of the Bussey Woods culprit remained a mystery even though $5000 was offered as a reward. That the killer had not bothered to conceal the bodies of their victims indicated the murderer might have been forced to leave the crime scene in a hurry. During the weeks that followed the Joyce killings, newspapers reported the arrest of several suspects, including Thomas Ainsley, a painter who lived in the same building as the children's mother in Boston. While Ainsley was reported "as being a hater of children" and an angry crowd gathered outside the police station seeking to lynch him, no evidence was found connecting him to the crime and he was released.

Then in early July, one John Stewart who lived in the vicinity of the Joyce family was arrested at Fort Independence on Castle Island after joining the army only days after the murder, giving the appearance that he was trying evade something. In reality, Stewart had deserted the military a few times after being paid a bounty to enlist, but fiercely protested his innocence of the murders and after the first court hearing, was released from custody on July 24 due to a lack of evidence. In March 1866 the investigation turned its attention to one Charles Dodge, alias "Scratch Gravel", who had boasted after being sent to prison for burglary that he had murdered the Joyce children. But a closer look by police determined that Dodge had actually been some five hundred miles away that day in June 1865.[6] The Joyce case eventually went cold, and every year that passed hopes faded that the brutal murders would ever be solved.

Five years after the Joyce tragedy, a sixty year old man by the name of Franklin B. Evans walked into the Boston office of the Traveler's Insurance Agency on August 16, 1870. He wished to obtain a life policy on himself for $1,500 and made the beneficiary his brother-in-law, Elias Evans of Derry, New Hampshire. Less than two weeks later, Elias notified the company that Frank Evans had drowned at Hampton Beach and wanted to collected his money, but the insurance company was of course suspicious, and sent an adjuster up to New Hampshire to investigate. Though Frank Evan's clothes had been found washed up on the shore, no body was found even though the sea was calm and clear that day, so there could be no death certificate. When the adjuster interviewed Elias and his family in Derry, he became convinced "that the whole affair was a fraud...and further refused to accept the allegations as satisfactory proofs of loss, and demanded the surrender of the policy."[7] Franklin Evans had vanished from Derry but he wasn't dead. The insurance fraud case remained unresolved until some two years later, when Evans turned up as a suspect when another young girl suddenly disappeared into the woods, this time in New Hampshire.

By June 1872, Frank Evans had moved to Northwood into the household of his sister Deborah and her husband Sylvester Day, their adult daughter Susan and her thirteen year old child, Georgianna Lovering. The girl's father had died in the Union army during the Civil War. As summer passed into autumn, on the morning of Friday, October 25, Evans asked "Georgie", as she was affectionately called by her family, to tend to his partridge traps in the nearby woods. Evans supposedly went off in a different direction to work. When she had not returned hours later, Georgianna's family became concerned and while searching the woods near their home, they discovered her apron and signs on the ground that a struggle had taken place. Near a fence, a broken comb identified as Georgie's was also found, but after that the trail went cold. When Frank Evans returned late that afternoon and was asked if he seen the missing child, he said he changed his plans that morning and instead visited the farm of the Roberts family for dinner. When the local Justice of the Peace discovered this alibi was a lie,

Evans was immediately detained by the authorities who "had him stripped to see if there was any evidence of blood on him. Not the slightest evidence could be found."[8]

The next morning, the search for Georgianna Lovering continued as hundreds of Northwood residents combed the woods while a heavy, bone-chilling rain fell down on them. In his diary now preserved at the New Hampshire Historical Society, Samuel Shepard James of Northwood noted: "Boys with others in the woods hunting after a lost girl Sylvester Day's grandchild." Nearly a week later on October 31, no progress had been in the investigation and a correspondent for the *Independent Statesman* of Concord commented that "the opinion is universal that the child has been murdered and concealed. Very strong suspicions are attached to a man by the name of Evans...the feeling against him is intense, and nothing but the presence of Sherriff Drew of Strafford, saved him from violence on Saturday." One can imagine a howling mob with torches and pitchforks looking for a good hanging tree, and it certainly must have been close to that.

During his initial questioning, Evans told Drew that he had plotted with a Mr. Webster of Kingston to abduct Georgianna Lovering, but when Drew interviewed this man, he denied all knowledge of the supposed kidnapping and proved he was not in Northwood the day the child vanished. Angered that his suspect had concocted yet another story to throw off the investigation, Drew continued to interrogate Evans late into the night of Friday, November 1st: "I want you to tell me whether that little girl is dead or alive." Evans hesitated for a moment, and then answered: "She is dead...I can't tell you but will go and show you where she is."[9] Taking this as a confession, Drew led the handcuffed Evans to his wagon and disappeared into the cold November night both hoping and dreading that the body of the missing child would be found.

At first, Evans had trouble finding the spot in the dark woods where he had concealed his victim, but eventually he led his captors to the base of an uprooted tree and simply said, "she is there." When the Sherrif Drew and his men sifted through the pile of leaves and mud, they were utterly horrified by what they saw. The *Independent Statesman* on November 7 reported the macabre discovery in gory detail: "The body was found wrapped in a cotton shirt, on removing which, the whole extent of the outrage was realized. This human fiend, after accomplishing his foul purpose...had removed the sexual organs of this little girl, fearfully lacerating the whole abdominal region, with a knife...This he had wrapped in his handkerchief and...according to confessions since made...concealed this portion of the body beneath a stone, whence he was compelled to produce it by Sheriff Drew. It was brought forward at the post mortem examination and declared by the physicians to correspond exactly with the parts removed from Georgianna Lovering, though this, of course, was a mere formality."

On the afternoon of Saturday, November 2, the official inquest was held and during the post mortem examination conducted by local physicians on the second floor of a local store, "marks of violence" and bruising consistent with strangulation were found on her throat, indicating that Ms. Lovering had been raped, strangled, and then mutilated after death. When news of this ghastly discovery rushed across Northwood, "stern, gloomy countenances, and gleaming eyes alone displayed the raging tumult of feelings...when, for the first time, the whole terrible truth of the affair was revealed." Frank Evans had already been secured in the jail at Exeter for his own safety and ordered to appear before a special grand jury scheduled to meet in January 1873.[10]

On Monday, November 4, Samuel James noted in his diary that there was "a little snow on the ground this morning" and the disgusted, angry citizens of Northwood attended the "funeral of the murdered child." As the nation learned of the sadistic crime, it was understandably categorized as "the most hideous crime ever perpetrated in New Hampshire." Within a few weeks, Georgianna's family distributed her image taken in the prime of life to local photographers such as W.N. Hobbs of Exeter, who sold copies of her likeness to preserve her memory and serve as a tragic, macabre memento of the crime.[11] This marked probably the very first time a murder victim in New Hampshire had been memorialized in this public fashion. New Hampshire authorities, however, had not yet begun the innovative but grisly practice of taking crime scene photographs and visually documenting the bodies of murder victims *in situ*, which would not be socially acceptable for decades to come. Among the very first crime scene photos in American history were made during the investigation of the Borden family murders in Massachusetts in 1892.

But naturally, there was great curiosity about the man who stood accused of such a brutal crime. According to newspaper reports, Franklin B. Evans was about sixty and a native of Strafford, though he had lived in Derry, Manchester, and around Boston during the Civil War before moving to Northwood. He was described as "weighing 135 pounds, 5 feet 8 inches in height, slim, gray hair" with "very large, full grayish whiskers. He has a rather strange eye, a little glaring." Another publication reported that when he was living in Manchester, Evans had attempted to join the local parish of Second Advent Church and become an itinerant preacher, "but his remarks were so foolish and he acted so much like a lunatic, that the members put him out, and he was generally renounced as a mean, sneaking hypocrite...All who knew him, however, declare that they never thought him fiendish enough to commit the crime for which he is now on trial." Thought his attempts to be a preacher failed miserably, Evans did apparently have one successful endeavor; he frequently supplied wild medicinal roots and herbs to New Hampshire physicians, and "his reputation for obtaining the medicinal products of the woods and fields was unsurpassed in this region, and...his rivals found it impossible to outstrip him in endurance or activity."[12] That he was able to conceal the body of Georgie Lovering so well reflected his extensive knowledge of the local woods.

In January 1873, Evans was arraigned for the Lovering murder and his trial began at the Exeter Town Hall on Monday, February 3, with Judges Charles Doe and Ladd presiding over the proceedings (New Hampshire law at that time required two judges to preside over a capital trial). According to an eyewitness, "seats had been provided...to the number of four hundred, and everyone was filled, and there were perhaps fifty standing. There were about a dozen women in the audience." After spending a few hours choosing the jury of twelve men, led by foreman Sewell Dow of Hampton, the Attorney General of New Hampshire opened his case and spoke until about six o'clock that evening, according to one reporter, "detailing the sickening circumstances of the crime, some of which are unfit for publication."[13]

The next morning at about nine, the trial resumed and the prosecution began calling its first witnesses. Among them was Sylvester Day, Georgianna's grandfather, who besides Frank Evans himself, was the last person to see her alive. According to Day, Evans had come to live with his wife, daughter, and granddaughter in June 1872. On the morning of October 25, he left his home at about eight thirty going towards Hill's, a neighbor where he was working, and at nine "Georgie" went out into the woods to check the partridge traps wearing an apron and a comb in her hair. When she didn't return after an hour, Mr. Day went into the woods with his daughter, who had just returned home from visiting her sister. When they found her apron hanging from a branch near the house, they knew immediately that something was wrong. "Georgie staid a little longer than I thought she would," according to Sylvester Day, "a half hour was time enough for her to go and come back." Other witnesses, including James Pender and John Mead, who both confirmed that they saw Frank Evans crossing a road on the morning of October 25, and he never went to Hill's farm to work as he told Sylvester Day.

But the most heart wrenching testimony came from Susan Lovering, who reminded the jury her daughter was only thirteen years, one month and thirteen days

160

old when she was murdered. As she told the hushed crowd that her dear "Georgie wore a black comb to keep her hair back and an apron, the witness exhibited the apron to the jury; she began to cry and was visibly overcome." It's not difficult to imagine that Susan Lovering cherished that apron for the rest of her life as a physical connection to the daughter she had lost forever. The next witness to testify for the prosecution was Sheriff Henry Drew, who repeated the story of Evans leading him to the body late on the night of November 1st. To this account, Drew added that "I asked him to tell me whether she was cold in death or not; he said, 'she is, and I've done wrong.'" Eben Parsley, one of the men who accompanied Sheriff Drew and Evans into the woods on that unforgettable night, asked Evans "how he could do the deed and he said the evil one got control of him."

One of the last witnesses to be called to the stand was Dr. Caleb Hanson, who had the grisly task of examining Georgianna's body. Hanson testified that the appearance of her eyes and protruding tongue made it clear that she had been strangled, and that her body had been "violated" after death.[14] The Attorney General then rested the state's case, and court adjourned until the next day, when the defense would attempt to convince the jury that Frank Evans was not guilty by reason of insanity. Despite the very real possibility that he would receive the death penalty for the crime he was accused of, "the prisoner sat through the day's proceedings and listened to the damning evidence against him in all its terrible minuteness without evincing feeling of any kind." But apparently inside his mind, Evans was overcome by fear or perhaps even some remorse, because at about eight o'clock on the morning of February 5, 1873 he attempted to commit suicide in his cell. "The keeper was absent from the room a minute," according to one report, "when he went back he discovered that Evans had taken one of his suspenders, tied it around his neck and attached the other end to a hook used for the purpose of hanging clothing. Just then the keeper disengaged him from the hook. Evans entered the court room this morning in iron. A red mark was seen on his throat where the suspenders ran."[15]

Evans' attorney, P. Webster Locke of Kingston, tried to demonstrate that Evans was insane, as we have observed many previous defendants claimed, assuming it might save them from the gallows. But this strategy backfired. The first witness for the defense was the accused man's son, Benjamin Evans, who had been wounded while serving in the Union army during the Civil War. He alleged that in the past several years his father had lived with him at various times and "acted strangely, as though he had no control of himself." In one instance, his father grabbed a lantern and threatened to dump the

161

fuel over the nearby stove and "said the Evil One had possession of him." Next to take the stand was one of Frank Evans' former landlords, Mary Ambudy, who only said vaguely that he had "manifested strange actions."

But in response, the prosecution called to the stand a series of expert witnesses who had extensive experience with mentally ill patients. While Dr. J.C. Eastman of Hampstead had known the accused for twenty-five years and described Evans as "peculiar man," Dr. Jesse Bancroft, Superintendent of the State Insane Asylum since 1857, "said nothing lead him to the conclusion that Evans was insane." Dr. John Tyler, head of the famed McLean Asylum in Massachusetts, spent an hour with Evans before the trial began and testified that "I saw no symptoms which led me to believe that he was insane. Finally, Dr. William Perry of Exeter had an interesting exchange with accused murderer: "I asked him what he wanted to do with the girl's body he cut out; he asked me how I knew he cut it out...he said there were many untrue stories...considering all the evidence as an expert, I discover not one particle of evidence of insanity; his object in the mutilation, in my opinion, to make anatomical examinations; I have seen nothing to contradict that he is perfectly sane."[16]

After this last witness left the stand, Evans' attorney delivered his closing remarks which attempted to instill doubts in the minds of the jury: "There is no question but he murdered the girl. There is a question yet undetermined. Is he sane? Would one of you meet him on the street and call him a sane man? We don't want the learning of the professors to warn us he is insane. Your duty to the State will be spoken of, but what a ghastly sight that will be that when he dangles by the neck...his life or death rests with you. In the name of God, be merciful! You must satisfy your conscience beyond a doubt!" In his closing argument, Attorney General Clark reminded the jury: "Who knew where the body was but the man who hid it? Can there be any doubt as to the murderer? My friend asks you to beware of punishing the prisoner on the account of the enormity of his crime. I pity the prisoner, but talk not of sympathy; if you do, talk it to the bereaved mother. This man of three-score and ten deprived of life a child of 13 as dear as yours or mine. Conscientious scruples need not interfere with you...and it is right to take the life of the guilty man now as when he was committing the act."

Finally, Charles Doe of Rollinsford, perhaps the most respected judge in New Hampshire judicial history, delivered the following instructions to the jury before they left the room to deliberate:

You and I may be opposed to capital punishment, but with that you and I have nothing to do here...There has been a great deal of public feeling...But I cannot too strongly impress upon you that if public opinion influences you or me at all, it is perjury for us. The counsel for the defendant admits, as well he must the killing of the girl. Insanity is a disease and nothing else in the eye of the law. It has been said that no man would do this deed in his right mind, and this is so in one sense. But the law is far more definite. Now, the question is, was the girl killed by the act of mental disease of this man? Was he compelled to do it by disease, or did he do it of his own free will?[17]

In a large part, these profound questions would be answered by Frank Evans himself months later. But his fate still had to be decided. Judge Doe finished his extensive instructions at about five o'clock on the evening of February 6, 1873 as darkness had already descended outside and the large hall was illuminated. The jury had only been deliberating for a half hour when the court was informed they had reached a verdict. Newspaper reporter John B. Clarke of Manchester described the tense scene with great vividness:

The judge orders the doors to be closed to prevent the ingress of the hungry crowd as he fears for the security of the floor. The prisoner menacled and guarded by two men, rises in the iron-railed enclosure to hear the verdict which is to fix the length of his stay on earth. The clerk rises and asks the customary question. Mr. Dow, the foreman, with some little hesitation...says: "We find the prisoner guilty of murder in the first degree!" The suspense of the last three days is ended...but no sound breaks the silence. The flickering gas jets throw light upon the face of Franklin B. Evans, but no change appears on his always dejected and nearly immovable face. In a few moments the clerk reads to the prisoner...the sentence of the court, that he be confined in the State Prison in Concord until the third Tuesday of February 1873 when he shall be hanged by the neck until dead.

In 1849, New Hampshire lawmakers had amended the capital punishment law to stipulate that a year must pass between the sentencing and execution of a convicted criminal to give the acting governor an opportunity to re-examine the details of each capital case and possibly commute the sentence to life imprisonment.[18] But no such mercy was given to Frank Evans, and in the wake of his conviction, his death sentence was lauded by the press. "New Hampshire Justice! The Northwood Murderer Convicted!" declared the evening edition of *Bangor Daily Whig* on February 6, 1873. But only days before his appointment with the hangman's noose, Franklin B. Evans would perhaps reveal the final secrets of his dark criminal past.

For most of his year-long stay in the State Prison in Concord, Evans prayed once a week with the prison chaplain, who told him he could expect no mercy from civil authorities and might save his soul from eternal damnation "only when he fully and thoughtfully confessed his guilt in the matter proved against him. This he refused to do, and yet would not plainly deny." It was not until close to eight weeks before his execution that Evans seemed to be more "inclined to speak of his guilt" and was urged by the chaplain and warden J.C. Pillsbury to make a "full and free statement of facts for his own good, making no statement he would not confirm on the scaffold." Only after "a great struggle" a few days before his execution was Frank Evans finally able to begin writing three confessions for three separate crimes that still are shocking in their audacity and candidness, confirmation Evans was "a man possessed of much shrewdness and cunning."[19]

In a letter to the Traveler's Insurance Company in Hartford, Evans admitted that he and his brother-in-law in Derry had indeed concocted "a plan of operation for defrauding your company" during the summer of 1870. After purchasing the life insurance policy on his own life for $1,500, he admitted "I went to Hampton Beach and made arrangement for board at the Granite State house. This was on the afternoon of the 24th of August. That evening I went out of the hotel, saying to the...clerk I was going bathing...I took off my clothing, leaving it all on the beach, and put on another suit provided for the purpose. I left my clothes lying on the beach at about ten o'clock that night." After hitching a ride all the way to northern Vermont to escape detection, he returned to Derry that their plot had been sniffed out by a suspicious insurance agent. Evans closed his letter: "I feel that I have done wrong in the matter, and want you to forgive me." Years after he had been executed in 1895, Evans' letter was included in an interesting book about various schemes to defraud insurance companies. The editors didn't forget to remind readers that Franklin B. Evans was "the hoary-headed scoundrel who expiated his crimes on the gallows at Concord, New Hampshire."[20]

Frank Evans' next chilling confession, however, revealed a clear motive for murdering Georgianna Lovering, though the post-mortem mutilation of her reproductive organs was indeed psychopathic. According to the man on death row:

> *I had for many years practised as a doctor. Wishing to qualify myself further in this practice...I bought a treatise on female diseases, and largely treating on child-bearing and*

midwifery, illustrated with drawings describing of the female system. Unfortunately,
Georgianna and her mother got possession of the book, but I soon recovered it. Georgianna
insisted on having and further perusing it. I declined, and she threatened to have me
arrested and sent to the State prison for an alleged rape. She had often done this before,
and now renewed her threats in much anger. My fears were much increased from an event
which occurred some six weeks before this. I altered a one dollar bill to ten dollars, and
succeeded in passing it. While I was working on this, Georgianna cam suddenly into the
room and detected me. She then threatened to expose me. Thus I found myself completely
in her power. Believing she would make good her threatening, my mind was much
agitated and tormented. In this state of mind about one month before her death, I first
thought of putting her out of the way…At length I became fixed in my purpose of
compelling her to exonerate me, or to take her life. In order to bring this about, I told her I
would give her the book if she would meet me in the woods at a certain place…at some
distance from her home. She assented, and on the morning of the fatal day, I left Mr.
Day's, telling the family I was going to Mr. Hill's…some few miles off. When she came I
talked with her for some time…trying to persuade her to do something to make me feel
secure. It was to no avail; – she persistently refused. Knowing that…I would most likely
be sent to State Prison on one or both of her complaints, I seized her by the throat. She
struggled but for a short time and was dead. I carried her body a long distance toward the
swamp, and when within a few rods of the place where I buried her, I separated the parts
found afterwards.[21]

Although Evans further confessed that his "feelings after the deed was done were
dreadful beyond description" and that he would have "given worlds…to have recalled
that hour," he did not hesitate to further mutilate Georgianna's character as he had
done to her defenseless body. He claimed that she "sometimes drank and was lewd in
conversation, often telling me of her shameful intercourse with three young men."
Perhaps he thought that casting doubtful aspersions on his victim's morality would
somehow make him less culpable, but it was all an illusion in his murderous mind.

   The public was not altogether surprised that Evans finally confessed to the crime
they were already convinced he had committed. But his admission to a much older
"awful transaction" was undeniable evidence that Evans had long targeted children as
his victims:

In the fall of 1850, I left my wife, having been living with her in Salem, Mass. And came
to Derry, N.H.. On arriving at the house of a Mr. Mills, late in the evening, I found the

door fastened. I heard in the house a moaning sound as of a child. I opened the window and got in. I found several children lying on the floor, and one girl sitting on the floor who seemed to be very sick. On examining her I concluded she could not live until next morning. Wishing to procure a body to examine for surgical purposes, I resolved to kill her, and took her to the woods, at some distance, and there strangled her. On examining the body I found one hip and part of the spine deformed, and partly on this account, but more because a feeling of remorse and terror seized me, I desisted...from my purpose of examining the body. I found a chestnut stump partly rotten, and turning it up placed the body under it and replaced the stump. I then wandered about the woods until morning. The place where I buried her was near the junction of two brooks. I searched for it a year afterwards but could not find it.[22]

Once the public learned of this "startling" confession, it was clear Frank Evans was a new breed of killer, one that New Hampshire had never seen the likes of before. While the term "serial killer" would not be coined for another century or so, Frank Evans crimes certainly fit the modern definition established in 2005 by the FBI's Behavioral Analysis Unit: "The unlawful killing of two or more victims by the same offender(s), in separate events."[23] Evans was also clearly a child predator, and the question still remains: If he had murdered two children twenty-two years apart, was Frank Evans perhaps responsible for other unsolved child murders during the two intervening decades? Many of his contemporaries thought so. But what evidence existed to implicate him in these other crimes?

Only about a week after Evans was arrested for the murder of Georgianna Lovering, there was already speculation that he was involved in the infamous Joyce killings of 1865. On November 9, 1872, the *Boston Daily Advertiser* claimed that "it is believed by any that he murdered the Joyce children...Evans, after the finding of the remains of the Lovering girl, asked Deputy Sheriff Drew if some persons in the room were Massachusetts officers, and if they wanted him for the murder of the Joyce children." These provocative comments peaked Drew's curiosity and he continued to question him further on the subject when he had the Northwood murderer cornered in a cell in Exeter. Drew told the press that "I traced him to Rhode Island and then back to Roxbury, Mass. His mention of Roxbury and the similarity of the two murders, suggested to me for the first time that he might have perpetrated the murder of the Joyce children." Drew reported the substance of his tantalizing conversation with Evans:

166

Evans-*Mr. Drew I was right there when that boy and girl were killed.*

Drew-*Was he stabbed, or not?*

Evans-*Yes, he was, several times.*

Drew- *Did the girl make much ado?*

E.- *Yes.*

D.-*More than the boy did?*

E.- *Yes.*

D.- *Why did she?*

E.- *She was raped. Don't ask me anymore. I have now told you.*

D.- *Was the act committed before he was killed?*

E.- *Yes. Mr. Drew I won't say anymore.*

D.-*Well, Frank, I guess you have.*

Evans was even familiar with the two-story home where the Joyce children had departed on the day they were killed. Drew told reporters that Evans' replies to his questions "were deemed by me of so much importance that I immediately reduced the substance of our conversation to writing."[24] Evans certainly did have a track record of being a child predator and he possessed intimate knowledge of the outrages committed against both children. Plus the murders happened in a wooded area, which Evans visited often to earn a living, and where he had murdered his confirmed victims. Certainly some of his knowledge of the Joyce crime could have been gleaned from newspaper accounts; but the circumstances of the murders in New Hampshire did appear to be eerily similar. And most perplexing, why did Evans himself mention the Joyce murders to authorities? It seems that he was looking for the attention, almost boasting about the crimes, as many serial killers do today.

There was another interesting anecdote from an eyewitness who was walking in the vicinity of the Bussey Woods in June 1865. An unidentified woman claimed that as they were walking on an adjacent road, "their attention was drawn to a man just emerging from a clump of bushes, but...when he was noticed, turned about and plunged into the woods, as if anxious to avoid them. This lady got a fair glimpse of the man as he turned away, and was struck with his sinister visage. On learning of the murder subsequently, she came naturally enough to think the man...was the perpetrator thereof." Seven years later, allegedly, when this same woman was walking by a shop in downtown Boston and saw Frank Evans face depicted on a pamphlet about the Northwood murder, she exclaimed: "That's the man!-that's the murderer of the Joyce children!"[25] Of course this story is circumstantial evidence at best, but what if she was right?

But not all were convinced that Frank Evans was linked to the Joyce affair. On February 8, 1873, the *Boston Journal* pointed out that Evans' comments "were drawn...interrogatively, and before he had been convicted of the crime for which he had been sentenced to be hung. It seems highly improbable that a man in his situation would have accumulated such a mass of testimony against himself, and but little credence is given to his story by the heads of the police department in this city." This logic makes sense, but the attitude of the police was perhaps reflective of the fact that one other man had already confessed to the gruesome crime and it was later proven he had been in another state when it happened. They were bound to be initially skeptical of any possible suspect.

The Joyce atrocity, however, wasn't the only crime Evans was suspected of having perpetrated during the 1860s. In February 1873, after he had been convicted of the Northwood murder, Evans received a visit from E.F. Pillsbury, an attorney from Augusta, Maine. Pillsbury had represented Lawrence Doyle, the Irishman who had been sentenced to life in prison for the murder of Laura Libby in Maine in 1862, though his lawyer was convinced Doyle was innocent. "Though he was anxious to do so," the *Farmer's Cabinet* reported with disappointment on February 19, 1873, Pillsbury "could not get one word from Evans that led him to believe that Evans had anything to do with the Maine child murder." If we are to believe Evans, he had a very strong motive to murder Georgianna Lovering because she was going to expose his counterfeiting activities or charge him with rape, whereas in the other murders, there was no apparent motive besides being consumed by psychopathic murderous lust.

There were also significant differences in the method of the Joyce and Libby killings in comparison to the Mills and Lovering murders. While Evans admitted that he strangled his two confirmed victims before he disposed of their bodies, ten years earlier Laura Libby was raped and had her throat slashed; the Joyce children had been stabbed numerous times in a furious attack, and grass had been stuffed in Isabella's mouth, suggesting that she was still alive when she was raped. In addition, the bodies of the Joyce children had been left where they had been killed, and no attempt was made to conceal their bodies. While this might have been because their killer hastily fled the scene to avoid capture, in the Mills and Lovering cases Frank Evans admitted he hid their bodies under the stumps of uprooted trees and in first case, the body was so well hidden that not even the murderer himself could find it a year later. In the Libby case, one Maine observer recalled "so ingeniously was the concealment of her body...that the merest chance revealed the grave."[26] There is no doubt that strangling and then cleverly hiding the remains of his victims in the woods were the hallmarks of Frank Evans' crimes.

While the speculation concerning the extent of Evans' heinous deeds captivated readers from Maine all the way to Milwaukee, preparations began for his scheduled execution in Concord on February 17, 1874.[27]   A few days before his execution, Evans arranged to sell his body for fifty dollars to Dartmouth College, as Thomas Powers and Josiah Burnham had done many decades before, to be publicly dissected after he was hanged. The gallows at the State Prison, which hadn't been used since 1869, was erected in the prison yard, painted blue, and "a new hemp rope twenty feet in length was used...so that no accident should occur at the execution." During his last night on earth, Evans was accompanied by two chaplains, "and every effort was made by the two clergymen to prepare the man for his doom, by making a clean confession of all his crimes. He reiterated in the most positive terms that he had confessed all knowledge of all the crimes of which he was guilty, and that if people did not believe it, he could not help it." Whatever secrets he still had, Evans would take them to the grave.

At seven o'clock on the morning of February 17, 1874, Frank Evans ate his last meal, a "hearty breakfast, consisting of three boiled eggs, two potatoes, bread, and a pint of tea, and seemed to relish the same as well as ever." At about eleven, he was escorted to the gallows, where his arms were strapped and a black hood was placed over his head. There was no opportunity to make a final parting statement; within a few seconds, Sherriff Odlin of Rockingham County, where the Lovering murder occurred, pulled the wooden lever "and the soul of Franklin B. Evans was launched into eternity. He fell about six feet and died without a struggle. In 19 minutes from the time he fell, the surgeons pronounced him dead, and after hanging ten minutes, the body was cut down and removed to Undertaker Crow's rooms, where a...very thorough post-mortem examination upon the body of Evans was made Tuesday evening."[28]

It is worth noting that Frank Evans also became the first person in New Hampshire's history to be photographed after being executed; a stereoscopic image meant to be viewed in a stereocard viewer, was taken of his corpse after it been transported to Dartmouth College to be dissected. A few years later, when Evans' skeletal remains were on display in one of the lecture halls at Dartmouth, a group of rowdy medical students who were disgruntled at the school's administration played a grisly joke by hanging Evans' skeleton in effigy from a flagpole on campus. According to one report, "it was with much difficulty taken down, amid the cheers and shouts of nearly the whole college who stood around the effigy."[29]

But for the people of New Hampshire and beyond, the deeds of Franklin B. Evans were no joke. The memories of the chilling murders he committed remained vivid for decades. In Northwood, when Eliott Cogswell wrote a history of the town, he was careful to mention that near Bow Lake "close by the line between Northwood and Strafford, was perpetrated the revolting murder of Georgianna Lovering." When describing the landscape of the Arnold Arboretum, one author from the late nineteenth century mentioned a "small cairn-like heap of stones, a pathetic little monument erected to commemorate a long-ago tragedy in this lovely region— the mysterious murder of the Joyce children...in 1865."[30] Over the past 140 years since Evans' execution, New Hampshire hanged ten more male criminals for their own horrific murders, but none of their crimes were as sinister or could be classified as serial killings like the crimes of Franklin B. Evans. Were five children all victims of one of America's first serial killers and child predators? Were there more victims? Like the ultimate fate of his evil, sadistic soul, these questions will likely always remain beyond the ability of historians to answer.

Endnotes: Chapter Thirteen

1. *Farmer's Cabinet*, November 14, 1850.

2. *Bangor Daily Whig*, May 12, 1864, March 31, 1870.

3. *Boston Traveller*, June 19, 1865.

4. *Boston Traveller*, June 19, 1865.

5. *Boston Journal*, June 19, 1865; *Boston Daily Advertiser*, June 20, 27, 1865; http://www.jphs.org/victorian/bussey-woods-murders.html.

6. *Boston Daily Advertiser*, June 20, 1865; *Boston Journal*, July 10, 1865; *Daily National Intelligencer*, July 25, 1865; *New York Times*, March 10, 1866; *Lowell Daily Citizen*, April 25, 1866.

7. John B. Lewis, Charles C. Bombaugh, *Strategems and Conspiracies to Defraud Life Insurance Companies An Authentic Record of Remarkable Cases* (Baltimore: 1896) 136-138.

8. *Independent Statesman*, November 7, 1872; *New York Times*, November 6, 1872.

9. *Independent Statesman*, November 7, 1872.

10. *Independent Statesman*, November 7, 1872.

11. *Independent Statesman*, November 7, 1872; To see this photograph, visit http://www.luminous-lint.com/app/image/952541188937095363289/

12. *The Northwood murder : a complete report of the trial of Franklin B. Evans for the murder of Georgianna Lovering at Northwood, October 25th, 1872, together with a portrait and sketch of the career of the murderer,* (Manchester: 1872) 2.

13. *The Northwood murder*, 3.

14. *The Northwood murder*, 4, 5.

15. *The Northwood murder*, 6.

17. *The Northwood murder*, 7; John Phillip Reid, *Chief Justice: The Judicial World of Charles Doe* (Cambridge: Harvard University Press, 1967).

18. *The Northwood murder*, 8; *Dover Gazette and Strafford Advertiser*, July 21, 1849.

19. *Independent Statesman*, February 19, 1874.

20. *Strategems and Conspiracies to Defraud Life Insurance Companies*, 137-138.

21. *Independent Statesman*, February 19, 1874.

22. *Independent Statesman*, February 19, 1874.

23. http://www.fbi.gov/stats-services/publications/serial-murder, accessed on July 6, 2011.

24. Bangor Daily Whig, February 8, 1873.

25. *Independent Statesman*, February 19, 1874.

26. Francis Gould Butler, *The History of Farmington, Franklin County, Maine...1776-1885* (Farmington: 1885) 241-242.

27. *Milwaukee Sentinel*, February 12, 1873; *Little Rock Daily Republican*, February 17, 1873.

28. *Independent Statesman*, February 19, 1874.

29. *New-Hampshire Patriot*, May 16, 1877; Robert N. Dennis collection of Stereoscopic Views, New York Public Library, MFY Dennis Coll 91-F39; also see http://www.flickr.com/photos/pantufla/297731385/#/

30. Edwin Bacon, *Walks and Rides in the Country Round Boston* (Cambridge: Houghton, Mifflin, & Co., 1898) 304.

CPSIA information can be obtained
at www.ICGtesting.com
Printed in the USA
BVOW07s1958070218
507552BV00006B/192/P